Adobe® Acrobat® 6
Complete Course

Ted Padova

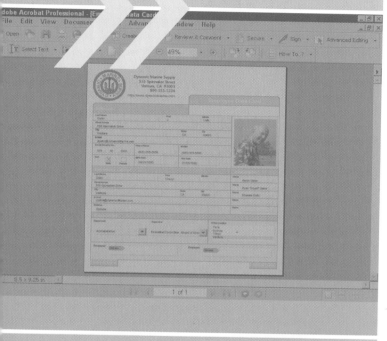

WILEY

Wiley Publishing, Inc.

Adobe® Acrobat® 6 Complete Course

Published by:
Wiley Publishing, Inc.
111 River Street
Hoboken, NJ 07030
www.wiley.com/compbooks

Published simultaneously in Canada

For general information on our other products and services or to obtain technical support please contact our Customer Care Department within the U.S. at 800-762-2974, outside the U.S. at 317-572-3993 or fax 317-572-4002.

Library of Congress Control Number: 2002111063

ISBN: 0-7645-1895-X

Manufactured in the United States of America

10 9 8 7 6 5 4 3 2 1

Credits

Publisher: Barry Pruett

Project Editor: Kezia Endsley

Acquisitions Editor: Mike Roney

Editorial Manager: Robyn Burnett

Technical Editor: Lori DeFurio

Interior Designers: Edwin Kuo, Daniela Richardson

Cover Designer: Anthony Bunyan

Production Coordinator: Maridee Ennis

Layout and Graphics: Beth Brooks, Carrie Foster, Joyce Haughey, Jennifer Heleine, LeAndra Hosier

Quality Control: Susan Moritz

Indexer: Sharon Hilgenberg

Proofreader: Linda Quigley

Special Help: Cricket Krengel, Adrienne Porter

Acknowledgments

I want to thank the people at Wiley Publishing, Inc. for their dedication and assistance in producing this publication — my Acquisitions Editor, Mike Roney, for his confidence and support, my Project Editor, Kezia Endsley, for her hard work and much assistance throughout the project, the background people like Rev Mengle and his production team, and special assistance provided as needed from Cricket Krengel and Adrienne Porter.

A very special thank you to my Technical Editor, Lori DeFurio, Developer Evangelist at Adobe Systems, for her keen eye and great assistance to ensure technical accuracy.

Much appreciation is extended to Dave Murcott and Brian Maffitt of Total Training for granting permission for distribution of video clips from their video series Total Acrobat.

Thank you also to Sherry Schafer for her art contributions of the tutorial images logo and the newsletter and Lisle Gates for again allowing me to use him as a subject for the photo contributions.

Bio

Ted Padova is author of the *Adobe Acrobat PDF Bible* (versions 4, 5, and 6), *Teach Yourself Visually Acrobat 5*, *Creating Adobe Acrobat PDF Forms*, and several other publications covering Adobe Photoshop and Adobe Illustrator. He is host of a collection of seven video CDs on Acrobat 6 training from Total Training (http://www.totaltraining.com).

» Table of Contents

Introduction

Welcome to Adobe Acrobat

Adobe Acrobat is one of the most amazing programs yet to be published by a software manufacturer. There are so many things you can do with Acrobat that the limits of the program are usually more related to the limits of a user's imagination than the program itself. Once you have a comprehensive knowledge of using the application, you can be certain it belongs on all computers after installing your operating system, your Internet connection, and the productivity tools you use. Regardless of the work you do on a computer, at one time or another Adobe Acrobat will be your constant work companion.

This book is designed to teach you how to use either the Adobe Acrobat Standard or Adobe Acrobat Professional software by performing tutorial steps to achieve results in constructing documents. Some tutorials result in creating a stand-alone document whereas other tutorials walk you through steps to build a document through several sessions. As you work through the sessions ahead, you learn to use much of what Acrobat offers you by performing tasks step-by-step to create documents similar to the way you produce electronic files in your own work environment.

Is This Book for You?

The answer to the question is definitely *yes* if you have little or no knowledge of using the Acrobat Standard or Acrobat Professional software. Regardless of the kind of work you do, if you work on a computer, Acrobat has its place among your software tools. There is no profession or workflow that exists in which using an Acrobat authoring application cannot help you.

What's in This Book?

The *Complete Course* series from John Wiley and Sons and Seybold Seminars Publications is designed for you the reader to learn a computer program by following the steps outlined in individual tutorials. In this series you learn by doing.

To present you with a real-world scenario, you will create and edit PDF documents commonly found in many companies such as an employee manual, an annual report, memos, multimedia presentations, and forms. The fictitious company called *Dynamic Marine Supply* produces products for a wholesale and retail market. Dynamic's management wants to reduce the amount of paper flow in the company by routing documents electronically. In this regard, Dynamic Marine intends to convert all analog documents including personnel forms, sales forms, policy and procedure manuals, accounting documents, management reports, and other similar documents to the Portable Document Format. Dynamic Marine wants to make their files accessible to employees so they can exchange files electronically while reducing paper workflow. They further want to use PDF as a delivery mechanism for presentations, document distribution via CD-ROMs, and a vehicle for reviewing and commenting on draft documents.

The sessions ahead are intended to use Dynamic Marine Supply as an example for how you go about setting up a PDF workflow environment and how to create, edit, and refine files for users of all Acrobat viewers. Through this mechanism, you'll learn about Adobe Acrobat and many of the things Acrobat can do for you.

Parts

This book is logically divided into sections referred to as Part I, Part II, and so on. There are eight parts in the book divided into distinctive categories supporting one or more categorical items. Eight parts of the book are printed in the pages ahead while Part IX is a bonus section on the CD-ROM. The focus of the sessions in the book is targeted at creating and exchanging electronic documents, whereas the bonus session covers printing PDF documents. Because Acrobat can do so many things, these parts are intended to give you an idea for sessions and tutorials related to some generic techniques specific to Acrobat. If you have a particular need in your organization, you can pick and choose the parts that apply most and devote more time to them. The contents include:

» Confidence Builder. Your Acrobat journey begins with a jumpstart into using the program without any background information. This is a hands-on section designed to familiarize you with Acrobat tools and editing features.

» **Part I: Course Setup.** This part includes the Project Overview.

» Project Overview. This is a narrative section providing you a little background information about Acrobat and distinctions between Acrobat viewers. The section covers some detail on the projects ahead in the tutorials as you move along in the book.

» **Part II: Getting to Know Adobe Acrobat.** This part introduces you to the Acrobat workplace and teaches you how to access tools and menu commands, and adjust preference settings.

» Session 1, "Customizing Acrobat," covers how to access toolbars, adjust your editing environment, change preferences, and access Acrobat help information.

» Session 2, "Opening and Saving Files," covers opening PDF documents in Acrobat, using the Save and Save As commands for updating edits, and optimizing files.

» Session 3, "Viewing and Navigating PDF Files," introduces you to PDF navigation and using viewing tools for zooming in on pages, using page thumbnails, and working with bookmarks.

» **Part III: Creating PDF Documents.** PDF documents are commonly converted from application documents created in many authoring programs. This part is dedicated to teaching you how to convert different file types and application documents to the Portable Document Format (PDF).

» Session 4, "Converting Application Documents to PDF," covers document file type conversions to the PDF format and introduces you to the PDF conversions from Microsoft Office programs.

» Session 5, "PDFs and Web Viewing," details Web page conversions from files stored locally on hard drives and Web pages on the Internet. Conversion to PDF from e-mail programs like Microsoft Outlook and Outlook Express is covered.

» **Part IV: Editing PDF Documents.** Once you create a PDF file, you need to know how to edit files for creating interactive documents or modify document content. This part teaches you many methods for changing initial views, appending pages to documents, and editing the page content.

  » Session 6, "Modifying Views and Pages," covers setting initial views and viewing files in different page layout modes.

  » Session 7, "Changing Document Pages," covers appending, replacing, and deleting pages in PDF documents.

  » Session 8, "Changing Document Content," shows you methods for adding text, changing text on pages, adding Web links, and copying and pasting page data.

» **Part V: Commenting and Reviewing.** For participation in any workgroup, the process of reviewing and commenting on files is a standard office practice. In this session you learn to use Acrobat's commenting tools and how to initiate and participate in e-mail-based reviews.

  » Session 9, "Using Comment Tools," teaches you how to use a number of tools designed for adding comments to PDF documents, how to create custom stamps, use the Commenting panel, and how to summarize comments.

  » Session 10, "Commenting and Reviewing," covers initiating an e-mail-based review, how to participate in a review, and how to use the review tracking tools.

» **Part VI: Adding Interactivity.** To make your files more dynamic you can add links, buttons, and interactive elements for the purpose of viewing and navigation. In this part you learn how to create interactive elements, import video and sound, and create presentation documents.

  » Session 11, "Creating Links and Buttons," covers page and document linking to aid users in viewing a collection of PDF files hosted on local hard drives, network servers, and the Internet.

  » Session 12, "Working with Multimedia," covers importing sound and video clips and covers how to create buttons for playing media.

  » Session 13, "Creating Presentations," covers file conversions from Microsoft PowerPoint to PDF and using Acrobat for presentations.

» **Part VII: Creating Acrobat PDF Forms.** One of the many useful purposes in using PDF documents is related to forms that circulate through offices and through Web hosting. In addition to the Acrobat tools, the Acrobat implementation of JavaScript adds extraordinary capabilities for creating interactive documents and forms. In this part you learn how to create PDF forms in Acrobat Professional, fill in forms in either Acrobat Standard or Acrobat Professional and add JavaScripts to PDF documents.

> » Session 14, "Editing and Filling In Forms," covers creating a PDF form in Acrobat Professional and filling in forms in any Acrobat viewer.

> » Session 15, "Creating JavaScripts," shows you how to create page templates and add a JavaScript. You learn where to look for JavaScripts and how to become more familiar with the Acrobat implementation of JavaScript.

» **Part VIII: Signing and Securing PDF Documents.** Acrobat offers you many security features for protecting documents using Acrobat security and through the use of digital IDs. In this part you learn how to encrypt files with Acrobat security and sign documents with a digital signature.

> » Session 16, "Securing Documents," shows you how to encrypt files against unauthorized viewing and protect files against editing.

> » Session 17, "Using Digital Signatures," covers how to create a digital ID, sign documents with a digital signature, and how to certify documents.

» **Part IX: Desktop and Commercial Printing.** PDF documents can be printed and routed through offices in analog form when hard copy is needed and you can prepare files for high-end commercial printing. This bonus chapter on the CD-ROM shows you how PDF documents are printed.

> » Session 14A, "Creating PDF Forms," is a bonus chapter included on the CD-ROM. Creating forms is a feature found only in Acrobat Professional. In this session, you learn to use Acrobat Propfessional for designing forms.

> » Session 18, "Printing PDF Documents," covers desktop printing, proofing color, preflighting jobs, and commercial printing.

> » Appendix A: "What's on the CD-ROM," covers a description of the CD-ROM's contents and how to install the tutorial files.

Learning More About Adobe Acrobat

Use of Adobe Acrobat is growing at impressive proportions. As of this writing, Adobe Acrobat is Adobe Systems number one growth product with sales growing at more than 40 percent year every year. Changes in the program and in the way techniques are used and employed are constantly subject for review. To keep abreast of current trends, you'll want to obtain information as it becomes available. You can find Acrobat related essays, articles, and news at many different Web sites.

Visit some Web sites: For starters, visit http://www.adobe.com. Adobe Systems is the first stop in your information search regarding Adobe Acrobat, Acrobat related solutions, and new release information. Stay connected with Adobe by visiting their Web site routinely. Be certain to make periodic stops at the Acrobat Web page to look for any maintenance upgrades to Adobe Reader, Acrobat Standard, and Acrobat Professional.

Visit http://www.planetpdf.com as well. One of the best sources of Acrobat-related information and tips, tricks, and techniques for using Acrobat can be found at the Planet PDF Web site. If you have a question, post it on the user forum. If you need a solution, search through the articles at Planet PDF. If you need a third-party software plug-in, search the Planet PDF Store.

Search the Internet: Many different users in the PDF community host Web sites where PDF documents, especially forms, can be found, and tips associated with creating PDFs are routinely published as free downloads. Search for Acrobat, PDF, or PDF forms in your Web browser and look around the thousands of search results you find.

Attend a conference: National and International seminars and conferences are held just about every week somewhere on the planet. Among popular conference programs offering PDF-related seminars and talks are Seybold Seminars (http://www.seyboldseminars.com), Open Publish (http://www.open-publish.com), and DigiPub Corporation's PDF Conference (http://www.pdfconference.com). The DigiPub bi-annual PDF Conference is entirely devoted to Acrobat and PDF. It is held in the eastern and western United States twice a year. Be certain to check any of the conference programs by visiting the Web sites. One conference can equip you with information that might otherwise take many months of dedicated study.

Send an e-mail: If you have a question about this book or want to suggest something for a future volume, send me an e-mail at ted@west.net. I receive over 20 e-mails daily regarding Acrobat and PDF from users around the world asking for help with a particular Acrobat solution. I still have more time on my hands, so you won't be sidestepped. Send an e-mail if you need help.

Resource Materials

There are many publications available to you for learning more about Adobe Acrobat. In particular, one of the largest collections of books in print is at Wiley and Sons. For starters, take a look at:

Adobe Acrobat 6 PDF Bible, by Ted Padova—A comprehensive reference manual for almost all that Acrobat can do is found in the *Acrobat PDF Bible*. Use this book to refer to techniques and features when you need a more amplified explanation for working with Acrobat.

Adobe Acrobat 6 For Dummies, by John Kaufeld—An introductory work on using Adobe Acrobat written for novice to intermediate users. In traditional Dummies book style, this publication offers easy-to-follow steps in using Acrobat.

Creating Adobe Acrobat Forms, by Ted Padova—If you want more information on creating Acrobat PDF forms and more information on JavaScript, this book is 600+ pages entirely devoted to Acrobat forms and written in a tutorial style with detailed text explaining all features related to forms.

Confidence Builder

This session is intended to help you get a jump-start into using Adobe Acrobat Standard or Adobe Acrobat Professional. In this session, you create a PDF document and edit it in Acrobat. You learn how to create a Portable Document File (PDF) with the Acrobat Distiller software, append pages to the file, and then add some interactivity. You learn how to modify pages, add a comment, and send your document to others for an e-mail review. The session is long but it is easily divided into logical segments. If you need to take a break, you can stop after any segment that ends with saving the file to update the edits.

TOOLS YOU'LL USE
Acrobat Standard or Acrobat Professional version 6.0 or greater, Acrobat Distiller version 6.0 or greater, Status Bar, Create PDF From File command, Pages panel, Add Watermark & Background command, Link tool, Stamp Comment tool, Send by Email For Review command, Initial View Properties, and the Save As command.

CD-ROM FILES NEEDED
cb_annualReport.ps, cb_cover.tif, cb_draft.pdf, cb_financial.pdf, and cb_highlights.pdf. The files are found in the Sessions/SessionCB/TutorialCB folder on the CD-ROM. A completed version of the project can be found in the TutorialCB_finals folder.

TIME REQUIRED
2 hours

Test Tutorial
» Getting Started with Adobe Acrobat

In this tutorial, you create a PDF document and open it in Acrobat. You then edit the document by appending pages and changing page content and add interactivity by creating links. You add a comment and send the file to a recipient for an e-mail review. The steps used in this tutorial are repeated and amplified in later sessions.

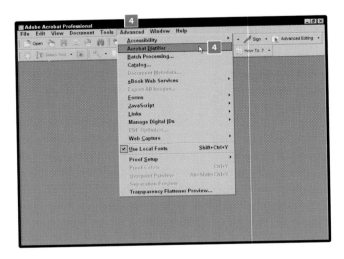

1. **Mount the CD–ROM located in the back of this book.**

2. **Drag the SessionCB folder from inside the Sessions folder to your desktop.**

<NOTE>
Windows users need to unlock files copied from the CD. When you copy the files to your hard disk from a CD, they are copied as read-only files. To unlock the files and disable read-only, right-click the SessionCB folder and select Properties from the context menu. Uncheck Read-Only, which allows you to now edit the files freely. You need to repeat these steps each time you copy a new session's folder from the CD.

3. **Launch Acrobat by double-clicking the program icon.**

<NOTE>
You can launch Acrobat through several means. You can open the Adobe Acrobat folder and double-click the program icon or a shortcut/alias on your desktop. Windows users can open Acrobat by opening the Start menu and choosing Acrobat from the options.

4. **Choose Advanced→Acrobat Distiller.**
   Acrobat Distiller opens in the foreground while Acrobat remains in the background.

<NOTE>
Acrobat Distiller is a separate program installed with Acrobat and executable from within the Acrobat program. The Acrobat Distiller software is used to convert a PostScript file to a PDF document. Distiller can be launched from within Acrobat or independently as a separate program. Distiller can also be called upon to convert a PostScript file to PDF by clicking the Create PDF task button and choosing From File from the options. When Distiller is launched from within Acrobat, Distiller opens in the foreground while Acrobat remains open in the background.

Test Tutorial
» Converting a PostScript File to PDF

There are several ways to convert authored application documents to PDF. One of the ways to convert to PDF is to first print a PostScript file to disk, and then convert the PostScript file to PDF with the Acrobat Distiller software. In this segment of the Confidence Builder, you learn to use the Acrobat Distiller software to convert a PostScript file to PDF.

5. **Click the pull-down menu in the Distiller window for Default Settings. Notice the different choices available for the Adobe PDF Settings. Choose High Quality from the options.**
    High Quality is used for printing high-quality images. Among other choices you have settings that are optimized for commercial printing, screen views, and creating the smallest file sizes used for Web hosting.

6. **Choose File→Open. Open the SessionCB folder and open the TutorialCB folder. Choose** cb_annualReport.ps **and click Open.**
    The target file is a PostScript file printed to disk from an authoring application that has been prepared for you. The Acrobat Distiller software converts the PostScript file to a PDF document, and the PDF is saved to the same folder where the PostScript file resides. The newly created PDF document can be opened in any Acrobat viewer. When you click the file and click Open, the Acrobat Distiller – Specify PDF File Name dialog box opens. In this dialog box, you navigate your hard drive for a folder destination and provide a filename for the converted PDF. By default, the filename appears as cb_annualReport.pdf.

7. **Leave the default filename as it appears in the Acrobat Distiller – Specify PDF File Name dialog box and click Save.**
    The file is converted to PDF and saved to your TutorialCB folder. If your preferences for Acrobat Distiller are not set to prompt you for a file destination, the file is automatically saved to the same directory as where the PostScript file resides. To view the preferences, choose File→Preferences and check the box for Ask for PDF file destination if you want to be prompted for a filename and destination.

8. **Click the Close button in the Acrobat Distiller window.**
    Acrobat Distiller quits while Acrobat remains open.

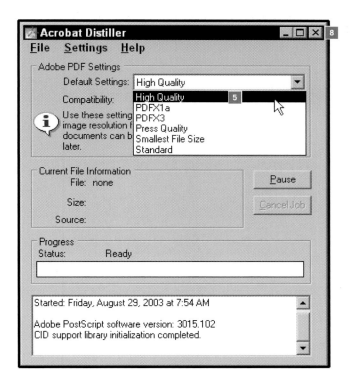

<NOTE>
If for some reason you experience difficulty converting the file to a PDF document, a converted file is located in the TutorialCB_Finish folder. Open the file cb_annualReportRaw.pdf and follow the remaining steps in this session.

<NOTE>
In Windows, the Close button is the top-right button in the title bar. On the Macintosh, the Close button is the top-left button in the title bar. You can also use the Control/Command+Q keyboard shortcut to quit Acrobat Distiller.

Test Tutorial
» Opening a PDF Document

Throughout this book you'll learn to work with PDF files in Acrobat. This segment teaches you how to open PDF files.

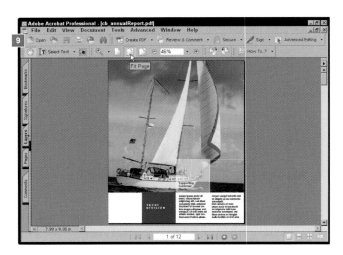

9. **Click the Open tool in the Acrobat Toolbar Well. Navigate to the TutorialCB folder and open the** cb_annualReport.pdf **file.** Notice Acrobat Distiller created the PDF file and automatically added the .pdf extension. The file was created in the same folder where the PostScript file resides.

Test Tutorial
» Navigating a PDF Document

Acrobat provides many means for page navigation and viewing. In this segment you learn to set a zoom level and scroll through pages with tools located in the Toolbar Well and in the Status Bar.

10. Click the Fit Page tool in the Acrobat Toolbar Well.

When you create a PDF document, the file opens at a zoom level that fits the PDF opening page within the width of the Acrobat Document pane. The viewing area for the PDF pages is called the Document pane. If you want to view more of the page within the Document pane, you need to adjust the zoom level. You can do this by either clicking one of the page views in the Acrobat Toolbar Well or adjusting a zoom percentage by entering a zoom value in the field box in the Toolbar Well or Status Bar.

11. Click the Next Page tool in the Status Bar.

The Status Bar contains navigation tools that enable you to move around a PDF document open in the Document pane.

12. Click the Next Page tool and again and repeat the step to move through all pages in the document.

13. Click the First Page tool in the Status Bar.

Acrobat returns you to the first page in the document.

14. Click the Previous View tool. Click the Next View tool.

Notice the last page you viewed in the file opens in the Document pane. The Previous Page tool and the Next Page tool take you to the last and next views in an open document or when a last or next view opens another file.

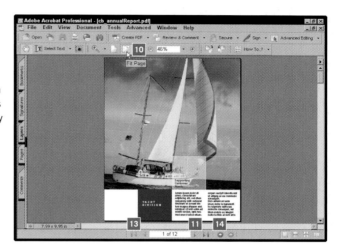

Test Tutorial

» Converting an Image File to PDF

In addition to using the Acrobat Distiller software, Acrobat can convert many file formats to PDF. In this segment you learn to use the Convert PDF From File command to convert image formatted files.

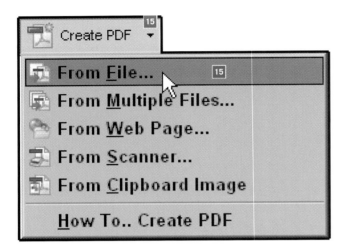

15. **Click the Create PDF task button and choose From File from the options. The Open dialog box opens.**
Certain file types can be converted to PDF documents directly from within Acrobat. In order to use the Create PDF From File command, a file has to be saved in a file format compatible with the Convert to PDF From File options.

< N O T E >
Once you establish a directory path when opening a PDF document as was accomplished in Step 6, the directory path remains absolute and Acrobat looks to this folder when you attempt to open another PDF file. Therefore, because you have opened a file in the TutorialCB folder, you don't need to relocate the folder to open the cb_cover.tif file.

16. **Choose All Files (*.*) from the Files of Type (Windows) or Show (Macintosh) pull-down menu. Click** cb_cover.tif. **Click Open. Click the Fit Page tool.**
The TIFF formatted file opens as a new PDF in the Document pane. The original file you opened remains open behind the most recently opened file.

Test Tutorial
» Appending Pages

You might need to create a single PDF document from several documents already in PDF format. In this segment you'll learn to insert pages in the open document from files located in your TutorialCB folder.

17. **Choose Window→Tile→Vertically.**
Both pages are shown in the Document pane. When files are viewed together in the Document pane, you can move pages between documents. The TIFF file is the cover page for the cb_annualReport.pdf document. You need to copy the cover page and append it to the annual report document.

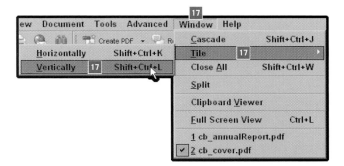

18. **Click the Pages tab on both documents.**
The Pages panel opens for both documents. In the Pages panel, you see thumbnail views of the document pages.

19. **Click the page thumbnail on the** cb_cover.pdf **document.**

20. **While holding down the mouse click, drag the cover page thumbnail to the top of page 1 in the** cb_annualReport.pdf **document.**
As you position the cursor in the Pages panel in the destination document, notice the cursor changes to a selection arrow with a + symbol. When you release the mouse button, the page is pasted into the destination document.

21. **Click the Close box on the cover file. Click No when you're prompted to save the file.**

22. **Click the Maximize button in the open document.**

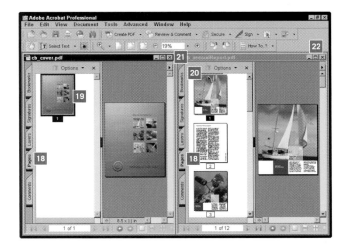

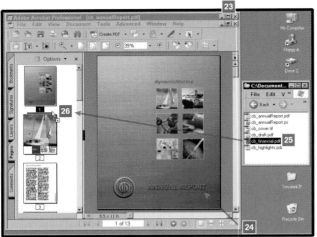

23. **Click the Maximize button in the Acrobat window.**

24. **Size the window down by dragging the lower-right corner of the window up and to the left. Click on the title bar in the Acrobat window and move the window aside (to the left in this example) so you can view your SessionCB folder.**

25. **Open the TutorialCB folder and click** `cb_financial.pdf`.

26. **While holding down the mouse click, drag the file below the first page thumbnail in the Acrobat window.**
    Notice the file is appended to the document when you release the mouse button.

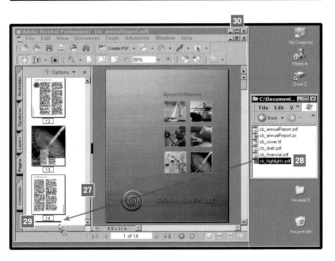

27. **Drag the scroll bar in the Pages panel down to scroll to the bottom of the page thumbnails.**

28. **Click** `cb_highlights.pdf` **in the TutorialCB folder.**

29. **Drag the file to the Pages panel below page 14.**
    The file is appended to the open document.

30. **Click Maximize to open the Acrobat window in a full-screen view. Macintosh users click the plus (+) button in the Acrobat window title bar to maximize the view.**

Test Tutorial
» Saving Files and Loading Toolbars

As you edit PDF documents you'll want to periodically save your work. Acrobat provides a tool in the Toolbar Well for saving documents. If you want to save a file with a new name or save a file to rewrite it and optimize the document, you use the Save As command. The default tools appearing in the Toolbar Well are only some of the many tools and toolbars you have available in Acrobat. As you approach each editing session, it's a good idea to open toolbars and dock them in the Toolbar Well. In this segment, you learn how to open toolbars and add them to the Toolbar Well.

31. **Choose File→Save As.**
    The Save As dialog box opens.

32. **Navigate to the TutorialCB_finish folder and save the file as**
    cb_annualReport_finish.pdf.

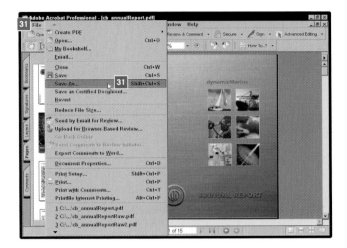

33. **Click the Advanced Editing task button.**
    When you click the Advanced Editing task button, the Advanced Editing toolbar opens as a floating toolbar in the Acrobat window.

34. **Open a context menu from the Toolbar Well (right-click in Windows or Control-click on the Macintosh) and choose Dock All Toolbars.**
    The Advanced Editing toolbar is docked in the Toolbar Well when you release the mouse button. Notice the context menu also displays a list of toolbars. Those toolbars with a check adjacent to the toolbar name are currently open in the Toolbar Well. Toolbars without check marks are hidden. Clicking a toolbar toggles it open or closed.

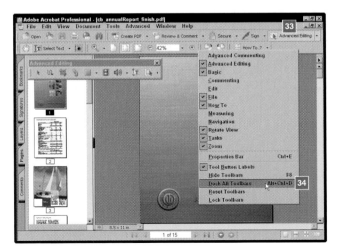

Test Tutorial
» Creating Page Links

In addition to the tools used for navigation in the Status Bar, you can add interactive elements to a PDF document to assist a user in navigating pages in open PDF documents and in navigating among a collection of different PDF documents. The Link tool is used to create hyperactive links. In this segment you learn how to add interactive links with the Link tool.

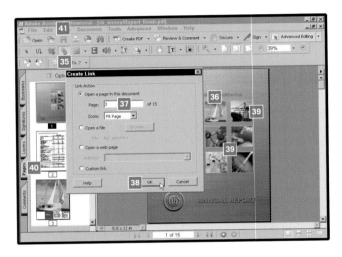

35. **Click the Link tool.**

36. **Draw a link rectangle around the first image thumbnail (top-left side of the thumbnail images on the cover page).**
    The Create Link dialog box opens.

37. **Type 3 in the field box below the Open a Page in This Document item.**
    By default, the radio button is selected for Open a Page in This Document.

38. **Click OK in the Create Link dialog box.**
    The rectangle you draw with the Link tool becomes the *hot spot* for the page link. To invoke the link action, you click the Hand tool and click the link. Page 3 opens in the Document pane after clicking the link.

39. **Repeat the same steps to add links for pages 5, 7, 9, 11, and 13 following an order down the first column and then down the second column of thumbnail images.**

< T I P >

The thumbnail images match the images on the respective pages. You can scroll the thumbnails in the Pages panel to see the pages that match the images on the cover page. Use the page numbers at the bottom of each page thumbnail if you are confused about setting the link to the correct page.

40. **Click the Pages tab to close the Pages panel.**

41. **Click the Save button to update your edits.**

Test Tutorial
» Adding a Watermark

Watermarks can be applied to a page or all pages in a file with a simple menu command. The document at hand is designed to be reviewed by members of a workgroup. The file is currently in draft form. So as not to confuse this file with a final document, you can stamp all pages with a watermark informing all your reviewers the file is still in draft form. In this segment, you learn how to add a watermark.

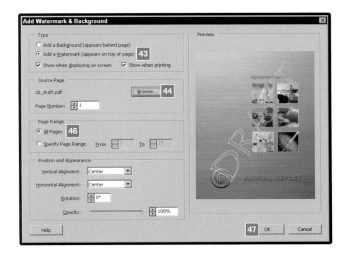

42. **Choose Document→Add Watermark & Background.**
    The Add Watermark & Background dialog box opens.

43. **Click Add a Watermark (Appears on Top of the Page).**
    As described in the text in the dialog box, a watermark appears on top of the page. Backgrounds appear behind page data.

44. **Click the Browse button.**
    The Open dialog box opens.

45. **Navigate to the TutorialCB folder and choose** cb_draft.pdf. **Click Open.**

46. **Ensure that the All Pages radio button is selected.**
    By default, All Pages is selected for you. Be certain the radio button is active before continuing. Notice that the preview area in the dialog box shows how the imported image appears on top of the text.

47. **Click OK.**
    The watermark is applied to all pages.

48. **Click Save to update your edits.**

Test Tutorial
» Adding a Stamp Comment

The annual report is intended to be circulated among selected coworkers for adding comments and finalizing the document meeting approval. To add a message asking reviewers to keep the document confidential, you can add a stamp comment. In this segment you learn how to add stamps with the Stamp tool.

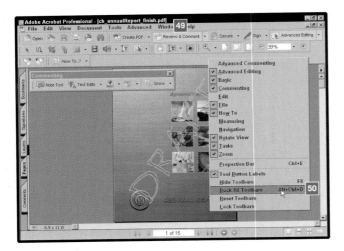

49. **Click the Review & Comment task button.**
Clicking the task button opens the Commenting toolbar.

50. **Open a context menu on the Toolbar Well (by right- or Control-clicking) and choose Dock All Toolbars.**

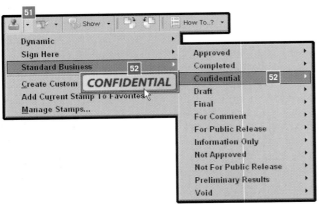

51. **Click the down-pointing arrow adjacent to the Stamp tool to open a pull-down menu.**

52. **Choose Standard Business→Confidential→Confidential.**
The Stamp tool is loaded with the selected stamp. Notice that the submenu shows a thumbnail view of a stamp.

53. **Click the Stamp tool in the document on the top-left side of the page.**

You can click to drop the stamp on the page or click and drag a marquee to define the size. When the stamp is placed on the page, a comment note pop-up window opens. Depending on any defaults you have for comment pop-up notes, the note color might be a color different than the note used in this example.

54. **Open a context menu by right-clicking (or Control-clicking) the note pop-up window title bar.**

55. **Choose Properties from the menu.**

The Stamp Properties dialog box opens. In this dialog box, you assign note properties for appearance settings, set the author and subject information, and examine the review history for comments shared in reviews. If you haven't changed defaults, the author's name is derived from your computer logon name. You can edit the author's name in the Stamp Properties dialog box to change the name to the text you add in the General Properties.

56. **Click the General tab.**

57. **Edit the Author field by typing your name.**

58. **Click the Close button.**

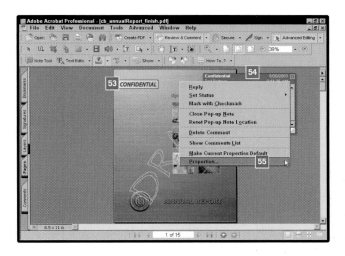

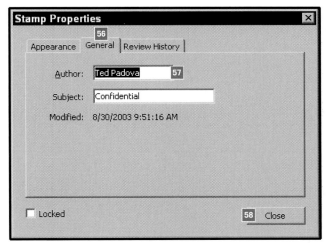

59. **Click the cursor in the note pop-up window and type a message. In this example I typed** Please keep this document confidential until we finalize it.

60. **Click the Save tool to update your edits.**

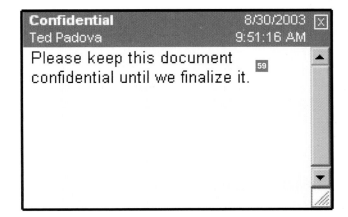

Test Tutorial
» Setting the Opening View

When you first opened the PDF after distilling it in Acrobat Distiller, the PDF page opened in a Fit Width view. Only a portion of the document page was displayed in the Document pane. You can establish the opening view of a PDF file and determine which zoom view the file will be displayed in when it's opened. Before saving a PDF as a final file, you'll often want to establish the opening view. In this segment, you learn how to control the page view when an Acrobat viewer opens a PDF.

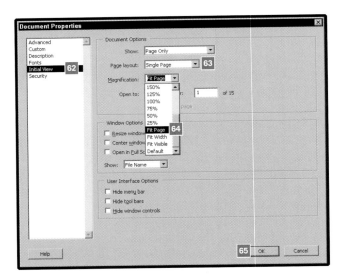

61. **Choose File→Document Properties.**
    The Document Properties dialog box opens.

62. **Click Initial View in the left pane.**

63. **Open the Page Layout pull-down menu by clicking the down-pointing arrow. Choose Single Page.**

64. **Open the Magnification pull-down menu and choose Fit Page.**

65. **Click the OK button.**
    Each time a user opens the file, the initial view opens the document in a single page layout view and fits the page completely in the Document pane. The changes you make in initial view take place only after you save the file.

66. **Choose File→Save As and save the file to the TutorialCB_finish folder. Click Yes when an alert dialog box opens.**
    When you choose File→Save As and save a file to the same folder using the same filename, Acrobat opens a dialog box informing you a file with the same name already exists in the target folder. It asks whether you want to replace the file. When you choose yes, you completely rewrite a file. By rewriting a file after several edits, the file is optimized and the result is a more efficient document with a smaller file size. As a matter of practice, always rewrite a file as your last editing step.

Test Tutorial
» Sending for E-mail Review

After you create a PDF document and edit the file, you might want to share your document with members of your workgroup for review and commenting. A nice new feature in Acrobat 6 is support for sending files for an e-mail review whereby recipients receive your document, add comment notes, and return the notes to you to be integrated into your original file. In this segment you learn how to start an e-mail review. For more on e-mail reviews, see Session 10.

67. Click the down-pointing arrow on the Review & Comment task button to open the pull-down menu.

68. Choose Send by Email for Review.

The Send by Email for Review dialog box opens. In this dialog box you add the addresses of the recipients you want to participate in the review.

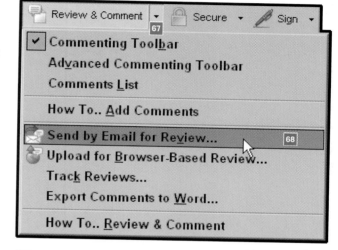

69. Type your e-mail address in the To field box.

If you have a colleague with Acrobat Standard or Acrobat Professional and want to try an e-mail review with another individual, use another e-mail address. If you want to test the process without participation from others, send the e-mail to yourself.

70. Click the Send button.

The Outgoing Message Notification dialog box opens.

71. Click OK to close the dialog box.

The Outgoing Message Notification dialog box informs you that the document in view in the Document pane is packaged for review and has been attached to your e-mail application.

72. Choose File→Quit to quit Acrobat.

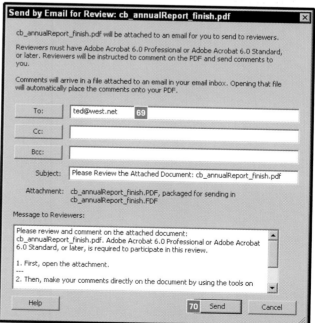

Part I
Course Setup

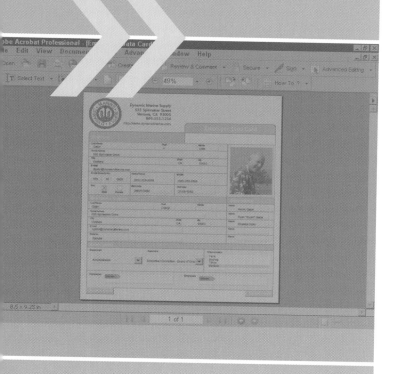

Project Overview

Understanding Acrobat Basics

Acrobat Viewers

Throughout this book references are made to Acrobat viewers. Whenever the term *Acrobat viewer* is used, you are informed that any Acrobat viewer application can view the PDF documents you create. If reference is made to Acrobat, the PDF can only be used by Acrobat Standard or Acrobat Professional. When there are distinctions between using Acrobat Standard and Acrobat Professional, the complete product name is mentioned. To help clarify things a little, you need to understand the various Acrobat viewers.

» **Acrobat Standard.** Acrobat Standard is a robust PDF editing program that offers most of the tools and commands you find in Acrobat Professional. Acrobat Standard requires purchase from Adobe Systems and is vastly different than the free Adobe Reader software. Throughout this book you find most of the tutorials addressing steps that can be performed with Acrobat Standard. A few features in a few of the tutorials ahead mention some tasks that can only be performed with Acrobat Professional.

» **Acrobat Professional.** Acrobat Professional offers you all the features, tools, and menu commands found in Acrobat Standard as well as an assortment of additional editing features that can only be performed with Acrobat Professional. Among the most obvious distinctions between the viewers is the commercial printing features and form tools that are not supported in Acrobat Standard.

» **Adobe Reader.** The free application from Adobe Systems is used to view and print PDF documents. Adobe Reader is not an authoring tool, and new data introduced into Adobe Reader cannot be saved. Adobe Reader cannot be used with the tutorials in the sessions ahead. However, the designs you create in Acrobat can be viewed and printed with the Adobe Reader software.

When you begin creating PDF documents, be aware of the limitations of the Acrobat viewers. Where more functionality is needed than is provided with Adobe Reader you might want to offer users help in guiding them to a viewer that can appropriately handle the files you author in Acrobat.

Acrobat Features

Because the tutorials in the following sessions provide instruction on using either Acrobat Standard or Acrobat Professional as your viewer, you should become aware of the many things that these viewers can do for you. For example:

» Create PDF documents from a variety of file formats.

» Create interactivity through links to other PDFs, other file types, and Web-hosted documents.

» Add interactive elements like hyperlinks, bookmarks, destinations, article threads, sounds, and movie files.

» Create accessible documents for visually- and motion-challenged users.

» Create digital IDs and electronically sign documents.

» Search through large volumes of PDF documents.

» Annotate and markup PDF documents for workgroup collaboration.

» Initiate and participate in e-mail-based reviews.

» Create online comments for Web-hosted workgroup collaboration.

» Convert Web pages and Web sites to PDF documents.

» Customize interactivity and data handling via JavaScript programming.

» Scan documents directly into Acrobat.

» Convert image scans to rich text via optical character recognition (OCR).

These are but some of the things you can do with Acrobat. When you think of Acrobat, it's hard to nail down the exact purpose of the program. It is a tool used by many people for many purposes.

Acrobat Tools

At the beginning of each session, you are informed about what tools are used in the tutorial. The reference to *tools* includes several items. For lack of a better term, whenever tools are mentioned, they can include any or all of the following:

» **Toolbars:** At the top of the Acrobat document window several toolbars are docked in the Toolbar Well. These items are tools used in Acrobat. A tool is selected by clicking it and using it in the document window. Some tools are nested in toolbars and can be accessed by clicking the down-pointing arrow within a tool group and clicking a command from the menu options.

» **Navigation Pane:** The Navigation Pane contains panels. To open a panel, click the panel name to expand it in the Navigation Pane. Each panel is referred to as a tool in the sessions ahead.

» **Menu Commands:** From the top-level menu bar, commands exist like most other windowing applications. Click menu names and click a menu command to gain access to a tool or editing feature.

» **Stand-alone Applications:** When the session begins, you are informed about all the Acrobat tools used in a given tutorial and any stand-alone applications. The listing for tools used in a session may also make reference to a stand-alone application that may include Acrobat Distiller or another program used in conjunction with Acrobat.

Project Description

The best way to learn a software application is when you use a program's tools and features to create documents for a purpose. Rather than poking around all the tools, menus, and commands in an application with the aid of a reference manual, you learn faster and more efficiently if you have some utilitarian purpose for the time you spend in a program. Throughout this publication you learn by creating documents that relate to files used in a *real-world* environment.

To help you move many of the features in Acrobat, you'll use a fictitious company where workflow solutions are intended to reduce the circulation of paper and move document distribution to a digital workflow. The result for the company is focused at reducing costs while creating a more efficient means of communication between employees. This is handled by eliminating much of the company's paper routing and distribution in analog form to electronic routing via Acrobat PDF files.

Because PDF files are used for so many purposes, the final documents you create serve multiple purposes. Acrobat is not like many other programs where you might assemble different documents into a single project or piece. Whereas a tutorial focused at page layout software might guide you through the production of a single document intended for commercial printing, your Acrobat journey results in several documents serving many purposes. The assembly of these documents provides you with a comprehensive knowledge for how the program works and the many things it can do for you.

Through the creation of files for the fictitious company, you need to give a little thought for how similar documents can be used in your own work environment. The first part of learning Acrobat comes in following directions to complete tutorials for the sample files, and the next step is applying these examples for your own purpose. In this regard, you'll want to make every effort to follow the steps in each session, and then try to apply your knowledge to your own work experience. Taking time to translate the learning you do on practice sessions to personal assignments will help you master Acrobat skills much faster.

The sessions that follow are divided into eight individual parts in the book and one part on the CD-ROM. Each part deals with a general category for producing Acrobat PDF documents for specific purposes. Although every effort has been made to work through sessions in a nonlinear form, there are times when you need to have a grasp of concepts from one session before you are able to complete tutorials in another session. Therefore, it is best to proceed starting at the beginning of the book and working through sessions successively.

Required Materials

To follow the tutorials in the book you need to have the proper software installed on an operating system compatible with the most recent version of Acrobat and all associated software applications. Recommendations for the software and hardware to be used include the following:

» Adobe Acrobat Standard or Acrobat Professional version 6.0 or greater—
The Adobe Acrobat installer CD-ROM includes both Acrobat and the Acrobat
Distiller software. Other applications in the form of plug-ins are automatically
installed with the Acrobat installation. After installing Acrobat, visit the
Adobe Systems Web site at http://www.adobe.com/products/acrobat. Select
the Downloads link at the top of the Web page and download the latest
maintenance upgrade. After downloading the file, install it on your computer
to upgrade your version of Acrobat if you see a maintenance upgrade
available.

» Internet Explorer 4+ or Netscape Navigator 4+—You need a Web browser
and Internet connection to download the necessary files. Use the latest version of either Microsoft Internet Explorer or Netscape Navigator. If you have
a version older than 4.x for either application, upgrade to version 4.x or
higher.

» Microsoft Office (2000 or greater)—Although not essential to complete most
of the tutorials, a few exercises use Microsoft Office products. If you want
to follow steps in the few tutorials using MS Office, you need to install
Microsoft Office on your computer.

» Windows Computer—A Pentium class III or 4 processor is recommended
with at least 128MB of RAM, a color monitor that displays 800×600 resolution or better, and 100MB of free hard drive space.

» Macintosh Computer—A Macintosh G4 computer with 128MB of RAM, a
color monitor that displays 800×600 resolution or better, and 100MB of free
hard drive space.

» CD-ROM drive—An external or internal CD-ROM drive is necessary to use
the tutorial files on the CD-ROM accompanying the book. CD-ROM files are
cross-platform and can be read using Windows and Mac OS X operating
systems.

» Microsoft Windows—A version of Microsoft Windows 98, 2000 or higher,
Windows NT with Service Pak 6 or higher, or Windows XP.

» Macintosh OS—Mac OS X (10.2 or above). MAC OS X is needed to install
Acrobat. Version 6 is not supported on Mac OS 9.

Tutorial Files

Tutorial files are contained in separate folders on the CD-ROM accompanying the book. Files are divided into two categories that include:

» **Session Folders**—The book is divided into 17 sessions and the Confidence Builder. Session folders are identified as Session01, Session02, and so on. The Confidence Builder folder is called SessionCB. Each session contains separate folders for all tutorials related to the session and folders with finished documents. You'll find in each Session folder three subfolders. The TutorialXX folder (where XX is the session number) contains the raw tutorial files you use to follow steps in each tutorial for a given session. The TutorialXX_finsh folder is used for files you save after following the tutorial steps. The TutorialXX_finals folder contains documents that appear in final form af the end of each session. To check your work, compare the files you save to the TutorialXX_finsh folder with the files contained in the TutorialXX_finals folder.

» **Tutorial Folders**—Each tutorial in a given session is found in the corresponding session number.

» **Tutorial Finals Folders**—To assist you in comparing the files you are instructed to create, there are completed files assembled precisely according to the tutorial steps. As you work on tutorial projects you are asked to save files to the Tutorial_finish folders. When you finish the tutorials, compare the files you save in the Tutorial_finish folders to those files found in the Tutorial_finals folders.

As a first step, be certain to open the readme file on the CD-ROM to check for any last minute changes. In the event anything changes from the time this manuscript is delivered to the printer and the final book is published, changes will be noted on the CD-ROM's readme file.

Part II
Getting to Know Adobe Acrobat

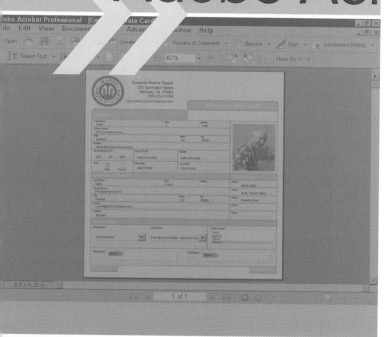

Session 1

Customizing Acrobat

Session Introduction

Acrobat authoring is performed in either Acrobat Standard or Acrobat Professional. In both programs you have many tools used for editing and modifying PDF documents. Tools are loaded from menu commands and docked in the Toolbar Well. Before you can begin an editing session, you need to know how to access tools and change preference settings. In this chapter you learn how to manage tools and set up your work environment.

TOOLS YOU'LL USE
Toolbar Well, Default toolbars, Advanced Editing toolbar, Commenting toolbar, Advanced Commenting toolbar, Navigation toolbar, Properties Bar, Default task buttons, eBooks task button, How To pane, Preferences dialog box, and the Hand tool.

<NOTE>
All the steps in each tutorial for this session can be performed in either Acrobat Standard or Acrobat Professional. All screen shots are taken with Acrobat Professional. When differences between the applications occur, they are reported in the tutorial's text.

CD-ROM FILES NEEDED
01_annualReportTab.pdf and 01_ceoLetter.pdf (found in the Sessions/Session01/Tutorial01 folder). Completed versions of each tutorial can be found in the Session01 folder inside the Tutorial01_finals folder.

TIME REQUIRED
90 minutes

Tutorial
» Getting to Know the Acrobat Tools

Acrobat has a number of tools that appear in the top level Toolbar Well as a default when you open the program. The tools are nested in different toolbars that can be removed (undocked) from the Toolbar Well. Additional tools are accessible from menu commands and are accessed by opening a context menu. In this tutorial you learn how to manage toolbars from menu commands and a context menu.

1. **Mount the CD–ROM located in the back of this book. Drag the folder called Session01 from inside the Sessions folder to your desktop.**

2. **Open your Program Files folder (Windows) or your Applications Folder (Macintosh). Open the Acrobat 6.0 folder (Windows) or the Adobe Acrobat 6.0 (Professional or Standard) folder (Macintosh). In Windows, open the Acrobat folder and double-click the** acrobat.exe **file. On the Macintosh, double-click the Acrobat 6.0 (Professional or Standard) program icon.** Acrobat launches.

< T I P >
In Windows, a program shortcut is installed on your desktop with your Acrobat installation. To launch Acrobat, double-click the shortcut icon. On the Macintosh, drag the program icon to the Dock. A program alias is copied to the Dock. Click once on the icon in the Dock to launch Acrobat.

3. **Click the Open tool in the Acrobat Toolbar Well.**
   The Open dialog box appears. In this dialog box you navigate your hard drive to find the location of the file you want to open. Navigation in the Open dialog box works like any other Open dialog box you use in other programs. Move around your hard drive by selecting the Look-In pull-down menu (Windows) or the From pull-down menu (Macintosh).

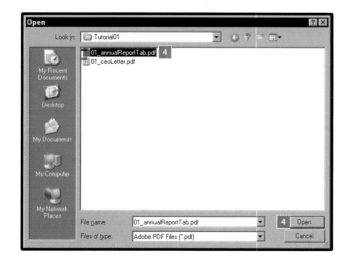

4. **Open the** 01_annualReportTab.pdf **file found in the Tutorial01 folder on your desktop. To do so, select the file and click the Open button in the Open dialog box.**
   The Session01 folder contains three folders. One folder is named Tutorial01, one folder is named Tutorial01_finish, and a third folder is named Tutorial01_finals. The Tutorial01 folder contains the raw PDF files you use in your tutorials. The Tutorial01_finish folder is used for files you edit in Acrobat and save. The Tutorial01_finals folder contains finished documents that show you the results of the tutorial steps. Use files found in this folder to compare your work. For this first session the Tutorial01_finish and Tutorial01_finals folders do not contain any files because you are not instructed to save a document in any tutorial.

5. When the file opens in Acrobat, you see the document in the Acrobat Window. The area where the document appears is called the Document pane.

6. To the right of the Document pane is the How To pane.

7. At the top of the Document pane is the Toolbar Well.

8. To the left of the Document pane is the Navigation pane where palette tabs are opened and closed. By default, the Navigation pane is collapsed when you open the tutorial file.

9. Click the Hide button to hide the How To pane.
   When you want to see a larger document view in the Document pane, you can hide the How To pane. Most often when editing in Acrobat, hiding the How To pane enables you to work more efficiently on documents.

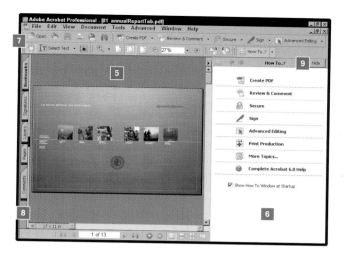

10. Select the Dynamic Zoom tool. From the Zoom toolbar in the Toolbar Well, click the down-pointing arrow to open a menu. Choose the Dynamic Zoom tool.

<NOTE>

The pull-down menu shown in the figure above contains five tools. The Loupe tool and Pan & Zoom Window are available only in Acrobat Professional. The Zoom In, Zoom Out, and Dynamic Zoom tools are available in Acrobat Professional as well as Acrobat Standard and Adobe Reader.

Expanding Toolbars

As you look at the toolbars in the Acrobat Toolbar Well, notice that several toolbars contain down-pointing arrows. Clicking such an arrow opens a pull-down menu. Additional tools can be selected from the menu items in each pull-down menu. The last item at the bottom of a pull-down is a command that expands the toolbar and shows all tools related to the toolbar in question. In the Zoom toolbar, the last item in the pull-down menu is Show Zoom Toolbar.

Select this command and the Zoom toolbar expands to show all the tools contained in the toolbar. When you expand a toolbar, it appears as a separate toolbar outside the Toolbar Well. Click the Close button marked by an X in the top-right corner of the toolbar (Windows) or the top-left corner of the toolbar (Macintosh) to hide the toolbar.

11. **Click and drag the Dynamic Zoom tool in the Document pane.**
    As you click and drag up, the document page zooms in. As you click and drag down, the document page zooms out. Practice zooming in and out of the page. Note that this tool requires you to click, keep the mouse button pressed, and then drag up or down to zoom in and out. You use other tools you select in toolbars by clicking the document page without dragging the mouse.

12. **Zoom in on the document page using the Dynamic Zoom tool. Select the Hand tool. Click and drag using the Hand tool.**
    The document page moves around the Document pane. The default tool when you open Acrobat is the Hand tool. Use this tool to move documents around the Document pane or when you want to click navigational buttons.

13. **Click the Fit Page tool.**
    The three tools adjacent to the Zoom tool pull-down menu are used to zoom in and out of a document page at different zoom levels. The first tool (beginning on the left side) is used to zoom to an actual size (100% view); the second tool (the Fit Page tool) results in fitting a page as large as can be seen in the Document pane without cutting off the edges. The third tool, called the Fit Width tool, fits the width of a page to the Document pane irrespective of the vertical size. Notice that the use of these tools requires you to click without dragging the mouse.

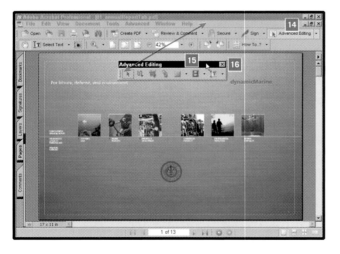

14. **Click the Advanced Editing task button to open the Advanced Editing toolbar.**
    Notice that the toolbar pops up in the Acrobat Window. The toolbar is referred to as a *floating* toolbar.

15. **Click and drag the toolbar to any location in the Acrobat Window.**
    To move the toolbar, you need to click the black title bar and drag to a new location. Clicking below the title bar selects a tool.

16. **Hide the Advanced Editing toolbar. Click the Close button in the top-right corner of the toolbar (Windows) or top-left corner of the toolbar (Macintosh).**
    The toolbar hides from view. To regain the toolbar, you click again on the Advanced Editing task button.

17. **Choose View→Toolbars. Move the cursor to the submenu and choose Advanced Editing.**

    The Advanced Editing toolbar opens as a floating toolbar in the Acrobat Window. Notice that toolbars are also accessed by menu commands. The Advanced Editing toolbar is accessed by clicking the Advanced Editing task button or by selecting the Advanced Editing menu command.

18. **Choose View→Toolbars→Advanced Commenting. The Advanced Commenting toolbar opens. Continue opening all toolbars in the list, including the Properties Bar.**

    As you open toolbars, the toolbars that are open contain a check mark in the Toolbars submenu. Those toolbar names without check marks are not yet open.

<NOTE>

All toolbars have the same names in Acrobat Professional and Acrobat Standard with the exception of the Measuring toolbar. Only Acrobat Professional offers you measuring tools. Inasmuch as all the toolbars have the same toolbar names, there are some tools contained in Acrobat Professional toolbars that are not available in Acrobat Standard.

19. **Hide all toolbars. Choose View→Toolbars→Hide Toolbars.**

    All toolbars are hidden in the Acrobat Window. To show the toolbars, press the F8 key on your keyboard. When you press the F8 key, all toolbars return to view.

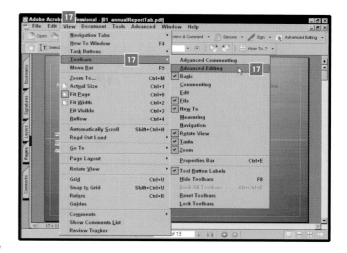

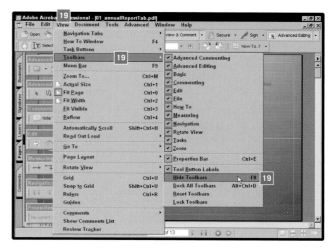

About Task Buttons and Toolbars

The Toolbar Well contains several toolbars containing an assortment of tools. In addition to the toolbars, Acrobat also provides you with task buttons contained in the Tasks toolbar that open other toolbars or offer you pull-down menu commands. Beginning with the Create PDF task button at the top of the Toolbar Well and the left side of the Tasks toolbar and continuing to the right across the toolbar to the Advanced Editing task button, you see five separate tools. Unlike other tools contained in toolbars, all of these tools can be displayed or hidden individually. Each task button contains a pull-down menu where you can choose menu commands specific to the task. You can open a toolbar for some task buttons, whereas other task buttons contain only menu commands. You open toolbars from a task button supporting a toolbar by clicking the task button. You open pull-down menus by clicking on a task button. Depending on whether the task button offers a toolbar or menu is evident when you click the button. The Tasks toolbar is opened from the View→Task Buttons submenu. You can choose to open all task buttons or hide the toolbar from this submenu. The remaining toolbars in the Acrobat Toolbar Well are accessed by choosing View→Toolbars and selecting the respective toolbar from a submenu command.

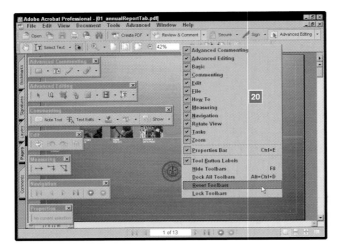

20. **Return to the default toolbars. Move the mouse cursor to an empty area where a toolbar is not displayed and right-click (Windows) or press the Control key and click (Macintosh) to open a context menu. Choose Reset Toolbars from the menu.**
At any time you want to return to the default view in the Toolbar Well, open a context menu and choose Reset Toolbars. All Acrobat versions return the toolbars back to the default position that appears when you first install the program.

21. **Open a context menu from the Toolbar Well and choose Advanced Commenting. Return to the context menu and choose Properties Bar.** Remember that a context menu is opened by right-clicking (Windows) or Control-clicking (Macintosh) the Toolbar Well. Notice that the context menu offers you the opportunity to open toolbars the same as when you choose View→Toolbars and make submenu selections for individual toolbars.

22. **Dock the toolbars. Open a context menu from the Toolbar Well and choose Dock All Toolbars near the bottom of the menu.**
When toolbars appear in the Toolbar Well, they are said to be *docked*. When you release the mouse button after making the menu choice, the Advanced Commenting and Properties Bar toolbars are docked in the Toolbar Well.

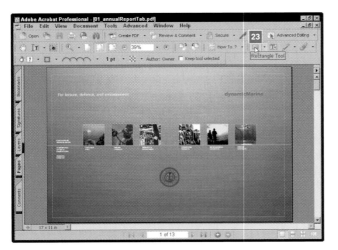

23. **Select the Rectangle tool. Its the red square in the Advanced Commenting toolbar.**
The Rectangle tool is a commenting tool and appears in the Advanced Commenting toolbar. Notice when you select a tool, the Properties Bar expands and offers you options choices from additional tools and pull-down menus related to the selected tool.

24. **Open a context menu by right-clicking (Control-clicking on the Macintosh). Choose Reset Toolbars.**

25. Choose View→Task Buttons→eBooks.

By default, all task buttons are visible in the Tasks toolbar except the eBooks task button. Notice when you select the task buttons menu, the submenu shows all task buttons. You can return to this menu to show and hide the task buttons.

26. Choose View→Task Buttons→eBooks again to hide this task button.

The eBooks task button disappears from the Tasks toolbar.

27. Drag a toolbar away from the Toolbar Well. Click the vertical bar adjacent to the left side of the Create PDF task button, hold the mouse button down, and drag away from the Toolbar Well.

Toolbars can be manually *undocked* from the Toolbar Well by clicking a *separator* bar along the left side of the toolbar and dragging it away from the Toolbar Well. The separator bar appears as a vertical blind on the left side of each toolbar. Conversely, toolbars can also be *docked* back into the Toolbar Well by dragging the separator bar on a toolbar and releasing the mouse button when a toolbar is positioned over the Toolbar Well.

28. Dock the Tasks toolbar. Click and hold the mouse button down on the separator bar and drag the toolbar to the Toolbar Well. Release the mouse button and drop the toolbar into the Well.

If you drag the toolbar to an empty area on the Toolbar Well, the toolbar drops into the same line as the target area. If you drag a toolbar to the Toolbar Well and see a black vertical line appear between rows of toolbars, the toolbar is dropped between two rows. You can dock toolbars above or below any existing toolbars.

29. Open a context menu on the Toolbar Well and choose Lock Toolbars from the menu.

When you lock toolbars, notice that the separator bars disappear. When toolbars are locked, you cannot move them from the Toolbar Well. If toolbars are floating in the Acrobat Window, the toolbars remain unlocked. This feature applies only to toolbars docked in the Toolbar Well.

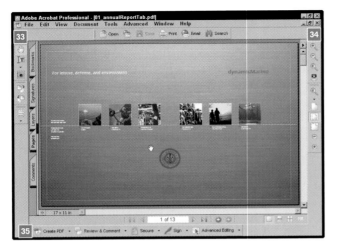

30. **Open a context menu on the Toolbar Well and choose Lock Toolbars to deselect the item (remove the check) from the menu options.**
Notice the separator bars reappear; the toolbars are now unlocked.

31. **Open a context menu on the Toolbar Well and choose Tool Button Labels.**
When you choose Tool Button Labels, the tool names disappear from the toolbars. You might hide labels when loading several toolbars to conserve room and keep the Toolbar Well small. The more toolbars you add to the Toolbar Well, the more room you lose for viewing document pages.

32. **Open a context menu and choose Tool Button Labels.**
Notice when you reopen the context menu, Tool Button Labels is unchecked. Choosing the menu command again places a check mark adjacent to the menu name. Check marks denote that a menu item is active.

33. **Click and drag a toolbar to the far left side of the Acrobat Window.**

34. **Drag another toolbar to the far right side of the Acrobat Window.**

35. **Drag a third toolbar to the bottom of the Acrobat Window.**
When you drag to any one of the three sides away from the Toolbar Well, be certain to drag a toolbar to the far-most edge of any side of the Acrobat Window. When you release the mouse button, the toolbar is docked to the target edge. If your workflow is better suited to using toolbars contained in areas other than the Toolbar Well, Acrobat affords you many options for docking toolbars.

36. **Open a context menu on the Toolbar Well and click Reset Toolbars.**
Note that when toolbars are docked on any side of the Acrobat Window, the Dock Toolbars menu command is grayed out. Acrobat considers a toolbar docked whether the toolbar is on the left, right, or bottom of the Acrobat Window and not appearing as a floating toolbar.

37. **Choose File→Close or click the Close button in the top-right corner (Windows) or top-left corner (Macintosh). If you are prompted to save the file, choose No.**

38. **Click the How To tool.**
The How To pane reopens and the view in the Acrobat Window returns to the original default view when you first opened the program.

<NOTE>
If you want to pause and take a rest, you can quit Acrobat and re-launch the program to follow the steps in the next tutorial.

Tutorial

» Getting Help in Acrobat

When you first launch Acrobat, a pane on the right side of the Acrobat Window appears in view. The pane is called the How To pane and it is used for quick access to help information. Acrobat offers you help information on several common topics. If you need help with one of the items listed in the How To pane, click an item and the pane contents change to display help information. In addition to the help options available in the How To pane, you can also access the complete Acrobat help guide where you can search topics and read help information. Help is only a click away in any Acrobat viewer. In this tutorial you learn how to obtain help from within your Acrobat viewer.

1. **Click the blue Create PDF button in the How To pane.**

   If you quit Acrobat, re-launch the program. By default the How To pane should open in view. If the pane is not visible, click the How To tool in the Acrobat Toolbar Well. Note that no document needs to be open when accessing help guides.

2. **Click the blue text *Create a PDF from a file*.**

   Another screen appears in the How To pane. The pane lists a step-by-step sequence for converting document files to PDF files. The window is scrolled by clicking on the down-pointing arrow at the bottom of the pane or by dragging the scroll bar on the right side of the pane.

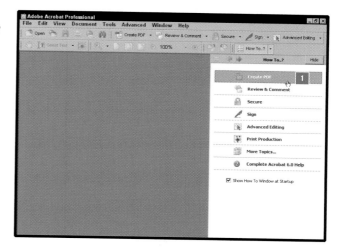

3. **Click the Back Button in the How To pane's toolbar.**

   The tools at the top of the How To pane enable you to navigate back and forth between views. On the top-left side of the toolbar is the Home Page button. Click this button to return to the opening page of the How To pane.

4. **Click the Home Page button.**

   You are returned to the How To pane home page.

5. **Click the text: *More Topics*.**

   The How To pane changes view. The list of topics are links to help information on assorted topics not covered when the home page is in view. Click any topic and step-by-step instructions are provided to guide you through different editing tasks.

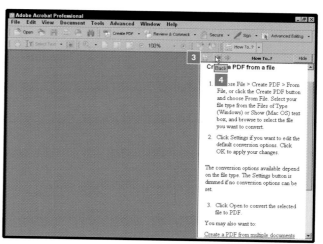

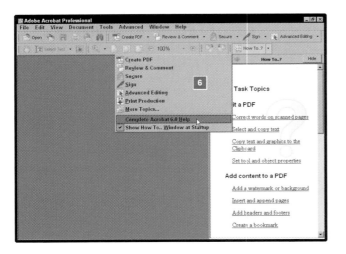

6. **Select the down-pointing arrow adjacent to the How To tool to open a pull-down menu. Select Complete Acrobat 6.0 Help from the menu.**

Inasmuch as the How To pane provides easy access to help information, the Complete Acrobat 6.0 Help is like a user guide that provides help on using tools, menus, and all the features available in your Acrobat viewer. The Complete Acrobat 6.0 Help document is a PDF document opening in a special Acrobat viewer window that opens on top of the Acrobat Window. You can click bookmarks in the guide to link to pages that are bookmarked, search for keywords to quickly find help on features, or open the document index to see an alphabetical listing of keywords that link to respective pages.

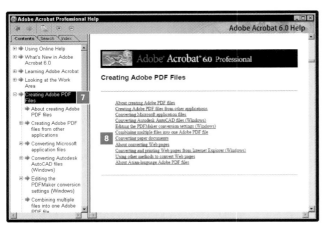

7. **Click Creating Adobe PDF Files in the Contents tab.**

The page changes in the help document Document pane to a contents page where links appear. The links open respective pages related to creating PDF documents from files. Click any link and the pages offer you a description for performing tasks used to convert files to PDF.

8. **Click Converting Paper Documents in the contents list.**

A page opens describing how to convert paper documents to PDF using a scanner along with the Adobe Paper Capture plug-in.

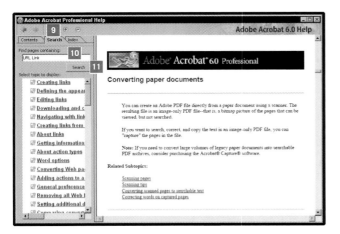

9. **Click the Search tab.**

The Search pane opens on the left side of the help document.

10. **Type URL Link in the Find Pages Containing box at the top of the Search pane.**

11. **Click the Search button.**

The search results are listed in the search pane. Click any item and the document pane changes to the page associated with the link.

12. Click the Index tab.

The index pane opens. The alpha characters appear in the list with a plus (+) symbol (Windows) or right-pointing arrow (Macintosh). Click the symbol/arrow and a list of topics open in a hierarchical order. If additional symbols/arrows appear, click them to expand the hierarchy. The relationship between the higher order items is referred to as a parent item. The items nested below parent topics are referred to as child items. Thus, you see a parent/child relationship in the pane when a plus(+) or right arrow exists adjacent to the text.

13. Click the plus symbol (Windows) or right-pointing arrow (Macintosh) next to the letter _C_ in the list.

The list expands displaying all index items begining with the letter C.

<NOTE>

When you click the plus (+) symbol, the symbol changes to a minus (-) (Windows). When you click a right-pointing arrow, the arrow changes to a down-pointing arrow (Macintosh).

14. Click the item called Case Sensitive (searches) in the index list.

Notice that when you click an item that contains child elements below the item, the list is expanded the same as when clicking a plus (+) or right-pointing arrow.

15. Click the text: _Doing a simple search of a document._

The Document pane in the Help document jumps to the page associated with the index item. To navigate back and forth between pages, click the arrows at the top of the help document.

16. Click the Print Topic tool in the help document.

The Print dialog box opens with the page range pre-selected from the page viewed in the help document. If you want a printed copy of the help information, click OK in the print dialog box.

17. Click Cancel in the Print dialog box.

18. Click the Close box in the help document.

The document closes.

<TIP>

If at any time during your progress through the tutorials in this book you feel confused or want more information on a given topic, open the Complete Acrobat 6.0 Help file. Click the Search tab and search for the information you want. Read over the help information to extend your Acrobat learning beyond what the tutorials offer you.

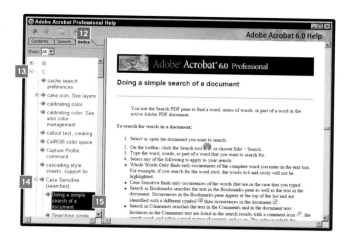

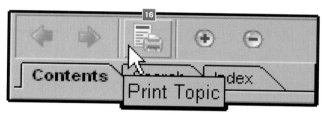

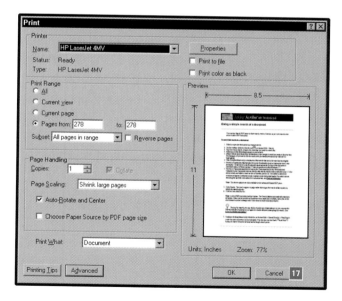

<NOTE>

Be certain your printer is properly configured and that you can print from Acrobat before attempting to print pages in the help document.

Tutorial

» Customizing Your Work Environment

With just a few tutorials covered thus far you should have a feel for the complexity of Adobe Acrobat and understand that there are a great number of tools to help you with many editing tasks. As you progress through the tutorials ahead, you'll want to customize your Acrobat work environment to suit the needs of each lesson. In this tutorial, you learn how to set up an environment for a specific editing job.

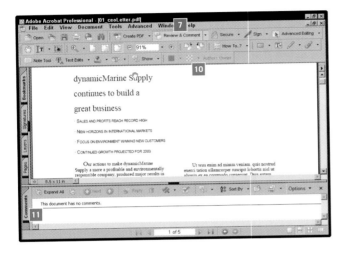

<NOTE>
When you begin a new session and open a toolbar, a floating toolbar opens. If you dock the toolbar using the context menu command or by dragging it, the toolbar docks in the Toolbar Well. If you close the toolbar and reopen it, the toolbar opens in the last state (in this case docked in the Toolbar Well).

<NOTE>
The first steps in many tutorials in the remaining sessions are devoted to setting up your work environment. Follow the steps to open the tools needed for editing sessions, and you can follow the remaining tutorial steps without struggling to find tools and palettes.

1. **Click the How To button to open the How To pane if it is not already open.**

2. **Uncheck the Show How To Window at Startup check box at the bottom of the How To pane.**
   More often than not, you'll want to keep the How To pane out of view to provide more viewing room for documents in the Acrobat Document pane. When you need to access help in the How To pane, click the How To button.

3. **Quit Acrobat. Re-launch the program.**
   As you re-launch the program, notice the How To pane is now hidden from view.

4. **Choose File→Open or click the Open tool in the Toolbar Well.**
   The Open dialog box appears.

5. **From the Tutorial01 folder, select** 01_ceoLetter.pdf.

6. **Click Open in the Open dialog box.**
   The document that opens in the Acrobat Document pane is a draft file that was designed for feedback from co-workers. To solicit feedback from other co-workers, the PDF author intends to use an e-mail-based review.

7. **Click the Review & Comment task button.**
   The Basic Commenting toolbar opens as a floating toolbar in the Acrobat Window.

8. **Open the pull-down menu on the Review and Comment task button and choose the Advanced Commenting toolbar.**
   The Advanced Commenting toolbar automatically docks in the Acrobat Toolbar Well.

9. **Open a context menu from the Toolbar Well and choose the Properties Bar.**
   In most editing sessions you'll find the Properties Bar helpful for changing attributes or editing text and objects.

10. **Drag the Properties Bar to the Toolbar Well.**

11. **Click the Comments tab to open the Comments palette.**
    Along the left side of the Acrobat Window are tabs that contain menus and tools to extend your Acrobat editing sessions.

12. **Close the document without saving.**

Tutorial

» Setting Preferences

In addition to opening tools and palettes for an editing session, the preference settings for your Acrobat viewer also help you customize your viewing and editing environment. Just as there are an abundant number of tools, preference settings are extensive and offer you many options for controlling the tool and viewing behavior. If something doesn't seem to work correctly in Acrobat, you can often adjust preference settings and make changes that affect your work environment. As you work through the tutorials ahead in this book we will return to the preference settings and make changes as needed. At this time it is important to understand how to open the Preferences dialog box and how to make changes to it. In this tutorial you learn to make some preference settings changes that affect tool behavior.

1. **Choose File→Open or click the Open tool in the Toolbar Well.**
   The Open dialog box appears.

2. **From the Sesson01/Tutorial01 folder, select** 01_ceoLetter.pdf.

3. **Click Open in the Open dialog box.**

4. **Choose Edit→Preferences (Windows) or Acrobat→Preferences (Macintosh).**
   The Preferences dialog box opens. The Preferences dialog box contains two panes. On the left side of the dialog box is a pane displaying a list of different preferences categories. On the right side of the dialog box are options pertaining to the category selected in the left pane. As you select different categories in the left pane, the right pane changes to reflect options for the selected category.

5. **Click General in the left pane.**

6. **Select the down-pointing arrow for Show tool and property button labels to open a pull-down menu.**

7. **Choose All Labels from the pull-down menu.**
   The labels for tools in the Toolbar Well can be expanded to show names as well as icons for each tool. If you need some help understanding the tool names, you can view the toolbars with expanded labels. The disadvantage in showing All labels is the tools occupy more room in the Toolbar Well. If you have many tools, the amount of room left over for page viewing is diminished.

8. **Check the Use Single-Key Accelerators to Access Tools check box.**
   As you become more familiar with Acrobat you can use keyboard shortcuts to access a tool. Rather than opening a toolbar via a menu command or context menu, you can simply press a key on your keyboard to access it.

9. **Click OK to close the Preferences dialog box.**

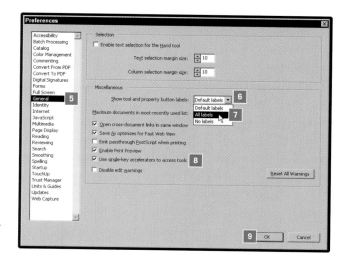

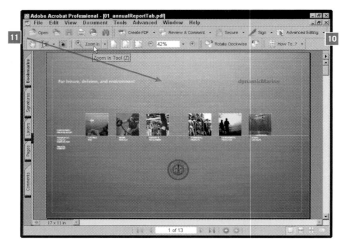

10. **Observe the Acrobat Toolbar Well.**

The tool labels are expanded. You can see the text added to the Open tool, the Zoom In tool, and the Rotate Clockwise tool. Some tools do not show the labels because Acrobat doesn't have enough room across the Toolbar Well to show all the labels.

11. **Click the separator bar for the File tools and drag away from the Toolbar Well to the Document pane.**

12. **Click the separator bar and drag the toolbar back to the Toolbar Well.**

Notice that when the toolbar is undocked from the Toolbar Well all the tool labels appear in the toolbar. By rearranging the toolbars, you can organize them so all the tool labels are in view.

13. **Press Control+K (Windows) or Command+K (Macintosh).**

The Preferences dialog box opens. As you begin new tutorials in the book, you'll be introduced to additional keyboard shortcuts that help you move along faster in your Acrobat editing sessions.

14. **Open the Show tool and property button labels pull-down menu and choose Default Labels.**

Notice that you return to the General category when you open the Preferences dialog box. Acrobat remembers your last category choice made in the left pane and continues to show the category options in the right pane until you select a new category.

15. **Click OK in the Preferences dialog box.**

16. **Press the Z key on your keyboard.**

The cursor changes to a magnifying glass with a plus symbol. The tool selected when you press the Z key on your keyboard is the Zoom tool. You can rotate through the zoom tools by pressing Shift+Z. Continue pressing Shift+Z and you see the cursor change to reflect the current selected tool.

17. **Press the H key on your keyboard.**

The cursor displays the Hand icon. When you press the H key, you return to the Hand tool. As a matter of first order for remembering keyboard shortcuts, try to commit using the H key for selecting the Hand tool to memory. You'll use this keyboard shortcut throughout the remaining sessions in the book.

< T I P >

To quickly access a reference for keyboard shortcuts, position the cursor over any tool in the Toolbar Well. Pause momentarily and a tooltip displays the tool name and the keyboard shortcut within parentheses. For example, when you position the cursor over the Hand tool, the tooltip pops up and displays: *Hand Tool (H)*. Press the character in the parentheses to access the tool with a keyboard shortcut.

» Session Review

This session covered the basics for getting familiar with customizing your work environment. You learned some of the relationships between tools, menus, and preferences. Answer the following questions to review your work. Answers for each question are found in the tutorial noted in parentheses.

1. How do you access a toolbar not in view in the Toolbar Well? (See Tutorial: Getting to Know the Acrobat Tools.)

2. Name two ways for docking toolbars in the Toolbar Well. (See Tutorial: Getting to Know the Acrobat Tools.)

3. How do you undock a toolbar from the Toolbar Well? (See Tutorial: Getting to Know the Acrobat Tools.)

4. How do you move a floating toolbar around the Acrobat Window? (See Tutorial: Getting to Know the Acrobat Tools.)

5. What happens when you lock toolbars? (See Tutorial: Getting to Know the Acrobat Tools.)

6. How do you return to a default view of the Toolbar Well? (See Tutorial: Getting to Know the Acrobat Tools.)

7. Which toolbar adds properties choices for other tools? (See Tutorial: Getting to Know the Acrobat Tools.)

8. What is the How To pane used for? (See Tutorial: Getting Help in Acrobat.)

9. How do you prevent the How To pane from opening when you launch Acrobat? (See Tutorial: Getting Help in Acrobat.)

10. How do you obtain help information on any topic? (See Tutorial: Getting Help in Acrobat.)

11. How do you expand a palette? (See Tutorial: Customizing Your Work Environment.)

12. How do you expand tool labels? (See Tutorial: Customizing Your Work Environment.)

13. How can you quickly observe a keyboard shortcut to access a tool? (See Tutorial: Customizing Your Work Environment.)

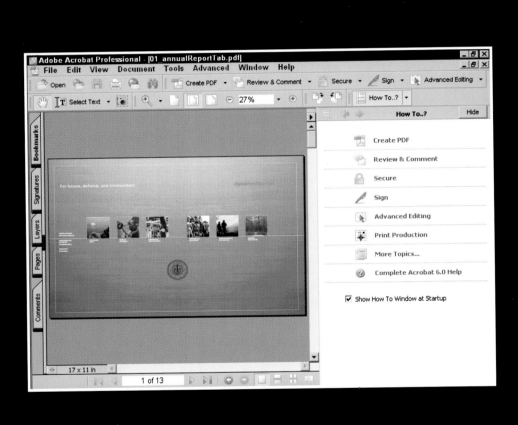

Session 2

Opening and Saving Files

Session Introduction

As you work in many Acrobat sessions, you might have a need to open several files and manage document views to work between files. After you complete editing your documents, you'll want to update your files and optimize them for the smallest file sizes. In this session you learn how to open PDF documents and save them.

TOOLS YOU'LL USE
Toolbar Well, the default toolbars, Open tool, Create PDF from Multiple Files command, Save tool, Save As command, and the Preferences dialog box.

< N O T E >
All the steps in each tutorial for this session can be performed in either Acrobat Standard or Acrobat Professional. All screen shots are taken with Acrobat Professional.

CD-ROM FILES NEEDED
02_boat.tif, 02_pulley.tif, 02_telescope.tif, 02_ceoLetterDraft.pdf, 02_employeeManual.pdf, 02_financialReport.pdf, 02_dynamicMarineLogo.ai, arrowLt.tif, arrowLtRollover.tif, arrowRt.tif, and arrowRtRollover.tif.

Tutorial files are found in the Sessions/Session02/Tutorial02 folder on the CD-ROM. Completed versions of each tutorial are found in the Sessions/Session02/Tutorial02_finals folder.

TIME REQUIRED
90 minutes

Tutorial
» Opening and Closing Documents

Acrobat has many tools and menu commands you can use to achieve the same results. With regard to opening files, you can use a tool, two menu commands, or the keyboard shortcuts. In this tutorial you learn how to open individual PDF documents and files saved in formats other than PDF.

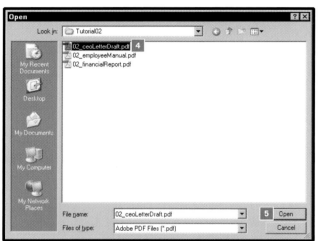

1. **Mount the CD–ROM located in the back of this book. Drag the folder called Session02 from inside the Sessions folder to your desktop.**

2. **Launch Acrobat.**

3. **Choose File→Open.**

4. **Select the file** 02_ceoLetterDraft.pdf **from the Tutorial02 folder.**

5. **Click the Open button.**

6. **Choose File→Close.**
   The PDF file closes.

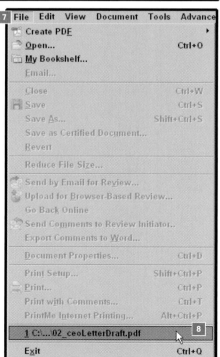

7. **Click File (Windows) or File→Open Recent Files (Mac).**
   Notice that the filename of your recently opened file appears at the bottom of the File menu (Windows) or at the bottom of the submenu (Macintosh). The total number of documents that can be displayed in the File menu (Windows) or the Recent Files submenu (Macintosh) is 10. This number is user-defined in the Preferences dialog box. For information about setting preferences for recently viewed files, see the tutorial called "Setting Preferences" later in this chapter.

8. **Select** 02_ceoLetterDraft.pdf.
   The file reopens in the Document pane.

9. **Press Control+W (Windows) or Command+W (Macintosh).**
   The open file closes. You also close documents by choosing File→Close or by clicking the Close button (X) in the top-right corner of the Acrobat Window (Windows) or by clicking the top-left circle icon (Macintosh).

10. **Click the Open tool.**

    You can also choose File→Open or press Control+O (Windows) or Command+O (Macintosh) to access the Open dialog box.

11. **Select** `02_ceoLetterDraft.pdf`. **Press the Shift key and click the last file,** `02_financialReport.pdf`, **as well.**

    When you select a file in the Open dialog box, press the Shift key, and then click another file, all the files listed between the selected files are selected as well. If you want to select files randomly in a non-contiguous order, press the Control key (Windows) or Command key (Macintosh) and click each file you want to add to the selection.

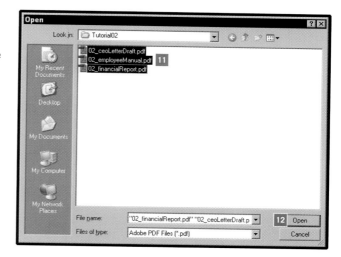

12. **Click the Open menu.**

    All the selected files open in the Document pane. The documents open on top of each other with the first file selected in the Open dialog box appearing in the foreground.

13. **Click the Window menu.**

14. **Select** `02_financialReport.pdf`.

    The document you select in the list of open documents appearing at the bottom of the Window menu moves to the front of the Document pane. You can open a maximum of 20 documents simultaneously in any Acrobat viewer. The total number of documents that can be shown in the Window menu is also 20.

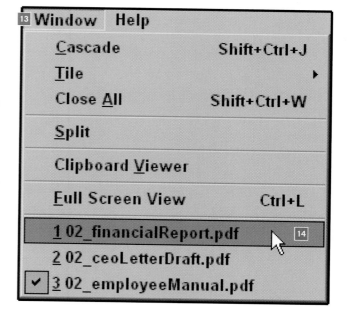

15. **Press Shift+Control+W (Windows) or Shift+Command+W (Macintosh).**

    All open documents close. You can also close all open documents by choosing Window→Close All. Note that closing a single document from a menu command is handled from the File menu, whereas closing multiple documents is handled from the Window menu.

Tutorial
» Opening Files Saved in Different Formats

The Open command can be used to open files other than PDF documents. When a file type is other than PDF, Acrobat performs a file conversion from the original file format to PDF format and then opens the file in the Document pane. Not all file formats can be converted to PDF, but Acrobat does support a wide range of original authoring formats. This tutorial sticks to converting image file formats to PDF using the Open command; you learn more about conversion to PDF from other file formats using different commands in Part III.

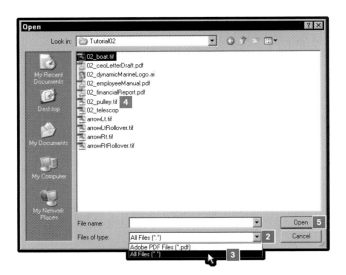

1. **Click the Open tool to access the Open dialog box.**
   Remember you can also use Control+O (Windows) or Command+O (Macintosh) or choose File➜Open to achieve the same result.

2. **Click the down-pointing arrow for Files of Type (Windows) or Show (Macintosh) to open a pull-down menu.**

3. **Click All Files.**
   The default file format shown in the pull-down menu is Adobe PDF Files (*.pdf) (Windows) or Adobe PDF Files (Macintosh). When the default menu command is selected, only Adobe PDF files appear in the Open dialog box. When you select All Files (*.*), all files in a given folder are displayed in the Open dialog box. Only certain file types can be opened in Acrobat. If you attempt to open a file type not supported by Acrobat, a dialog box shows you a message informing you the file type is either not supported or the file has been corrupted.

4. **Select** 02_pulley.tif.

5. **Click the Open button.**

6. **The file is converted to PDF and opens in the Document pane.**

7. **Press Control+W (Windows) or Command+W (Macintosh).**

8. **Click No in the dialog box that asks if you want to save changes before closing the file.**

9. **Click the Open tool.**

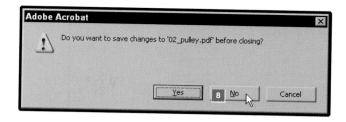

10. **Click All Files from the pull-down menu for Files of Type (Windows) or Show (Macintosh).**

11. **Click** 02_boat.tif.

12. **Control-click (Windows) or Command-click (Macintosh) the** 02_dynamicMarineLogo.ai **file.**

13. **Control-click (Windows) or Command-click (Macintosh) the** 02_pulley.tif **and** 02_telescope.tif **files.**

14. **Click the Open button.**
    The four files are converted to PDF and open as separate documents in the Document pane.

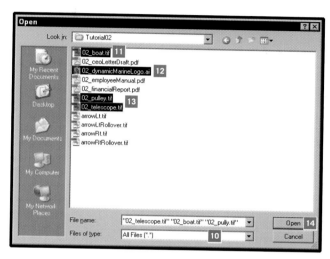

15. **Click the Window menu.**
    Notice the four documents appear at the bottom of the Window menu. The files are listed according to the filename used when the file was saved.

16. **Press Shift+Control+W (Windows) or Shift+Command+W (Macintosh).**

17. **Click No in the warning dialog box asking if you want to save the file. Repeat clicking No until all the files are closed.**
    Acrobat prompts you to save each file. You need to successively click No in the warning dialog box to close each file without saving.

Tutorial
» Saving Files

Like almost any program you use on Windows or on Macintosh OS X, you save files from the Save command in the File menu. As you edit PDF documents, the files become bulky and store more information than necessary each time you save the file. When you rewrite a file to your hard drive, Acrobat compresses the file and produces a smaller PDF. In this tutorial you learn the differences between using the Save and Save As commands.

1. **Click the Create PDF task button.**
   When you click the Create PDF task button, a pull-down menu opens. The menu commands are used for converting different file types to PDF. When you convert an image file to PDF, the same result occurs as when using the Open command.

2. **Click From Multiple Files.**
   When you choose File→Open and open several non-PDF files, each file is converted to PDF as a separate document. When you use the Convert PDF From Multiple Files command, files are converted to PDF and each file appears as a separate page in a single PDF document.

   After clicking the From Multiple Files command, the Create PDF from Multiple Documents dialog box opens.

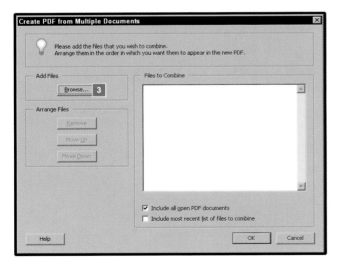

3. **Click Browse in the Create PDF from Multiple Documents dialog box.**
   Clicking the Browse button opens the Open dialog box. Use either Control/Command-click or Shift-click to select multiple files to convert to PDF.

4. **Click** `arrowLt.tif` **in the Open dialog box.**

5. **Shift-click** `arrowRtRollover.tif`.
   You should see four files selected. They selected files include: `arrowLt.tif`, `arrowLtRollover.tif`, `arrowRt.tif`, and `arrowRtRollover.tif`. Be certain that all four files are selected before proceeding.

6. **Click Add.**
   Acrobat returns you to the Create PDF from Multiple Documents dialog box. The files are listed in the Files to Combine window.

7. **Click** `arrowLt.tif`.

8. **Click the Move Up button.**
   The list you see in the Files to Combine window shows you the order for how the files will appear in the resultant PDF document. If you want to rearrange the page order, you select files in the Files to Combine window and click the Move Up or Move Down buttons.

9. **Click** `arrowLtRollover.tif`.

10. **Click the Move Up button.**

11. **Click OK.**
    The files are converted to a single PDF with the files appearing in the page order determined in the Files to Combine window.

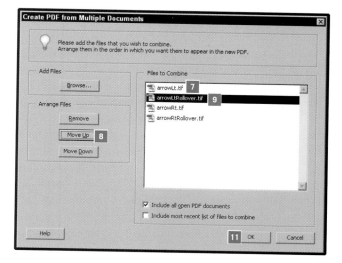

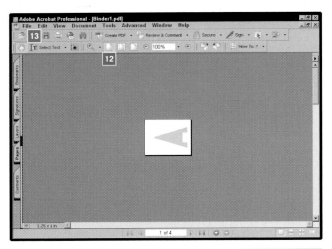

12. **Click the Actual Size tool.**

13. **Click the Save tool.**
    Notice the Status Bar at the bottom of the Acrobat window shows you that you are viewing page 1 of 4 pages.

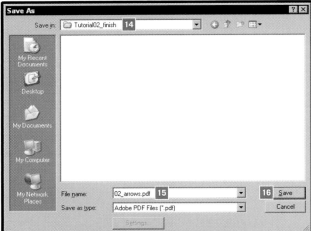

14. **Navigate to the Tutorial02_finish folder.**

15. **Type** 02_arrows.pdf **in the File name (Windows) or Save As (Macintosh) field box.**

16. **Click Save.**
    The file is saved to your hard drive in the Tutorial02_finish folder.

17. **Choose File→Close, or press Control/Command+W.**

18. **Click the Open tool, or press Control/Command+O, or choose File→Open. Navigate to the Tutorial02 folder and open** 02_employeeManual.pdf.

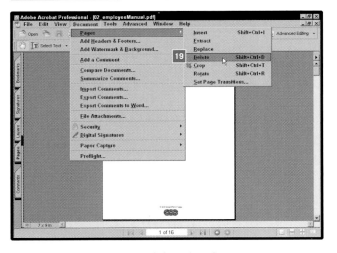

19. **Choose Document→Pages→Delete.**
    The Delete command opens the Delete Pages dialog box where you specify the pages you want to delete from a file.

20. **Click OK in the dialog box.**

    The page in view is automatically targeted for deletion in the Delete Pages dialog box. You can change the page number by entering values in the From and To boxes. In this example, the first page is targeted for deletion.

21. **Click OK in the warning dialog box that appears.**

    A warning dialog box opens asking you to confirm the deletion. Click OK and the page is deleted.

22. **Choose File→Save As.**

23. **Navigate to the TutorialO2_finish folder.**

24. **Name the file** `02_employeeManual_finish.pdf` **and click Save.**

<NOTE>

In this session you'll find a file called `02_employeeManual_finish.pdf` in the TutorialO2_finals folder and a duplcate copy of the document in the TutorialO2_finish folder. The duplicate copy is intentionally contained in the TutorialO2_finish folder to instruct you on methods and resons for overwriting existing files. If you overwrite the file and want to compare your results, compare your file to the file contained in the TutorialO2_finals folder.

25. **Click Yes in the warning box that appears.**

    A warning dialog box opens informing you that a file with the same name already exists in the folder where you are saving the document. When you click Yes, Acrobat rewrites the file and optimizes it for the smallest file size. If you click the Save button, the file is not optimized.

26. **Choose File→Close or press Control/Command+W.**

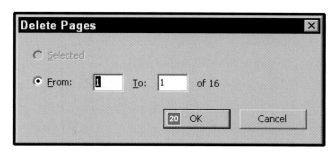

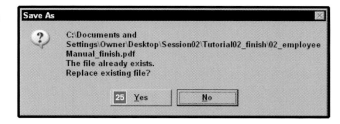

Optimizing PDF Documents

As you add or delete pages or add or remove data from pages, Acrobat keeps track of your edits. Each time you click File→Save, the file is updated to save the current edits. The Save command, however, keeps redundant and unnecessary information, which results in larger file sizes. If you make frequent edits, use the Save As command. When you use Save As and overwrite a file with the same name, the file is completely rewritten and optimized, resulting in a smaller file size.

You are forced to use Save As and rewrite the file to your hard drive. This behavior is a method of reminding you to use Save As

and rewrite a file to optimize it. Acrobat keeps unnecessary data in a PDF file each time you save the file to update your edits. When you use Save As, the unnecessary data is eliminated from the file. As a matter of practice, you should use File→Save As as a last step in an editing session to be certain your saved file is optimized and results in the smallest file size.

Tutorial
» Setting Preferences

You have options for choosing among a few preferences that relate to opening and saving files. The preferences enable you to customize your work sessions in regards to the number of files you keep in view as recent files and using optimum settings for reducing file sizes. Be certain to visit the Preferences dialog box regularly to double-check your settings.

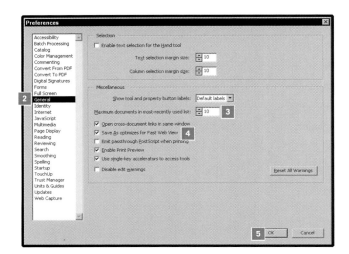

1. **Choose Edit→Preferences (Windows) or Acrobat→Preferences (Macintosh).**
   You can also use Control+K (Windows) or Command+K (Macintosh) to access the Preferences dialog box.

2. **Click General.**

3. **Type 10 in the Maximum Documents in Most-Recently Used List box.**
   The default number of documents that appear in the most-recently used list is five. You can edit the field box by typing values from 1 to 10. This preference is used for your own personal needs. If the menu list is too long for your monitor to comfortably display a long list of files, change the value according to what looks best to you.

4. **Ensure that the Save As Optimizes for Fast Web View box is checked.**
   By default the check box is enabled. If you find that the check box is disabled, be certain to check the box. When you use File→Save As, the file is optimized resulting in the smallest file size.

5. **Click OK.**

» Session Review

This session covers opening, closing, and saving files. You learned how to open PDF documents, convert image formatted files to PDF, and how to combine files to produce a single PDF document with multiple pages. You learned how to save files and how to rewrite files to optimize them. You learned about a few preference options related to viewing recently viewed documents and optimizing files to produce the smallest file sizes. Answers for each of the following questions are found in the tutorial noted in parentheses.

1. How do you open several PDF documents listed in a non-contiguous order? (See Tutorial: Opening and Closing Documents.)

2. How do you move a document forward in the Document pane when several files are open in Acrobat? (See Tutorial: Opening and Closing Documents.)

3. How do you open the last viewed file without using the Open tool or Open menu commands? (See Tutorial: Opening and Closing Documents.)

4. Which dialog box is used to open several files and combine them in a single PDF document? (See Tutorial: Opening Files Saved in Different Formats.)

5. How do you change the page order of files combined into a single PDF document before the PDF file is created? (See Tutorial: Opening Files Saved in Different Formats.)

6. Name three tools and/or menu options used for saving PDF documents. (See Tutorial: Saving Files.)

7. When are the Save tool and the Save menu item disabled? (See Tutorial: Saving Files.)

8. How do you rewrite a PDF file? (See Tutorial: Saving Files.)

9. How do you determine the number of recently viewed files that appear in a menu? (See Tutorial: Setting Preferences.)

10. How do you determine whether your files are optimized when using the Save As command? (See Tutorial: Setting Preferences.)

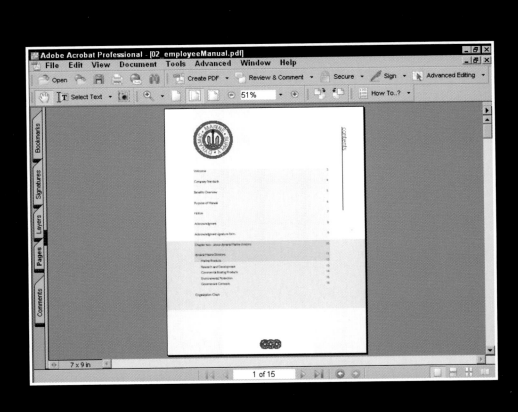

Viewing and Navigating PDF Files

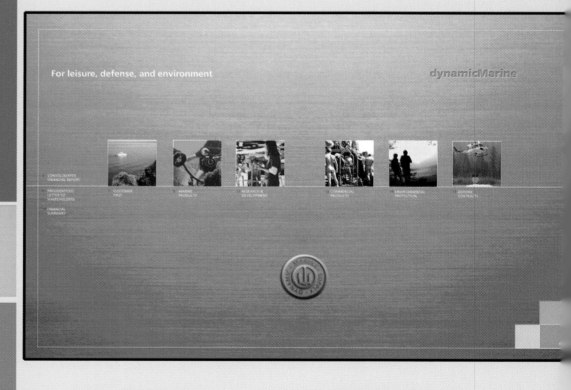

Tutorial: **Using Page Viewing Tools**

Tutorial: **Saving Initial Views**

Tutorial: **Using Zoom Tools**

Tutorial: **Using the Pages Palette**

Tutorial: **Working with Bookmarks**

Session Introduction

Navigating through a PDF document and between several PDF files are tasks you will perform frequently. Acrobat provides you with many viewing options to help you scroll through pages and facilitate editing your PDFs. The more you know about all of Acrobat's viewing options, the faster you can move through the editing phases. In this session you learn many ways to view PDF files in Acrobat viewers.

TOOLS YOU'LL USE

Navigation tools, Zoom tools, Hand tool, Window menu, Status Bar, Page Layout tools, Pages palette, and Bookmarks palette.

CD-ROM FILES NEEDED

03_annualReport.pdf, 03_employeeManual.pdf, and 03_employeeManualBookmarks.pdf.

Tutorial files are found in the Sessions/Session03/Tutorial03 folder on the CD-ROM. Completed versions of each tutorial are found in the Sessions/Session03/Tutorial03_finals folder.

TIME REQUIRED

2 hours

Tutorial
» Using Page Viewing Tools

Acrobat offers you many ways to display PDF documents in the Document pane. You might want to view multiple documents during an editing session, change different view options, or navigate quickly through PDF pages. In this tutorial you'll learn how to view PDFs in the Document pane and understand how Acrobat treats many display options.

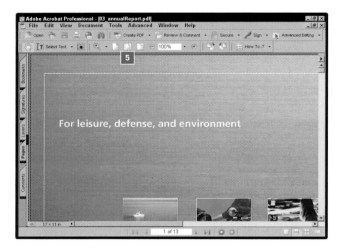

1. **Mount the CD–ROM located in the back of this book.**

2. **Drag the Session03 folder from inside the Sessions folder to your desktop.**

3. **Launch Acrobat.**

4. **Choose File→Open or click the Open tool. Open the 03_annuaReport.pdf document in the Tutorial03 folder.**
   When the PDF document is open, the document is displayed at the default view in the Document pane. Depending on how the open view options were established by the PDF author, the view can be zoomed in to a large view or zoomed out to a smaller view. As you view PDFs, you can change the view after opening the file.

   <NOTE>
   Depending on your monitor resolution and size of your monitor, your view in an Actual Size view (100%), Fit Page view, and other views may appear differently than the figures used in this tutorial. All figures for this book were taken on a monitor with the resolution set to 800x600.

5. **Press Control/Command+0 or click the Fit Page tool.**
   The default view for the open document is set to a 100% view. The zoom for the view is an Actual Size view. If you want to view the PDF with pages completely in view in the Document pane, you can change the view with keyboard shortcuts. Control/Command+0 is a keystroke combination you'll use frequently to change the view to a Fit Page view, whereby the entire page fits within the Document pane.

   <NOTE>
   Fit Page can also be applied with a tool in the Zoom toolbar. Click the Page icon appearing in the middle of the three page icons in the Zoom toolbar to view the open file in a Fit Page view. If you place the cursor over an icon and pause briefly, a tooltip displays text indicating which tool is used when you click the mouse button.

6. **Click the down arrow located below the scroll bar on the right side of the Acrobat window several times to scroll the page.**
   When the page changes to a new page, notice the page break in the document is visible in the Document pane. The current view is set for a Continuous view. Acrobat provides you with several page layout view options that can be changed in a menu command or in the Status Bar.

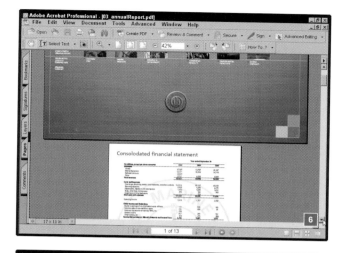

7. **Click the Continuous Facing Pages tool in the Status Bar.**

8. **Press the Page Down key on your keyboard to scroll pages.**
   Notice the Document pane displays the PDF with facing pages.

9. **Click the Single Page tool in the Status Bar.**
   Notice the pages snap to a single page view in the Document pane.

10. **Click the Next Page tool in the Status Bar to navigate to the second page.**

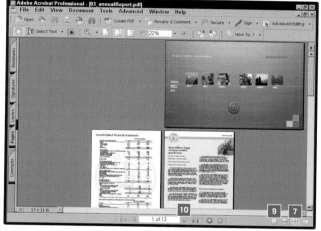

11. **Open a context menu by right-clicking (Windows) or Control-clicking (Macintosh). Choose Next Page.**
    Notice you can navigate through pages forward and back using the context menu commands.

12. **Click the Last Page tool in the Status Bar.**
    The last page in the PDF file opens.

13. **Click the Close button (top-right corner of the document window) to close the document. (Top-left corner of the document window on Macintosh.)**

14. **Click the Open tool and open the** 03_employeeManual.pdf **file from the Session03 folder.**

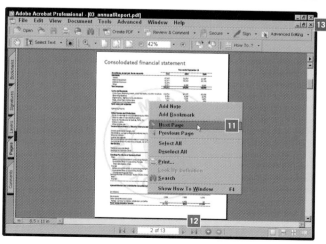

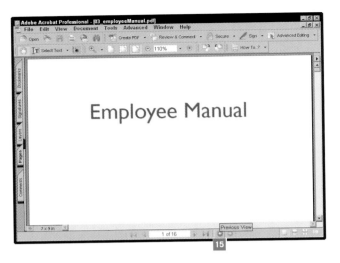

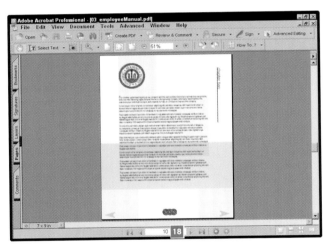

15. **Click the Previous View tool.**

    Notice the current open document closes and the last view in the previously viewed document opens in the Document pane. The Previous View tool shows you the last view whether the last view was in the current active PDF document or was in another file.

16. **Click the Next View tool. Click the Fit Page tool.**

    Notice you return to the 03_employeeManual document. When you click the Fit Page tool in the Zoom toolbar, the page is shown in a Fit Page view.

17. **Click the mouse cursor in the text box in the Status Bar where the display reads 1 of 16.**

    When you click the text box, the text is highlighted. Any value you type in the box replaces the highlighted value.

18. **Type** 10 **in the box and press Enter (Windows), Return (Macintosh), or Enter on your numeric keypad.**

    Page 10 opens in the Document pane. Type any page number in the Status Bar and you can immediately jump to a specific page.

19. **Leave the** 03_employeeManual.pdf **document open to complete the next tutorial.**

Navigating Views in PDF Documents

Acrobat provides you with several tools and menu commands to navigate pages in PDF documents. In the Status Bar you have all the tools needed to move back and forth between pages and view previous and next views.

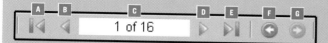

From the left, the tools include:

A. **First Page tool:** Opens the first page in the open PDF document. When the first page is in view in the Document pane, the First Page tool is grayed out.

B. **Previous Page tool:** Opens the preceding page. When you view the first page in a document, the Previous Page tool is grayed out.

C. **Page number view:** The display reads *n of n*, whereby the first value is the current page of the document and the second value is the total number of pages. Enter any number within the document's page range to view that page. If you type a page number out of the page range, Acrobat opens an alert dialog box informing you the page does not exist and no page navigation occurs.

D. **Next Page tool:** Opens the next page. When you view the last page in a PDF file, the Next Page tool is grayed out.

E. **Last Page tool:** Opens the last page in a document. When you view the last page in a PDF file, the Last Page tool is grayed out.

F. **Previous View tool:** Opens the previously viewed page. A previous view can be the open document or the last page viewed from another file. If you open a file and don't change views, the Previous Page tool is grayed out. If a page other than the opening page has not yet been viewed, the tool is grayed out.

G. **Next View tool:** Opens the next viewed page after viewing the previous view. A next view can be the open document or the next page viewed from another file. The tool is active only after using the Previous View tool. If a Previous View has not been used, the Next View tool is grayed out.

In addition to the tools available in the Status Bar, you can access the Navigation toolbar by choosing View→Toolbars→Navigation or by opening a context menu on the Toolbar Well and choosing Navigation from the menu commands.

The Navigation toolbar contains the same tools found in the Status Bar with the exception of the Page number view. The tools are: A – First Page tool, B – Previous Page tool, C – Next Page tool, D – Last Page tool, E – Previous View tool, and F – Next View tool.

Acrobat also provides you with four page layout views. Choose View→Page Layout and choose from one of the four views listed in a submenu or click one of the page layout tools in the Status Bar. The different layout views include:

A. **Single Page:** Shows single pages only. When you navigate pages, the pages snap to a page view showing a single page regardless of how you view the zoom level.

B. **Continuous:** Scrolling pages displays a continuous flow of pages where a portion of one page can be viewed in the Document pane along with a portion of another page. When zoomed out you can see multiple pages in the Document pane. The pages don't snap to single page views.

C. **Continuous—Facing:** Displays pages in a continuous flow of facing pages. When zoomed out you can see multiple facing pages.

D. **Facing:** Displays facing pages that snap to view like single page views. A maximum of two pages are shown in the Document pane. When zoomed out, only two pages are shown in the Document pane at one time.

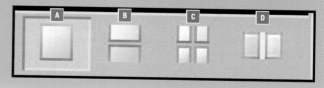

Tutorial
» Saving Initial Views

When you open a PDF document, the first view you see is referred to as the Initial View. Initial Views display page layout, zoom levels, page modes, and window controls. A PDF author can save an Initial View when authoring PDF documents, or files can be saved with fixed views. In this tutorial you learn how to set the defaults for Initial Views and how to override defaults by saving Initial Views.

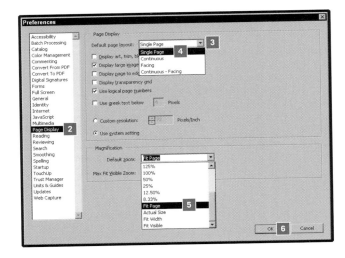

1. **Choose File→Preferences (Windows) or Acrobat→Preferences (Macintosh).**
   The 03_employeemanual.pdf document should be open in the Document pane.

2. **Click Page Display.**

3. **Click the down-pointing arrow to open the Default Page Layouts pull-down menu.**

4. **Choose Single Page.**

5. **Open the Default Zoom pull-down menu and click Fit Page.**

6. **Click OK.**
   By setting your viewing preferences for the Initial View, you determine which page layout view and zoom level you want to use. These settings apply to any PDF document unless the PDF author has determined a default view for the document.

7. **Close all documents by pressing Shift+Control+W (Windows) or Shift+Command+W (Macintosh). Reopen the 03_employeeManual.pdf file.**
   Notice the document opens with a Fit Page view and the page layout mode is Single Page.

8. **Choose File→Document Properties.**

9. **Click Initial View.**
   Notice the Page Layout and Magnification menu items are set at the Default menu selection.

10. **Press Esc (Escape key) on your keyboard.**
    You can cancel out of any dialog box in Acrobat by pressing the Esc key; this works on both Windows and Macintosh OS.

11. **Close the 03_employeeManual.pdf document. Click the Open tool. Open the file 03_annualReport.pdf.**
    Notice the file opens in a Continuous page layout view and the zoom level is 100%. You can see the percent of zoom level in the Zoom toolbar.

12. **Choose File→Document Properties.**

13. **Click Initial View.**

    Notice the Page Layout menu selection is set to Continuous and the Magnification is set to 100%. Regardless of which viewing options the users choose, this document always opens according to the settings established in the Document Properties dialog box.

14. **Open the Show pull-down menu. Choose Page Only from the menu selections.**

15. **Open the Magnification pull-down menu and choose Fit Page.**

16. **Click OK.**

    The settings established in the Initial View can be saved when you save the PDF document. Each time a user opens the PDF, these new settings override the user's preference settings.

17. **Choose File➔Save As.**

18. **Navigate to the Tutorial03_finish folder and save the file as** `03_annualReport_finish.pdf`. **Close the file by pressing Control/Command+W.**

19. **Open the** `03_annualReport_finish.pdf` **document in the Tutorial03_finish folder.**

20. **Choose File➔Document Properties. Click Initial View.**

21. **Select Single Page for the Page Layout and select Fit Page for the Magnification. Click OK.**

22. **Choose File➔Save As. Save the file to the Tutorial03_finish folder and overwrite the last save you made to the file.**

23. **Close all documents by pressing Shift+Control+W (Windows) or Shift+Command+W (Macintosh).**

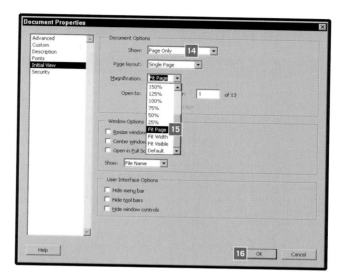

Tutorial
» Using Zoom Tools

Acrobat supports a maximum page size of 200 by 200 inches. You might have large documents or drawings whereby you need to examine detail, or you might have layouts and designs with small type that need to be viewed in varying zoom sizes. Acrobat viewers afford you many options for using zoom tools and menu commands to change views. In this tutorial you learn how to zoom in and out of document pages.

1. **Choose File→**`03_annualReport_finish.pdf` **(Windows) or File→Open Recent File→**`03_annualReport_finish.pdf`.
   The last files you opened are listed as recently viewed files. If you don't see the files listed in a menu, use the Open tool and open the `03_annualReport_finish.pdf` document in the Tutorial03_finish folder. When you open the file, the default view is Fit Page with a Single Page layout view.

2. **Click the down-pointing arrow adjacent to the Zoom In tool.**

3. **Click Dynamic Zoom from the pull-down menu options.**

4. **Place the cursor in the center of the document page and click and drag up toward the Acrobat Toolbar Well.**
   The document page zooms in. To zoom out with the Dynamic Zoom tool, click the mouse button and drag down. The Dynamic Zoom tool enables you to jump to zoom levels quickly regardless of the size of your images or PDF documents.

5. **Press Control/Command+ – (minus sign).**
   The page zooms out in the Document pane. Each time you press Control/Command+ – (minus sign), the page zooms out at fixed zoom levels.

6. **Click the down-pointing arrow to open the fixed zoom menu commands.**

   The menu shows you fixed zoom sizes. When you use keyboard shortcuts to zoom in (Control/Command+ +) or Control/Command+ –), the zooms jump to the preset zoom levels and some zoom levels in between the presets.

7. **Click 400%.**

   The page is zoomed to a 400% view.

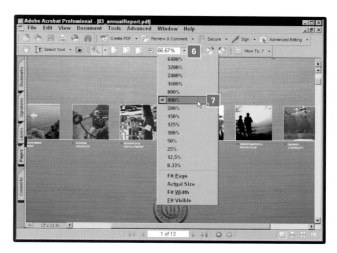

8. **Click the minus (-) icon on the Zoom toolbar.**

   The page zooms out to a 300% view. Notice the zoom level is in between the 400% and 200% preset zoom levels.

9. **Press Control/Command+0 (zero).**

   The page returns to a Fit Page view.

10. **Open the Zoom pull-down menu.**

11. **Choose Zoom In.**

<TIP>

For a quick temporary access to the Zoom In tool, press Control/Command+Spacebar. To access the Zoom Out tool, first press Control/Command+Spacebar, and then press the Alt/Option key. The symbol inside the magnifying glass icon changes from a + (plus sign) to a – (minus sign) when you change from the Zoom In tool to the Zoom Out tool. Release the keys and you return to your previous editing tool.

12. **Place the Zoom In tool on the top-left side of the marine logo. Click and drag a marquee rectangle around the logo.**

    The page zooms to the size defined by the marquee rectangle drawn with the Zoom In tool.

13. **Click the Fit Page tool.**

    The page returns to a Fit Page view.

<NOTE>

The following zoom tools are available only to Acrobat Professional users. Acrobat Standard users should look over the steps in the tutorial and close the file when you come to the end of this tutorial.

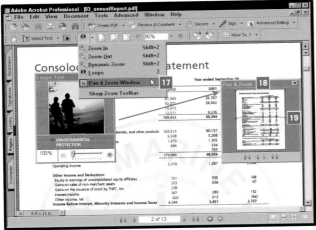

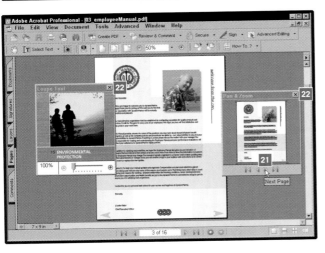

14. **Click the Loupe tool in the Zoom toolbar pull-down menu.**

15. **Click one of the photo images.**

    Acrobat Professional has a Loupe tool used for examining a small area on a document page while the page view in the Document pane remains at a fixed view. You can click the Loupe tool on another part of the document and the zoom appearing in the Loupe Tool window changes according to the area where you click the cursor. The Loupe Tool window is used for zooming in from 100% to 6400%. You can size the Loupe Tool window by dragging the lower-right corner in or out. As you click or click and drag the cursor around the Document pane, the Loupe Tool window shows a zoom view in relation to the cursor position.

16. **Press the Page Down key to navigate to the second page in the document.**

    Notice the Loupe Tool window retains the zoom level on the first page while the second page opens in the Document pane.

17. **Open the Zoom tool pull-down menu and choose Pan & Zoom Window.**

    The Pan & Zoom window opens.

18. **Click the Pan & Zoom title bar and drag the window to the right side of the Document pane.**

19. **Click the lower-right handle on the red keyline border in the Pan & Zoom window and drag up.**

    Notice as you resize the red rectangle, the page zooms to the view defined by the rectangle. The Pan & Zoom window page thumbnail remains at a Fit Page view.

20. **Select** `03_employeeManual_finish.pdf` **from the Recently Viewed files list.**

    If you don't see the `03_employeeManual_finish.pdf` file in the list, click the Open tool and open the file from the Tutorial03_finish folder.

21. **Click the Next Page tool in the Pan & Zoom window twice to navigate to Page 3.**

    Notice the same navigation tools are available in the Pan & Zoom window as you have available in the Navigation toolbar. Also notice that the original zoom acquired in the Loupe Tool window remains unchanged even though the active document has changed.

22. **Close the tool windows by clicking the Close button in each window.**

23. **Close all documents by pressing Shift+Control+W (Windows) or Shift+Command+W (Macintosh).**

Tutorial
» Using the Pages Palette

Clicking tools to navigate pages is like clicking hypertext link buttons. Acrobat has many tools and features that link to page views. As an additional navigation tool, the Pages palette offers you a visual thumbnail view of pages and provides you a means of quickly moving around your documents. In this tutorial you learn some of the features found in the Pages palette.

1. **Open the** `03_annualReport.pdf` **document.**

2. **Click the Pages tab.**
   The tabs on the far left of the Acrobat window are expanded and collapsed by clicking a tab or by pressing the F6 key. The container for these palettes is called the *Navigation pane.* If you press F6 the first time, the Bookmarks palette opens. If you click a tab and click again on the same tab to close the palette and press the F6 key, the last palette you viewed opens in the Navigation pane.

   < N O T E >
   Users of previous versions of Acrobat will remember that page tuumbnails were viewed in the Thumbnails palette. This palette in Acrobat 6 is called the Pages palette. Although features have been added to the Pages palette, viewing page thumbnails in the Pages palette is similar to viewing page thumbnails in the Thumbnails palette in earlier versions of Acrobat.

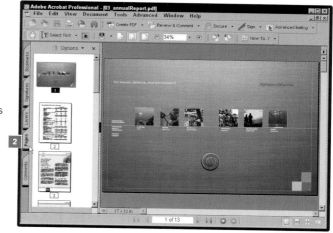

3. **Click the scroll bar and drag down to view page eight.**
   The same window controls you have in the Acrobat window for scrolling pages are also available in the palettes docked in the Navigation pane. Click the scroll bar and drag up or down or click the up or down arrows to scroll page thumbnails.

4. **Click page 8 in the Pages palette.**
   Notice a single click of the mouse button changes the page view in the Document pane to the page clicked in the Pages palette.

5. **Place the cursor in the Pages palette between the page thumb-nails and right-click (Windows) or Control-click (Macintosh) to open a context menu.**

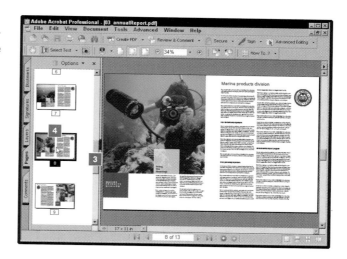

6. **Choose Enlarge Page Thumbnails from the menu.**

7. **Return to the context menu and select Enlarge Page Thumbnails again and repeat the steps a third time.**
   With each selection of the menu command, the page thumbnails are enlarged. To reduce the size, open the same context menu and click Reduce Page Thumbnails.

8. **Drag the separator bar to the right approximately two-thirds across the Acrobat window.**
   As you move the separator bar to the right, the Pages palette increases in size while the Document pane reduces in size.

9. **Move the Pages palette scroll bar down so that the page 10 thumbnail is in view.**
   Notice as you scroll pages in the Pages palette, the thumbnail views change while the page in the Document pane remains fixed at the last page view.

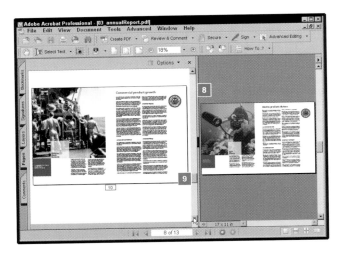

10. **Open a context menu in the Pages palette and choose Reduce Page Thumbnails. Repeat reducing page thumbnails three more times.**

11. **Drag the separator bar to the far-right side of the Acrobat window.**

12. **Click page 7. Shift-click page 8.**
   You select a contiguous range of pages when you click and press the Shift key and click another page. All pages between the selected pages are included in the selection. To select a non-contiguous range of pages, press Control/Command-click and click each page you want to include in a selection. Selected pages have a dark border around their thumbnails.

13. **Click page 7 and drag the selection between page one and two.**

14. **Wait until you see a separator bar appear between the target pages and then release the mouse button.**
   The pages are reordered in the document. As you can see, you can easily use the Pages palette like a slide sorter. You can adjust page views and move pages around to reorder them.

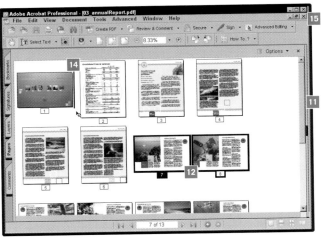

15. **Close the document.**

16. **Click No when prompted if you want to save changes.**

17. **Reopen the** 03_annualReport.pdf **document.**

18. **Click the Pages tab.**
   Notice the Pages tab returns to the default width. The expanded width you made in steps 8 and 11 are not retained as a new preference.

19. **Close the document.**

Tutorial
» Working with Bookmarks

Yet another navigational tool at your disposal includes bookmarks. Unlike the navigation tools discussed thus far in this session, bookmarks are user-defined. You create bookmarks in either an authoring program that exports to PDF with bookmarks preserved in the PDF or you create bookmarks in Acrobat Standard or Acrobat Professional. In this tutorial you learn how to create bookmarks and navigate to bookmarked pages.

1. **Open the** `03_employeeManual.pdf` **file from the Tutorial03 folder.**

2. **Click the Next Page tool to open the Contents page.**

3. **Click the Bookmarks tab.**

4. **Click the down-pointing arrow to open the Options menu.**

5. **Choose New Bookmark.**

   A bookmark captures the current page view. In this example the document is open on page 2 and the view is a Fit Page view. The bookmark captures page 2 and the Fit Page view. As you create bookmarks, remember that you always first set the desired view, and then create the bookmark.

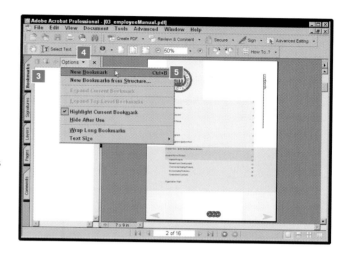

6. **Type** contents **for the bookmark name.**

   When you create a bookmark from the Options menu command or by using the keyboard shortcut Control/Command+B, the bookmark is created with a default name *Untitled*. Acrobat highlights the name in the Bookmark palette for you. You can change the *Untitled* name by typing words on your keyboard. There is no need to select the name or insert the cursor to change the name as long as you don't unselect the word *Untitled* when it first appears.

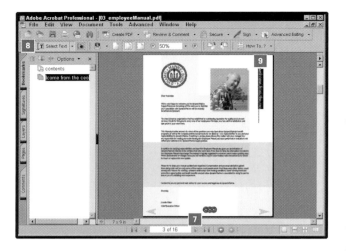

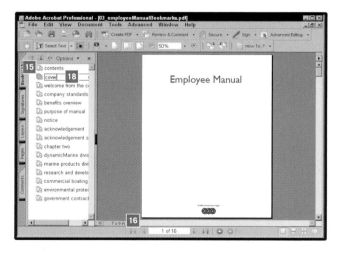

7. **Click the Next Page tool or press Page Down on your keyboard to open page 3.**

8. **Click the Select Text tool.**

9. **Drag the cursor down across the vertical type:** *welcome from the ceo.*
   Be certain the text is selected.

10. **Press Control/Command+B.**
    Using the keyboard shortcut to create a bookmark is the same as using the Options menu command. In this step, the bookmark name is derived from the selected text. As you create bookmarks, you can shorten your steps by selecting text when the text selection is what you want to use for a bookmark name.

11. **Click the Next Page tool or press Page Down.**

12. **Select the vertical text** *company standards* **on page 4.**

13. **Press Control/Command+B to create another bookmark. Repeat the same steps and create bookmarks on the remaining pages in the document.**

14. **Close the file without saving and open the file** `03_employeeManualBookmarks.pdf`. **This file contains bookmarks so you can easily follow the remaining steps in this tutorial.**

15. **Click contents in the Bookmarks palette.**
    Notice the contents page opens in the Document pane. The contents bookmark is selected after you click it. Leave the bookmark selected in the Bookmarks palette.

16. **Click the First Page tool to navigate to the first page in the document.**
    The page changes in the Document pane; however, the bookmark remains selected.

17. **Press Control/Command+B.**
    A new bookmark is created directly below the selected bookmark.

18. **Type cover for the bookmark name.**

19. Click contents.

The contents page opens in the Document pane. The page viewed in the Document pane has no effect on reorganizing bookmarks. However, you do need to select a bookmark before moving it into the Bookmarks palette. When you select a bookmark, Acrobat opens the view associated with the bookmark.

20. Click and drag the contents bookmark below the cover bookmark and move the cursor slightly to the right. Wait until you see a red down-pointing arrow before releasing the mouse button.

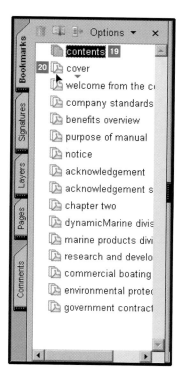

21. Click the welcome from the ceo bookmark. Press Shift and click the acknowledgement signature bookmark.

All bookmarks between those you clicked are added to the selection.

22. Click the bookmark icon to the left of the welcome from ceo bookmark and drag up and left until you see a small flag appearing below the contents bookmark.

When you see a red down-pointing arrow appear below a bookmark, the selected bookmark is targeted for placement directly below another bookmark. When you move the cursor slightly to the right and see the flag appear, the bookmark(s) is targeted for nesting as a child bookmark below a parent bookmark.

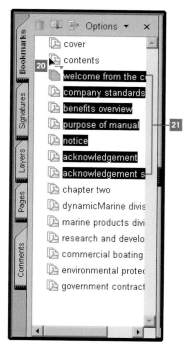

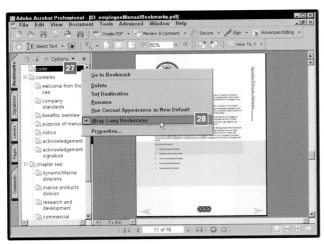

23. **Release the mouse button.**

    The selected bookmarks are indented within the contents bookmark. The contents bookmark is a parent bookmark and all the indented bookmarks directly below the contents bookmark are its children.

24. **Click the dynamicMarine divisions bookmark.**

25. **Shift-click the government contracts bookmark.**

26. **Click the dynamicMarine divisions bookmark and drag up and to the right of the chapter two bookmark to nest the group as child bookmarks below the chapter two parent bookmark.**

27. **Click a bookmark.**

    Click any bookmark in the Bookmarks palette.

28. **Open a context menu and choose Wrap Long Bookmarks.**

    The bookmark names are word-wrapped in the palette so you can see the entire bookmark name.

29. **Click the – (minus) icon (Windows) or down-pointing arrow (Macintosh) adjacent to each parent bookmark.**

    The bookmarks collapse in the bookmark pane. To expand bookmarks, click the + (plus)/arrow symbol. Note: when you click a – (minus), the icon changes to a plus (Windows) or when you click a down-pointing arrow, the arrow changes to a right-pointing arrow (Macintosh).

<TIP>

Bookmarks can be nested in many subgroups with different parent/child relationships. When you expand a bookmark with several nested levels, you might see the first level expand while the remaining levels remain collapsed. To expand all levels, press Control/Option and click a collapsed bookmark. All subordinate bookmarks are expanded. To collapse all, press Control/Option and click again on the first level parent bookmark.

30. **Press Control/Command+D.**

    The Document Properties dialog box opens. Alternatively, you can choose File→Document Properties to achieve the same result.

31. **Click Initial View. Open the Show pull-down menu and click Bookmarks Panel and Page.**

    When you set the Show menu choice to show Bookmarks Panel and Page and save the PDF document, the file opens with the Bookmarks pane open.

32. **Click OK and choose File→Save As. Save the file to the Tutorial03_finish folder and overwrite the file. Close the file after saving.**

» Session Review

Acrobat provides you with many tools, menu commands, and palettes for viewing and navigating files and pages in PDF documents. As you work with Acrobat's editing tools, you need to know how to move around a document and how to handle multiple document views. In this session, you learned navigation methods that are used in all subsequent sessions. To help you review this session, try to answer the following questions. Answers are found in the tutorial noted in parentheses.

1. Which keyboard shortcut do you use to fit a page completely in the Document pane? (See Tutorial: Using Page Viewing Tools.)

2. How do you snap pages to view without seeing partial pages on the top and bottom of the Document pane? (See Tutorial: Using Page Viewing Tools.)

3. How do you access the Navigation toolbar? (See Tutorial: Using Page Viewing Tools.)

4. Which page layout views can show you four pages simultaneously in the Document pane. (See Tutorial: Using Page Viewing Tools.)

5. Which keystroke is used to dismiss dialog boxes? (See Tutorial: Using Page Viewing Tools.)

6. Which tool enables you to zoom in on a page without changing the zoom level in the Document pane? (See Tutorial: Using Zoom Tools.)

7. How do you quickly zoom into a specific area on a page? (See Tutorial: Using Zoom Tools.)

8. Which keys are used to temporarily access the Zoom In and Zoom Out tools? (See Tutorial: Using Zoom Tools.)

9. How do you force a page to always open at 100% view? (See Tutorial: Saving Initial Views.)

10. How can you jump to a specific page in a PDF document? (See Tutorial: Using Page Viewing Tools.)

11. How do you jump to a page using thumbnails? (See Tutorial: Using the Pages Palette.)

12. How do you change the size of page thumbnails? (See Tutorial: Using the Pages Palette.)

13. How do you reorder pages in a PDF document? (See Tutorial: Using the Pages Palette.)

14. How do you create a bookmark name without typing the name in the Bookmarks pane? (See Tutorial: Working with Bookmarks.)

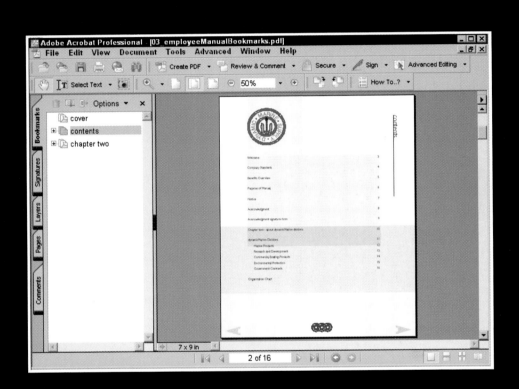

Part III
Creating PDF Documents

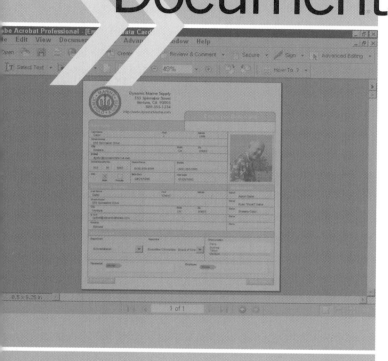

Converting Application Documents to PDF

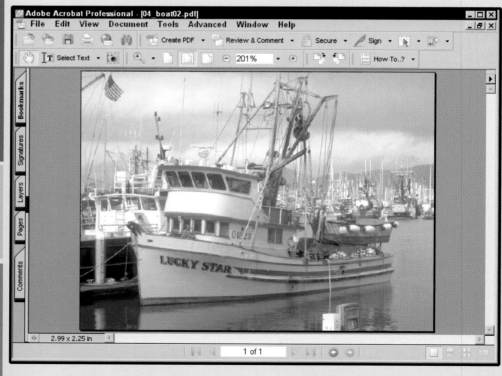

Session Introduction

Acrobat is not intended to be a word processing program, an illustration program, a layout application, or any other type of original authoring program. It is designed to convert files originated in other programs to the PDF format. In order to open a file in Acrobat, the document needs to be a PDF or a file saved in a format compatible for converting to PDF. In this session, you learn how to convert a variety of program documents to the Portable Document Format.

TOOLS YOU'LL USE
Microsoft Office version 98 or greater, PDFMaker, Acrobat Distiller 6.0 or greater, Convert to PDF From File command, Convert to PDF From Multiple Files command, Convert to PDF From Clipboard Image command (Windows only), and the Snapshot button.

<NOTE>
If you don't have Microsoft Office installed on your computer, you can review the session and try to understand how some of Acrobat's conversion tools are used. For other programs you use in your workflow, be certain to look over converting to PDF with Acrobat Distiller and using applications that support PDF conversion.

CD-ROM FILES NEEDED
04_boat01.bmp, 04_boat02.tif, 04_president.jpg, 04_pulley.png, 04_ceoLetter.doc, 04_employeeManual.ps, 04_financialDocument.xls, 04_memo.doc, 04_orgChart.ai, and 04_presentation.ppt.

Tutorial files are found in the Sessions/Session04/Tutorial04 folder on the CD-ROM. Completed versions of each tutorial can be found in the Sessions/Session04/Tutorial04_finals folder.

TIME REQUIRED
2 hours

Tutorial
» Converting Image Files to PDF

In Session 2 you learned how to convert files saved in the TIFF format to Adobe PDF. Acrobat supports many file formats for conversion to PDF from within Acrobat. In addition to converting to PDF, you also have options for assigning attributes during conversion. In this tutorial, you learn how to convert several file types to PDF, learn how to adjust conversion settings, and understand which file formats are acceptable for conversion with Adobe Acrobat.

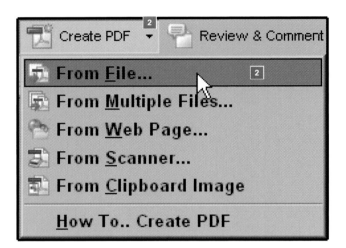

1. **Mount the CD–ROM located in the back of this book. Drag the folder called Session04 from inside the Sessions folder to your desktop. Launch Acrobat by double-clicking the program icon.**

2. **Click the Create PDF task button and choose From File.**
   When you click the Create PDF task button, the pull-down menu opens.

3. **Navigate to the Session04 folder on the Desktop and open the Tutorial04 folder.**

4. **Open the pull-down menu for Files of type (Windows) by clicking the down-pointing arrow or Show (Macintosh).**

5. **Click TIFF Files (*.tif or *.tiff) from the pull-down menu options.**
   When you select a specific file type in the Files of type (Windows) or Show (Macintosh), only the files of the type selected in the pull-down menu are shown in the Open dialog box.

Image Compression

In the Adobe PDF Settings dialog box, you have choices for file compression. Files compressed with different settings result in smaller file sizes. Among the choices are ZIP compression and different levels of JPEG compression. ZIP is a *lossless* compression scheme, which means you can compress a file to reduce the size without any image loss or degradation. With JPEG, you have several choices for the amount of JPEG compression to be applied to an image. The quality suffers the more you compress the file. JPEG compression is known as a *lossy* compression scheme and creates smaller file sizes by throwing away some image data. The more you compress the file, the more data is eliminated from the

image, which can result in a visibly degraded image. Acrobat informs you of the image quality to be retained respective to the choice you make in the Conversion Options dialog box. JPEG (Quality : Low) is the lowest quality and the highest compression. Conversely, JPEG (Quality : High) is the highest quality and the lowest compression. If in doubt about the amount of compression to apply to an image, you can open a file and choose a compression level. Examine the image on-screen. If it looks degraded, close the file without saving and open it with another compression level. What you see on-screen is what appears in Acrobat when viewing files on your monitor.

6. **Choose** 04_boat02.tif **from the Open dialog box.**

7. **Click the Settings button in the Open dialog box.**
   The Adobe PDF Settings dialog box opens.

<NOTE>

When the All Files (*.*) option is selected from the pull-down menu, all file types are listed in the Open dialog box. If you want to limit your search for a file to a given file type, select the desired file format. Only files matching that format are listed in the Open dialog box. However, the Settings button is not available when you choose All Files (*.*). If you want to adjust settings such as image compression, color management, and other attributes with certain image formats, select the format from the pull-down menu to enable the Settings button.

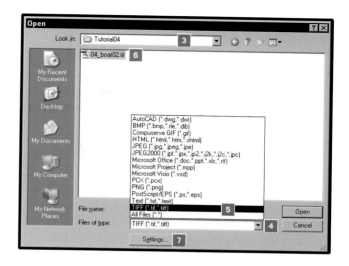

8. **Click JPEG (Quality : Maximum) from the Color pull-down menu.**

9. **Click OK to close the Adobe PDF Settings dialog box.**

10. **Click Open in the Open dialog box.**
    The file opens in a Fit Page view with the settings you specify in the Adobe PDF Settings dialog box. This example shows you how to convert a TIFF file to PDF. There are many file formats supported by Acrobat. For a description of the supported formats, see Table 4-1.

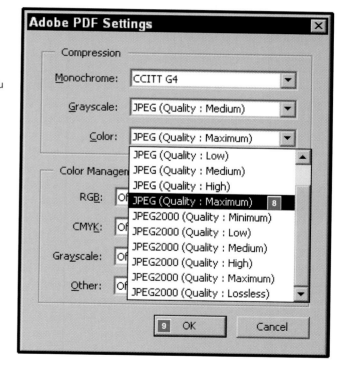

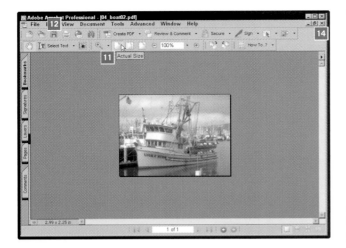

11. **Click the Actual Size button.**

    When you convert an image file to PDF, don't be alarmed at the quality you see when the file first opens in the Document pane. For smaller files, the Fit Page view can be a much larger zoom level than a 100% view. Clicking the Actual Size button shows you how the image looks at a 100% view.

12. **Click the Save button.**

13. **Save the file as** 04_boat02.pdf **to your Tutorial04_finish folder.**

14. **Click the Close button to close the file (top-left corner on Macintosh).**

<NOTE>

When you need image files converted to PDF, use the Open command or the Create PDF From File command found in either the Create PDF task button or in the File→Create PDF submenu. Using the Create PDF From File or Open command is especially helful when converting digital camera images that need to be integrated into PDF documents. Once in PDF form, images can be copied and pasted into other PDF documents.

<NOTE>

Attributes such as file compression can be assigned to all file types listed previously with the exception of CompuServe GIF, HTML, and TEXT. When any of the other file types is selected, the Settings button in the Open dialog box becomes active.

Table 4-1: File Formats Acceptable to Create PDFs

File Extension	File Type
[1]AutoCAD (*.dwg, *.dwt)	AutoDesk AutoCAD files are supported in Acrobat Professional on Windows only.
BMP (*.bmp, *.rle, *.dib)	Bitmap (bmp). Common format from paint programs and also can be saved from Photoshop. Can be 1-bit, 4-bit, 8-bit, or 24-bit color depths. Often used as a format for importing images in Office programs.
Compuserve GIF	Graphic Interchange Format (GIF). Common format for Web-hosted images.
HTML (*.html, *.htm, *.shtml)	HyperText Markup Language (HTML). Scripting language used for creating Web pages. When opening an HTML file, the Web page is converted to PDF.
JPEG (*.jpg, *.jpeg, *.jpe)	Joint Photographic Expert Group (JPEG). Yields small file sizes by compressing images. Also a common format used for images in Web pages.
JPEG2000 (*.jpf, *.jpx, *.jp2, *.j2k, *.j2c, *.jpc)	JPEG2000 is a more recent JPEG format offering you more compression options than earlier versions.
[1]Microsoft Office (*.doc, *.ppt, *.xls, *.rtf)	Microsoft Office programs. The PDFMaker macro is installed in Office applications if Office is installed before you install Acrobat.
[1]Microsoft Project (*.mpp)	PDFMaker also supports converting Microsoft Project files.
[1]Microsoft Visio (*.vsd)	Another program that uses the PDFMaker Macro, Visio files can be converted to PDF with Adobe PDF layers preserved in the resultant PDF document.
PCX (*.pcx)	PCX isn't an acronym for anything. It was originally a file extension used with PC Paintbrush—the oldest paint program for DOS/Windows. Some old archival documents might be saved in this format.
PICT (Macintosh only)	Picture (PICT). Native to the Macintosh, the PICT format is the Mac counterpart to PCX and commonly used for screen images and multimedia.
PNG (*.png)	Portable Network Graphics (PNG). Another format used for Web graphics. Enables saving 24-bit images without compression.
PostScript/EPS (*.ps, *.eps)	Files printed to disk as PostScript files are distilled in Acrobat Distiller. If you open an EPS or .ps file in Acrobat, Distiller is automatically launched by Acrobat and converts the PostScript/EPS to PDF.
Text (*.txt, *.text)	Text (TXT). ASCII text saved as text only from word processors or from text editors. All formatting for text styles and characters is lost with ASCII files. Acrobat cannot open documents saved from word processors in formats other than ASCII except Microsoft Word using the PDFMaker Macro.
TIFF (*.tif, *.tiff)	Tagged Image File Format (TIF). A common graphic image format used by graphic artists and designers. Portable to all professional level layout and illustration programs.
All Files (*.*)	When this selection is made from the pull-down menu, all file types listed above are seen in the Open dialog box.

[1]Requires original authoring programs in order to convert document files to PDF.

Tutorial
» Converting Clipboard Data to PDF (Windows Only)

Data you copy to the Clipboard can be converted to a PDF document. The data must be accessible to Acrobat in order to convert to PDF. If you copy data to the Clipboard from some authoring programs, Acrobat might not recogize the data. Anything you copy to the Clipboard while working in Acrobat is accessible. In this tutorial you learn how to create PDFs from data copied to the Clipboard from within Acrobat.

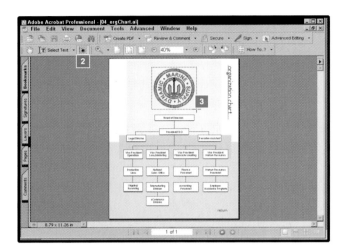

1. **Click the Open button and open the** 04_orgChart.ai **file from the Tutorial04 folder.**

    The file opens in Acrobat. This file is an Adobe Illustrator document saved in the native .ai Illustrator format.

2. **Click the Snapshot button.**

    The Snapshot button copies a document page or a selected region of a page to the Clipboard. To copy a page, you use the Snapshot tool and click anywhere on the page. To copy a por- tion of a page, click and drag a marquee with the Snapshot tool around the area you want to copy.

3. **Click and drag a rectangular marquee around the logo at the top of the page.**

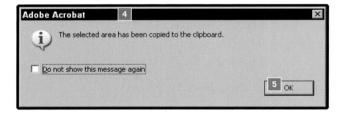

4. **Release the mouse button. An alert dialog box opens informing you that the selected area has been copied to the Clipboard.**

5. **Click OK in the alert dialog box.**

Converting Adobe Illustrator Files to PDF

When you use the Open file command or the Create PDF From File command and open an Adobe Illustrator .ai file, the file may con- tain an Adobe PDF compatible file within the Illustrator document. Whether the PDF compatible file exists depends on how the file was saved from Illustrator. Each time you save a file from Adobe Illustrator, the Native Format Options dialog box offers you an option to *Create a PDF Compatible File.* If you enable the check box for creating a compatible PDF document, the Illustrator file is recog- nized as a PDF document. Hence, no file conversion is necessary.

When you use the Open command or the Convert to PDF From File command and convert a file, you need to save the file to side-step converting it again. Likewise, the file doesn't appear in the Recently Viewed Files list unless the file was saved after conversion.

With Adobe Illustrator files that have been saved with a Compatible PDF File, you can open the file, close it, and the file appears in the Recently Viewed Files files without saving it from Acrobat.

6. **Click the Create PDF task button.**

7. **Choose From Clipboard Image.**
   The Clipboard data is converted to PDF and a new page opens in the Document pane.

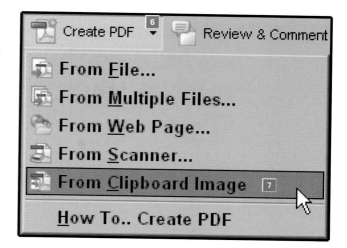

8. **Click the Actual Size button.**
   To see the image at 100% size, zoom out of the view by clicking the Actual Size button.

9. **Click the Save button. Save the file as** 04_logo.pdf **to the Tutorial04_finish folder.**
   Because the file has not been saved, the Save dialog box opens; supply a filename and select a destination. Click Save and the file is written to the target folder.

10. **Click the Close button to close the document (top-left corner on Macintosh).**

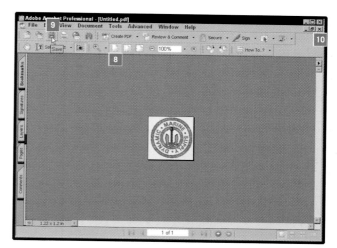

Converting Screen Images to PDF (Macintosh)

The Create PDF From Clipboard Image command is not available on Macintosh. However, Macintosh users are not left out when you need to capture a screen and save it to a PDF file. There are several keyboard shortcuts you can use to capture screen shots, dialog boxes, foreground data, and specific regions of the display on your monitor. To convert what you see on your monitor to PDF for a full-screen capture, press Command+Shift+3. Mac OS intervenes and captures the current monitor view. The file is automatically saved as a PDF document. You can open the file in Acrobat, or open it in Adobe Photoshop or Adobe Photoshop Elements where you can crop out excess data or edit the image. From Photoshop, save the file as a Photoshop PDF and you can open it in Acrobat without any further file conversion. For capturing other screen views such as dialog boxes, selected areas of your screen, and so on, use the Grab tool. Refer to your user manual to discover how to use the Grab tool.

Tutorial
» Converting Microsoft Word Files to PDF

In any office environment, one of the most common authoring applications used is Microsoft Word. For authoring documents, MS Word can handle most of what an office worker needs, including memos, letters, forms, and certain page layouts. If you have a number of office workers in your company and need to send documents to users who don't have Word installed, you can easily convert to PDF and have users review your Word files in an Acrobat viewer. In this tutorial you learn how to convert Microsoft Word files to PDF.

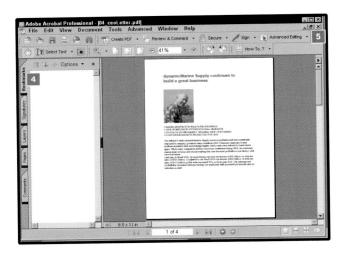

1. **Click the Create PDF task button. Choose From File.**

2. **Open the Tutorial04 folder and select** 04_ceoLetter.doc.

3. **Click Open.**
   Acrobat launches Microsoft Word automatically and Word opens the document. In a few moments, the Word file is converted to PDF and opens in Acrobat.

   <NOTE>
   You must have Microsoft Word installed on your computer to convert Word files to PDF. If you do not have Microsoft Word installed on your computer, you can skim over the tutorial to see how Word documents are created from MS Word. When Word document conversions are used in later sessions, you can open corresponding PDF files from the Tutorial04_finals folder and observe the results of files converted to PDF from Microsoft Word.

4. **Click the Bookmarks tab.**
   Notice that the Bookmarks palette is empty. You can have Acrobat automatically create bookmarks from Word styles; however, to do so requires you to make choices for the PDF conversion. These options are found in either Acrobat or Microsoft Word.

5. **Click the Close button and close the PDF document without saving it.**

6. **Launch Microsoft Word by double-clicking the program icon. Open the file** 04_ceoLetter.doc **from the Tutorial04 folder.**

7. Choose Format and click Styles and Formatting (Windows) or View→Formatting Palette (Macintosh).

The Style Sheets are listed in the Styles and Formatting pane (Windows) or the Formatting palette (Macintosh).

8. Scroll through the Styles and Formatting palette by dragging the scroll bar to observe the style sheets contained in the document.

The first few lines of text use the MainHead style and the sub-heads in the document are defined with the SectionHeads style. These styles can be converted to bookmarks and can link the Bookmark names to the pages where the heads appear in the resultant PDF document. In order to convert styles to bookmarks, you need to make some adjustments in the PDF conversion settings.

9. Choose the Adobe PDF menu.

Notice Microsoft Word contains two menus (Windows only) for Acrobat commands (Adobe PDF and Acrobat Comments). These menus are installed when you install Acrobat on your computer. In addition to the menus, there are three tools positioned in the Word toolbar that are also installed with Acrobat. On the Macintosh, the menus don't appear, but you have similar options with tools installed in the toolbar.

10. Choose the Change Conversion Settings command.

The Acrobat PDFMaker dialog box opens. In this dialog box, you make choices for options associated with the PDF conversion.

11. Check Add Bookmarks to Adobe PDF.

In order to convert the Word styles to bookmarks you need to check this option.

12. Check Enable Accessibility and Reflow with Tagged PDF.

Checking this box creates a tagged PDF and preserves the underlying structure of the document. In addition to making the document accessible for interpretation with screen readers used by people with vision and motion challenges, tagged PDF documents retain more of the content structure such as paragraph formatting, tables, and the like. If you need to export PDF text back to a program like Microsoft Word for updating or future editing, retaining the structure makes your formatting job in Word much easier.

13. Click the Bookmarks tab.

After you set the options for adding bookmarks, you need to specify which styles are converted to bookmarks.

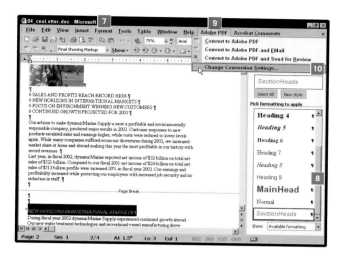

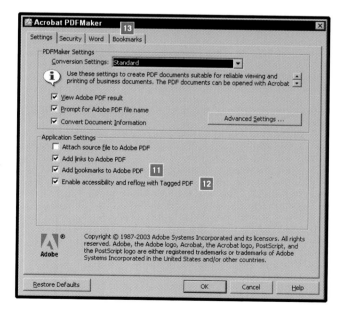

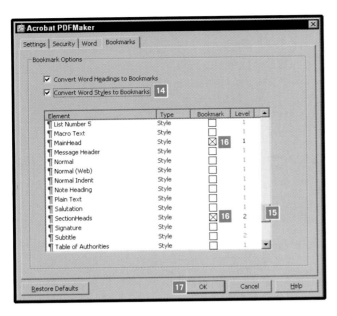

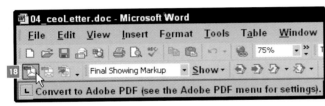

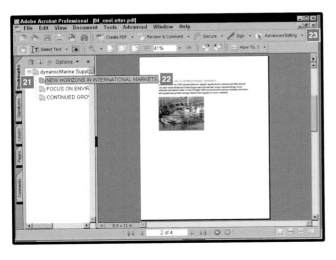

14. **Check Convert Word Styles to Bookmarks.**
    Checking this box instructs Word to convert the style sheets to bookmarks. However, you're only half finished after checking this box. The next step is to select which styles you want to convert.

15. **Scroll the scroll bar down toward the bottom of the list.**

16. **Check the box under the Bookmark heading for the two styles used in this document. They are MainHead and SectionHeads.**
    Be certain the check box is enabled for both items.

17. **Click OK.**

18. **Click the Convert to Adobe PDF button in the Word toolbar.**
    The same conversion occurs as when you use Convert PDF From File. The PDFMaker Macro runs through a routine and ultimately opens the resultant PDF in Acrobat.

< N O T E >

Whether the resultant PDF opens in Acrobat is determined in the Adobe PDFMaker dialog box. By default the check box for View Adobe PDF result is enabled. Keep the box checked if you want to view PDFs immediately after conversion.

19. **Type** 04_ceoLetterBookmarks.pdf **for the filename and save the file to the Tutorial04_finish folder.**
    When you click the Create Adobe PDF tool in Word, you are prompted to save your file in the Save Adobe PDF File As dialog box. Type a filename and navigate to a location to save your file just like you would when using a Save or Save As dialog box.

20. **The PDF opens in Acrobat.**

21. **Click the Bookmarks tab.**
    Notice that the PDF contains bookmarks derived from the style sheets used in Microsoft Word.

22. **Click the first child bookmark.**
    The second page in the document opens in the Document pane. As you can see, all the bookmarks link to the respective headings.

23. **Click the Close button to close the document. (Top-left corner on Macintosh.)**

Tutorial
» Setting Conversion Options in Acrobat

Many conversion settings in the Adobe PDFMaker dialog box in Microsoft Word can also be addressed from within Adobe Acrobat. You have options in Acrobat to set default conditions for conversion to PDF. These are available from most of the file types that Acrobat recognizes when you open a file or use the Convert PDF menu commands. In this tutorial you learn how to change conversion settings in Acrobat.

1. **Press Control/Command+K.**
   Alternatively, you can choose Edit➔Preferences. In either case, the Preferences dialog box opens. In the Convert to PDF preferences pane, you make choices for the conversion settings you want to use with many file formats.

2. **Choose Convert to PDF to access these settings.**
   On the right side of the Convert to PDF preferences pane, you see a list of all the acceptable formats.

3. **Click Microsoft Office.**

4. **Click the Edit Settings button.**
   The Adobe PDF Settings for Supported Documents dialog box opens.

5. **Check the box for Enable Accessibility & Reflow (Microsoft Office 2000/XP Only).**
   Notice this setting is permitted only with Microsoft Office running in Microsoft XP and Windows 2000. Users of other operating systems need to address this setting in Microsoft Word.

6. **Check the box for Add Bookmarks and Links to Adobe PDF File.**
   Be aware that the bookmark options need to be determined in Microsoft Word when you save your Word files. Enabling this check box does not convert styles that are not marked for conversion in Word.

7. **Check the box for Convert Entire Excel Workbook.**
   An Excel workbook may contain several sheets. When the check box is enabled, all worksheets are converted and each worksheet is placed on a separate page. When you enable adding bookmarks to the Adobe PDF file for Excel conversions, each worksheet is bookmarked.

8. **Click OK to close the Adobe PDF Settings for Supported Documents dialog box.**
   Acrobat returns you to the Preferences dialog box.

9. **Click OK in the Preferences dialog box.**
   The settings you make in the Preferences dialog box remain fixed until you change them. All future conversions use these preference settings. Leave these settings at the new default to follow the steps in the next tutorial.

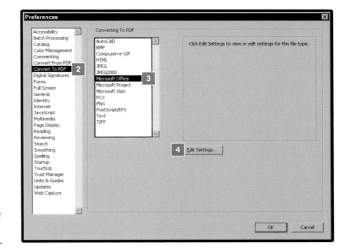

Tutorial
» Converting Multiple Files to PDF

Acrobat supports multiple file conversions from files saved from different authoring programs. The file formats still have to be compatible with those listed in the Convert to PDF preferences. Any one or all the files can be converted and assembled into a single PDF file. In this tutorial you learn how to convert multiple file types with a single menu command.

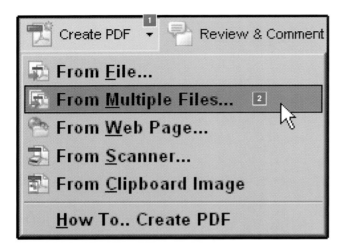

1. **Click the Create PDF task button.**

<NOTE>

In order to follow steps in this tutorial you need to have Microsoft Office installed on your computer.

2. **Choose the From Multiple Files command.**
   The Create PDF from Multiple Documents dialog box opens.

3. **Click Browse.**
   The Open dialog box opens. In this dialog box you select the files you want to convert to PDF and combine the pages in a single document.

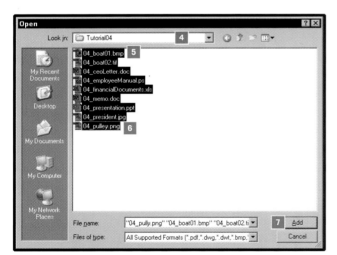

4. **Open the Tutorial04 folder by clicking the Look in pull-down menu and navigate your hard drive to find the Tutorial04 folder.**

5. **Click** 04_boat01.bmp.
   You are selecting the first file in the list.

6. **Press Shift and click** 04_pulley.png.
   All files between the first and last file you select are included in the selection.

7. **Click Add.**
   Acrobat returns you to the Create PDF from Multiple Document dialog box.

<TIP>

This tutorial details creating a single PDF document from multiple files. If you want to convert different files saved in different formats to separate PDF documents, click From File in the Create PDF pull-down menu and select all the files you want to convert. Click OK and Acrobat converts each file to a separate PDF document.

8. **Click** 04_employeeManual.ps.

9. **Click Remove.**

    The 04_employeeManual.ps document is a PostScript file. The file can be converted using the From Multiple Files command, but converting PostScript files is discussed in the "Using Acrobat Distiller" tutorial later in this chapter. For now, eliminate this file from the list.

10. **Click** 04_ceoLetter.doc.

    Before converting the files to a PDF document you can arrange the order as you want them to appear in the PDF document. In this example, I want the two Word files at the top, followed by the image files, the financial documents, and the presentation file at the end of the document. Notice the file formats include several image file formats, Microsoft Word files, a Microsoft Excel file, and a PowerPoint Presentation file.

11. **Click Move Up.**

    Keep clicking Move Up until the file moves to the top of the list.

12. **Click** 04_memo.doc.

13. **Click Move Up until the file appears below the** 04_ceoLetter.doc **file.**

14. **Click** 04_pulley.png. **Click Move Up until the file appears below** 04_boat02.tif.

15. **Uncheck the two check boxes at the bottom of the dialog box if either one is enabled.**

    In the event you start with another file open in the Document pane, disabling the check box for Include All Open PDF Documents disregards all open documents in Acrobat. The second item, Include Most Recent List of Files to Combine, includes your recently viewed files in the resultant PDF. By disabling both check boxes, you are assured that only those documents listed in the Create PDF from Multiple Files dialog box are used to produce the PDF.

16. **Click OK.**

    Acrobat takes a few minutes to convert all the files to PDF. Eventually, the document opens in Acrobat with the default name: Binder1.pdf. As yet the file is not saved.

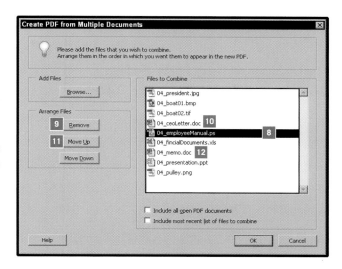

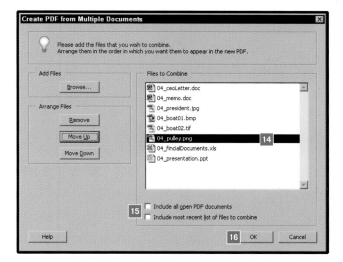

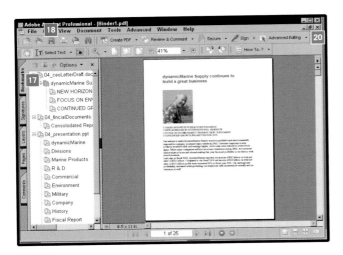

17. **Click the Bookmarks tab.**

    Notice the document contains bookmarks derived from the Microsoft Office files that were converted. The Word document, Excel document, and PowerPoint document all produced book-marks in the PDF file.

18. **Click the Save button.**

19. **Navigate to the Tutorial04_finish folder and save the file as** 04_annualReportDraft.pdf.

20. **Close the document.**

Converting to PDF from Layout Programs

Although Microsoft Office applications and others are supported by Acrobat for conversion to PDF using the From File or From Multiple Files menu commands, there are a number of applications that are not supported with the Acrobat tools. However, converting many professional authoring programs like layout programs and illustration programs doesn't require Acrobat conversion tools because most of these programs offer you direct exports to PDF from the host program. How PDF exports occur from layout programs varies a little, but all the high-end professional programs do support creating PDFs without the need for using commands in Acrobat. Table 4-2 lists the programs most used for page layout and the tools needed to export to PDF.

Table 4-2: PDF Conversion Methods for Layout Applications

Program	Description/Method of PDF Conversion
Adobe FrameMaker	Commonly used by many technical writers and publication authors, FrameMaker is designed for work-groups collaborating on publications developed by an individual or several individuals on a mutual project. FrameMaker has built-in support for Save As PDF that prints a file to disk and distills the file in the background.
Adobe InDesign	Adobe InDesign supports PDF creation from within the program. InDesign is written on core PDF tech-nology and saves directly to the PDF format via an Export command. InDesign supports advanced PostScript features such as transparency and layered documents.
Adobe PageMaker	In version 7.x, PageMaker to PDF support is built into the program. Earlier versions of PageMaker can export to PDF via a PageMaker addition. To acquire the addition, you can download it free from Adobe's Web site. All versions of PageMaker print PostScript files and distill the files in the background with Acrobat Distiller.
QuarkXPress	Version 6 of QuarkXPress supports PDF creation without the addition of QuarkXTensions. Earlier versions of QuarkXPress require you to download a Quark XTension from Quark's Web site. With the XTension you can import PDF documents and export to PDF where Distiller is run in the background to convert the XPress document to PDF.
Microsoft Publisher	Microsoft Publisher is the only layout program in this group that doesn't internally support PDF cre-ation. Publisher files need to be printed to disk as PostScript and distilled in Acrobat Distiller.

Tutorial
» Using Acrobat Distiller

Many popular computer programs support direct exports to PDF. Program exports to PDF combined with Acrobat's tools for PDF conversion offer you a huge array of opportunities for converting files created in the most widely used programs. However, there are times when you might need to convert a document whereby you can neither export directly to PDF nor does Acrobat support PDF conversion. In these situations, you have another option through the use of Acrobat Distiller. Acrobat Distiller converts to PDF files that are printed to disk as PostScript. In this tutorial you learn about printing PostScript files and using Acrobat Distiller for PDF conversion.

1. **In Acrobat, choose Advanced→Acrobat Distiller.**
   Acrobat Distiller opens in front of the Acrobat window.

<NOTE>
There are several ways to access Acrobat Distiller. You can double-click the application icon as Distiller is a separate program installed in your Acrobat folder. You can use the Create PDF From File command or Create PDF From Multiple Files command. Acrobat Distiller is launched automatically when you select a PostScript file to convert to PDF. You can also drag a PostScript file on top of the Distiller window or on top of the Acrobat window. In etiher of these cases, Acrobat Disitller launches automatically and/or begins con-version to PDF.

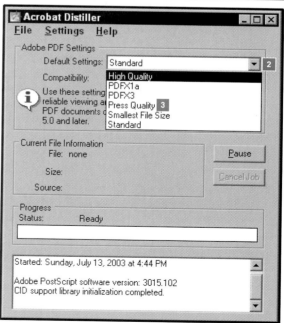

2. **Click the down-pointing arrow to open the Default Settings pull-down menu.**
   A list of Adobe PDF settings shows you the default settings installed with Acrobat. The options you see for PDFX1a and PDFX3 are available only in Acrobat Professional.

3. **Choose Press Quality.**
   Press Quality produces the highest quality PDF document and renders the PDF suitable for commercial printing.

4. **Choose File→Open.**
   The Open dialog box appears.

5. **Open the Tutorial04 folder and click** `04_employeeManual.ps.`
   The PostScript file is converted to PDF by Acrobat Distiller using the Press Quality Adobe PDF settings. The PDF file is saved to the same folder from where the PostScript file was opened. In this example the PDF is saved to the Tutorial04 folder.

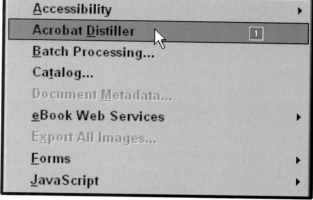

Printing PostScript Files

When you print a PostScript file, you are actually saving a file to disk. Rather than print to a printing device you print to your hard drive. Any program capable of printing is capable of having the authoring document converted to PDF when printing PostScript and using Acrobat Distiller for the PDF conversion.

On Windows, open your Print dialog box from any authoring program and choose File→Print. In the Print dialog box be certain to select a PostScript printer as your target printer. Desktop color printers of a non-PostScript type won't produce a file suitable for distillation. After selecting a PostScript printer, check the box for Print to File. When you click OK in the Print dialog box, the file is written to your hard drive as a PostScript file. In addition to using a PostScript printer, you can also use the Adobe PDF Printer that is installed when you installed Acrobat. If you use the Adobe PDF printer, you can print the file to PostScript or uncheck the box for Print to File. A PDF is produced by Distiller automatically.

On Macintosh, you have a few choices for creating PDF documents from programs not supported with Create PDF From File or by exporting directly to the PDF format. Built into Macintosh OS X is the capability to save any file from a Print dialog box to PDF. However, saving to PDF in the Print dialog box results in a low-quality PDF document. If you want to use Adobe PDF settings for High Quality, Press Quality, PDF/X, or Standard, be certain to print the file to your hard drive as a PostScript file. Check the box for Save as File in the Output Options and select PostScript as your format. The file is written to your hard drive. Open Acrobat Distiller and select an Adobe PDF setting. Open the PostScript file and Distiller converts the file to PDF.

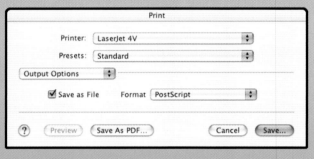

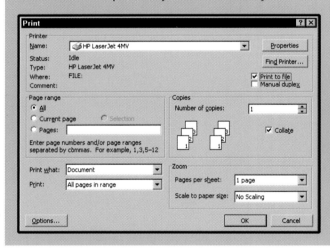

Understanding Adobe PDF Settings

When you first open Acrobat Distiller and plan to convert a PostScript file to PDF, your first decision is to choose Adobe PDF settings that are suited for the kind of output your PDF is intended. A PDF designed for Web viewing, for example, requires a different PDF than one intended for commercial printing. Among the differences between Web viewing and commercial printing is the resolution of images where Web views require much less resolution than PDFs designed for print. During the process of distillation, Acrobat Distiller Adobe PDF settings are used to perform tasks like reducing image sizes.

Image resolution changes, as well as a host of other settings, are made in the Adobe PDF Settings dialog box. By default you have preset settings available by selecting options in the Default Settings pull-down menu. The default settings provided to you when you install Acrobat include:

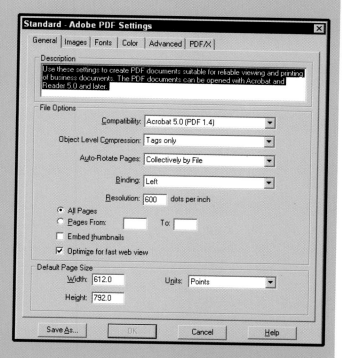

» **High Quality:** These settings are designed for high-quality printing, but not necessarily for commercial printing like printing color separations.

» **PDFX1a (Acrobat Professional only):** PDF/X is a subset of the PDF format designed for use with high-end commercial printers.

» **PDFX3 (Acrobat Professional only):** PDF/X-3 is a more recent upgrade to the PDF/X format and is also used for high-end printing.

» **Press Quality:** Notwithstanding the PDF/X options, this setting is also used for high-end printing and prepress.

» **Smallest File Size:** This setting produces the smallest file sizes, suitable for screen viewing and Web hosting. You should check results to be certain images are not visibly degraded when using this setting.

» **Standard:** The default for most PDF conversion you perform for office programs and files suited for desktop printers.

The default sets that are provided with your Acrobat installation can be changed and edited and new custom Adobe PDF settings can be added to the pull-down menu choices. To edit an Adobe PDF setting or create a new set, click Settings and click Edit Adobe PDF Settings. The Adobe PDF Settings dialog box opens after making the menu choice.

There are six tabs (five in Acrobat Standard) that offer a host of options for how PostScript files are converted to PDF. The range of options and all the settings available to you are beyond the scope of this book. To learn more about the Adobe PDF settings, see the Acrobat Help Guide. You'll find a detailed description of all the options you can select in the Adobe PDF Settings dialog box.

For general use, select the Standard settings for files used around the office, use Smallest file size for files intended for screen views, and use High Quality for color proofs and printing. If you prepare files for commercial prepress, be certain to read the descriptions in the Acrobat Help Guide for PDF/X and using Press Quality settings.

» Session Review

There's much more to PDF conversion than was covered in this session, but you should have a basic understanding for how many authoring program documents are converted to PDF. This session covered a lot of material. To review the session, try to answer the following questions. Answers are found in the tutorial noted in parentheses.

1. How do you create smaller file sizes for images converted to PDF? (See Tutorial: Converting Image Files to PDF.)

2. What's image compression? (See Tutorial: Converting Image Files to PDF.)

3. Which compression scheme produces lossless compression? (See Tutorial: Converting Image Files to PDF.)

4. What is PDFMaker used for? (See Tutorial: Converting Microsoft Word Files to PDF.)

5. How do you create bookmarks in PDFs when converting Microsoft Word files? (See Tutorial: Converting Microsoft Word Files to PDF.)

6. Where do you change conversion settings in Acrobat? (See Tutorial: Setting Conversion Options in Acrobat.)

7. What is the benefit of creating tagged PDF files? (See Tutorial: Setting Conversion Options in Acrobat.)

8. What is the Snapshot button used for? (See Tutorial: Converting Clipboard Data to PDF.)

9. How do you convert several files to a single PDF document? (See Tutorial: Converting Multiple Files to PDF.)

10. How do you create a PostScript file? (See Tutorial: Using Acrobat Distiller.)

11. How do you change Adobe PDF settings? (See Tutorial: Using Acrobat Distiller.)

12. How do you create a PDF if your layout program doesn't export to PDF? (See Tutorial: Using Acrobat Distiller.)

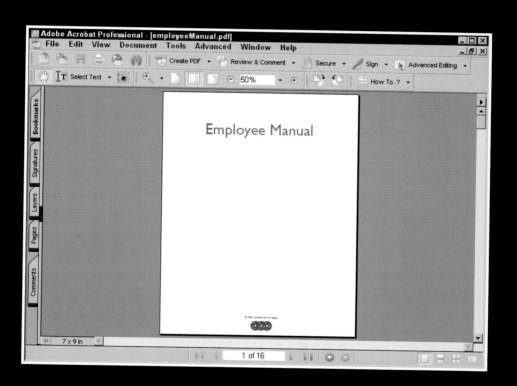

PDFs and Web Viewing

Tutorial: **Converting Local Web Pages to PDF**

Tutorial: **Converting Web Hosted Pages to PDF**

Tutorial: **Creating PDFs from Internet Explorer (Windows Only)**

Tutorial: **Creating PDFs from Microsoft Outlook or Outlook Express (Windows Only)**

Session Introduction

In addition to the PDF conversion options you learned in Session 4, Acrobat offers you many options for converting Web pages to PDF and file conversions for e-mailing PDFs. In this session you learn how to convert Web pages to PDF from Acrobat and Microsoft Internet Explorer and Microsoft Outlook and Outlook Express.

TOOLS YOU'LL USE
Microsoft Internet Explorer (Windows), Microsoft Outlook or Outlook Express (Windows), PDFMaker, the Create PDF From Web Page command.

CD-ROM FILES
05_webPages folder, index.html, and 05_memo.doc (found in the Sessions/Session05/Tutorial05 folder)

TIME REQUIRED
60 minutes

Tutorial
» Converting Local Web Pages to PDF

As you learned in Session 4, you use the Create PDF From File command to convert many file formats to PDF. In addition to the file formats discussed in Session 4, you can also convert HTML documents to PDF. In this tutorial you learn how to convert Web pages residing on your hard drive to PDF.

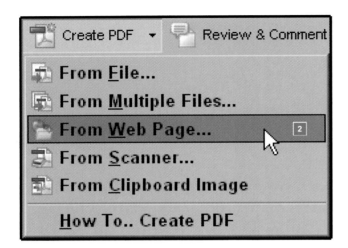

1. **Mount the CD–ROM located in the back of this book. Drag the folder Session05 from inside the Sessions folder to your desktop. Launch Acrobat by double-clicking the program icon.**

<NOTE>
The Tutorial05 folder contains a subfolder titled 05_webPages, which is where an HTML document and supporting files are contained. Be certain to keep the path between the HTML document and supporting files together.

2. **Click the Create PDF task button and choose From Web Page.**
The Create PDF from Web Page dialog box opens.

3. **Click Browse.**
The Select File to Open dialog box opens.

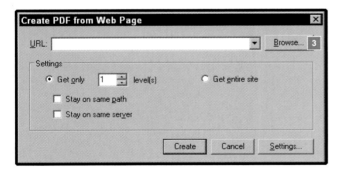

4. **Open the 05_webPages folder inside the Tutorial05 folder.**

5. **Choose** 05_index.html.

6. **Click Select.**
   Acrobat returns you to the Create PDF from Web Page dialog box.

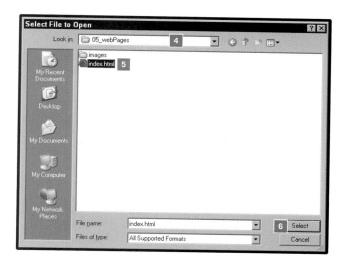

7. **Click Create.**
   As the HTML file is converted to PDF, Acrobat displays the Download Status dialog box. Wait until the dialog box disappears and the PDF conversion is completed. The converted document opens in the Document pane.

<NOTE>
The Web page contains Flash animation and sound. New features in Acrobat 6 enable you to convert Web pages to PDF while preserving animation from many media formats.

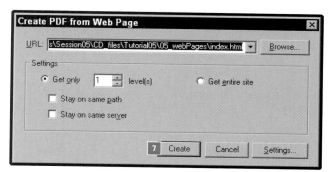

8. **Click the Fit Page button.**
   Notice the PDF contains a bookmark to the page. As you convert multiple pages to PDF, each page is bookmarked with a structured bookmark.

9. **Click the Save button.**

10. **Save the file to the Tutorial05_finish folder as** 05_index_finish.pdf.

11. **Close the document by clicking the Close button.**

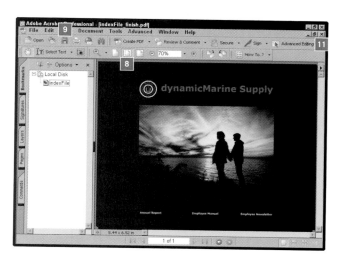

About Structured Bookmarks

When you convert Web pages to PDF, you have an option in the Web Page Conversion Settings dialog box to create bookmarks. To enable bookmark creation, click the Settings button in the Create PDF from Web Page dialog box. The Web Page Conversion Settings dialog box opens.

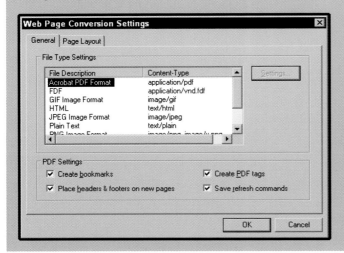

Click Create Bookmarks and click OK. When you return to the Create PDF from Web Page dialog box and click Create, the Web pages are linked to structured bookmarks appearing in the Bookmarks palette.

Structured bookmarks are different than the bookmarks you cre-ated in Session 3 in that a structured bookmark enables you to perform a number of page-editing tasks. You can, for example, move a structured bookmark in the Bookmarks palette, and the page associated with the bookmark is also moved among the PDF pages to the same respective location. You can delete a struc-tured bookmark and delete the page associated with the book-mark. Additional options include extracting pages, viewing Web links, and opening linked Web pages in your Web browser. These options are all available in the context menu you can access from any structured bookmark.

Tutorial

» Converting Web Hosted Pages to PDF

Create PDF from Web Page is accessed via the Create PDF task button, the Create PDF From Web Page tool in the Toolbar Well, or by choosing File→Create PDF From Web Page. Regardless of which method you use, the Create PDF from Web Page dialog box opens. You can open files that are located on your hard drive or network server, or you can convert Web pages hosted on the Internet. Instead of clicking the Browse button, you can type a URL in the URL field box and convert any Web page you can access in a Web browser to PDF. In this tutorial, you learn how to convert Web pages hosted on Web servers to PDF.

1. **Click the Create PDF from Web Page tool in the Acrobat Toolbar Well.**
   The Convert PDF from Web Page dialog box opens.

2. **Type a URL address for the Web page you want to convert.**
   You need to be certain you have an active Internet connection and type a URL that opens a Web page in your Web browser. Enter any Web address you want in the URL field box.

3. **Enter 1 in the Get Only field box.**
   By default the Get Only field box captures 1 level. If you change the number, Acrobat continues to download Web pages at the number of levels you specify in the field box. Each Web site is different and the number of levels and pages associated with each level varies greatly between Web sites. In some cases, the number of Web pages that get converted to PDF can be extraordinary. To begin a capture of a Web site, start with one level. As you want to convert more pages, you can add levels to your capture.

4. **Click the Create button.**
   The Download Status dialog box opens and closes after the page is converted to PDF and opens in the Document pane. If you want to append pages to your document by converting additional Web pages, you can click any URL link and the Web page associated with the link opens in your Web browser or is appended to your current open document.

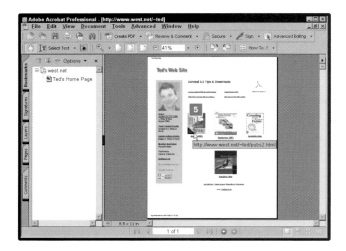

5. **Click a link on the Web page you converted to PDF.**
   The Specify Weblink Behavior dialog box opens. Be certain the first page you captured contains URL links to other Web pages. If you don't find a link to another Web page, capture another site by starting at step 1 in this tutorial.

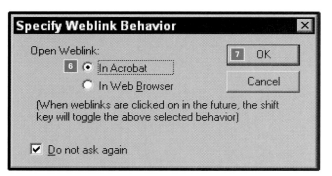

6. **Click the radio button for In Acrobat.**
   When you click a URL link, the Specify Weblink Behavior dialog box opens. You can choose to view the linked Web page in your Web browser or you can convert the Web page to PDF and append it to the current document.

7. **Click OK.**
   The Web page is converted to PDF and appended to the open file.

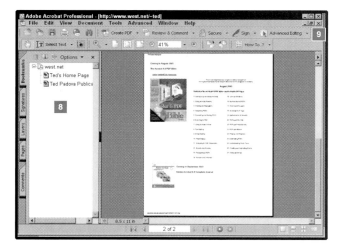

8. **Observe the Bookmarks palette.**
   Notice an additional page is added to the first Web capture and another structured bookmark is created in the Bookmarks palette.

9. **Close the document.**
   Click No when prompted if you want to save the file.

Tutorial

» Creating PDFs from Internet Explorer (Windows Only)

The methods described in the previous tutorials presume that you are working in Acrobat and want to convert Web pages while in an Acrobat editing session. If you don't have Acrobat open and you're browsing the Internet, you can convert Web pages to PDF from within Microsoft Internet Explorer (on Windows only). You might want to archive research data found on Web sites, capture your own Web site for creating files for print or for setting up a review session to solicit colleague opinions on a Web site revision, or catalog PDFs so you can easily search the content. Rather than return to Acrobat and use the Convert to PDF From Web Page command, you can convert pages viewed in your Web browser to PDF. In this tutorial you learn how to convert Web pages from within Microsoft Internet Explorer.

1. **Launch Microsoft Internet Explorer by double-clicking the program icon.**

2. **Choose File→Open.**
   Rather than search the Internet, open a file locally on your hard drive. Clicking the Open command enables you to open a Web page stored on your hard drive.

3. **Click Browse.**
   The Microsoft Internet Explorer dialog box opens.

4. **Navigate to the Session05 tutorial folder and open the Tutorial05 folder. Open the 05_webPages folder and double-click the 05_index.html file.**

5. **Click Open.**
   You are returned to the Open dialog box.

6. **Click OK.**
   The Web page opens in Microsoft Internet Explorer.

7. **Click the down-pointing arrow on the Adobe PDF toolbar to open a pull-down menu.**
   Notice in Microsoft Internet Explorer (Windows only) a tool and menu are installed in the Explorer toolbar. The tool is the Convert Web Page to PDF tool installed in the Explorer toolbar when you install Acrobat. Adjacent to the toolbar is a pull-down menu also installed with your Acrobat installation.

8. **Choose Preferences.**
   The Adobe PDF Preferences dialog box opens.

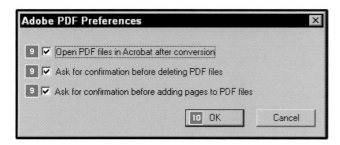

9. **Enable all check boxes in the Adobe PDF Preferences dialog box.**
   By default the check boxes should be enabled. If you find an item unchecked, be certain to check the box before beginning. The options include:

   » **Open PDF Files in Acrobat After Conversion.** When the check box is enabled, the Web page converted to PDF is opened in Acrobat. If Acrobat is not open, the program is launched and the file opens in the Document pane.

   » **Ask for Confirmation Before Deleting PDF Files.** If you convert a Web page and save the file, and then convert a file using the same name, the new file replaces the old file. When the check box is enabled, Acrobat informs you in an alert dialog box that a file with the same name already exists and asks if you want to replace the file. You can click No in the dialog box and use another filename to avoid overwriting files.

   » **Ask for Confirmation Before Adding Pages to PDF Files.** If you don't want to inadvertantly append pages to an open PDF document, check the box.

10. **Click OK.**

11. **Click the Convert Web Page to PDF tool in the Explorer toolbar.**
    Alternatively, you can open the pull-down menu adjacent to the Convert Web Page to PDF tool and click the Convert Web Page to PDF menu command. The Convert Web Page to Adobe PDF dialog box opens.

12. **Navigate to the Tutorial05_finish folder.**

13. **Type** 05_dynamicWebPage.pdf **for the filename and click Save.**
    Explorer displays the Converting Web Page dialog box and shows you the status of the conversion progress. In a few moments, the PDF opens in Acrobat.

14. Click Close.

Notice the Save button is grayed out in the toolbar since the PDF is already saved to your Tutorial05_finish folder.

15. Quit Internet Explorer by choosing File→Quit.

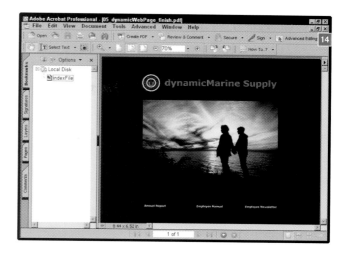

Web Page Conversion on the Macintosh

Support for PDF viewing in Acrobat on the Macintosh is much less than what you find on Windows in the first release of Acrobat 6. Macintosh users should frequent Adobe's Web site and look for a maintenance upgrade when made available that supports similar features on Mac OS. Until that time, you can convert to PDF on the Macintosh using Mac OS X built-in features for PDF conversion. If you use Microsoft Internet Explorer, Netscape Navigator, or Apple's Safari, you easily create PDF documents through the Print dialog box.

In any browser, choose File→Print. The drop-down menu contains a button used for PDF conversion.

Click Save As PDF and the Save to File dialog box opens. Type a name in the Save As field box and navigate to the folder where you want to save the PDF. Click Save and the Web page is converted to PDF.

Tutorial
» Creating PDFs from Microsoft Outlook or Outlook Express (Windows Only)

Another method of PDF conversion is available directly from within Microsoft Outlook or Outlook Express. You create PDF documents from all supported formats that are acceptable when using the Create PDF From File command. Rather than open Acrobat, you can convert different file formats to PDF and attach the PDF document to an e-mail message. In this tutorial, you learn how to convert to PDF from within Microsoft Outlook.

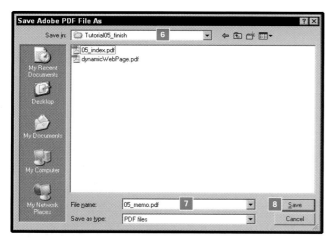

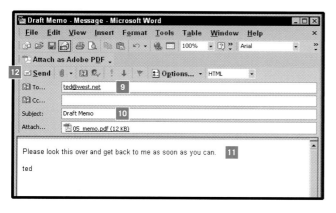

1. **Launch Microsoft Outlook or Outlook Express by double-clicking the program icon.**

2. **Click New in the program toolbar or choose File→New→Mail Message.**

3. **Click the Attach as Adobe PDF button.**
   The Choose File to Attach as Adobe PDF dialog box opens.

4. **Navigate to the Tutorial05 folder.**

5. **Click** 05_memo.doc.
   The 05_memo.doc file is a Microsoft Word file. You need to have Microsoft Word installed. When you open the file, the PDFMaker macro discussed in Session 4 performs the conversion to PDF. The first stop in the conversion process is to specify a filename and target destination in the Save Adobe PDF As dialog box.

6. **Navigate to the Tutorial05_finish folder.**

7. **Type** 05_memo.pdf **in the Filename field box.**

8. **Click Save.**
   The file is converted to PDF and is automatically attached to your e-mail message as a file attachment.

9. **Type your own e-mail address in the message line.**

10. **Type** Draft Memo **in the Subject line.**

11. **Type a message in the message window.**

12. **Click the Send button.**
    Double-click the file attachment in your e-mail message and the PDF opens in Acrobat.

13. **Close all files by pressing Shift+Control+W.**

» Session Review

In this session you learned how to convert Web pages and documents to PDF from within Microsoft Outlook or Microsoft Outlook Express. To review the PDF conversion methods from these programs, answer the following questions. Answers are found in the tutorial noted in parentheses.

1. Which tools are used to create PDFs from HTML documents stored on a hard drive? (See Tutorial: Converting Local Web Pages to PDF.)

2. What are some differences between bookmarks and structured bookmarks? (See Tutorial: Converting Web Hosted Pages to PDF.)

3. What tool is used to convert Web-hosted HTML files to PDF? (See Tutorial: Converting Web Hosted Pages to PDF.)

4. How do you append Web captures to PDF documents? (See Tutorial: Converting Web Hosted Pages to PDF.)

5. Which program formats are supported when converting files to PDF from e-mail programs? (See Tutorial: Creating PDFs from Microsoft Outlook or Outlook Express.)

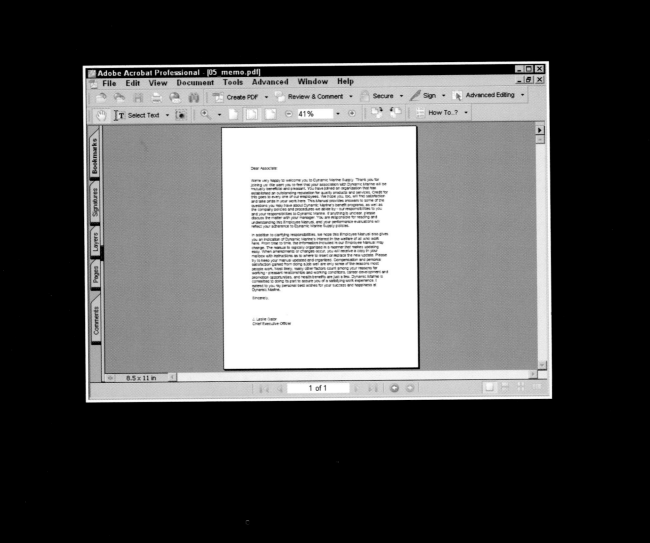

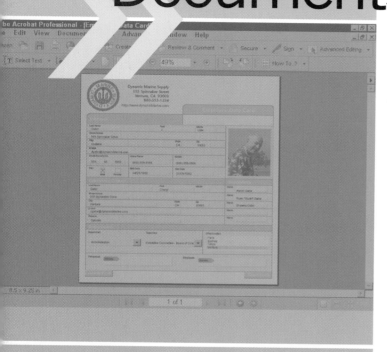

Part IV
Editing PDF Documents

Session 6

Modifying Views and Pages

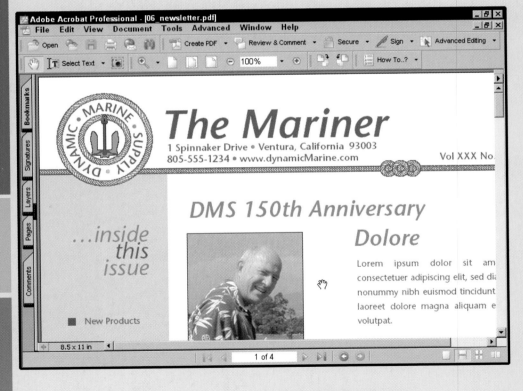

Tutorial: **Saving an Opening View**

Tutorial: **Setting Page Modes**

Tutorial: **Adding Document Properties**

Tutorial: **Adding Page Numbers**

Tutorial: **Adding a Background**

Session Introduction

For major document editing you need to return to the original authoring application, make edits, and convert to PDF. However, there are several editing tasks that you can successfully accomplish in Acrobat. In this session you learn how to establish initial views, change document properties, and modify page content using headers and footers and watermarks and backgrounds.

TOOLS YOU'LL USE
Document Properties, Initial View, Add Headers & Footers command, Add Watermark & Background command

CD-ROM FILES NEEDED
06_newsletter.pdf and 06_background.pdf (found in the Sessions/Session06/Tutorial06 folder)

TIME REQUIRED
90 minutes

Tutorial
» Saving an Opening View

When users open PDF documents, the first view they see is the initial view established according to each individual user's preferences. To create consistent opening views across all the PDFs you distribute, you can save an initial view according to the way you think your files are best displayed in an Acrobat viewer Document pane. When saving PDF documents with an initial view, you override all user preferences, and you can be confident that your files appear with the same zoom view on any user's computer. In this tutorial you learn how to save PDFs with fixed initial views.

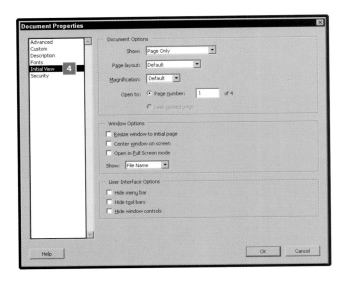

1. **Mount the CD–ROM located in the back of this book. Drag the folder Session06 from inside the Sessions folder to your desktop. Launch Acrobat by double-clicking the program icon.**

2. **Open the file 06_newsletter.pdf from the Tutorial06 folder.**

3. **Choose File→Document Properties.**
   The Document Properties window opens.

4. **Click Initial View in the left pane.**
   When you click Initial View, the right pane of the Document Properties dialog box contains three categories for setting up an initial view. The Document Options offer selections for page, page layout, and zoom views as well as an option for opening a file on a user-selected page number. The Window Options area contains options for displaying the Acrobat window and choices for how the title is displayed in the Acrobat viewer Title Bar. The User Interface Options area offers choices for hiding menus, tools, and palettes. All choices made in this pane can be saved so that every user who opens your file sees the same initial view.

5. **Click the down-pointing arrow adjacent to Page Layout.**

6. **Choose Single Page.**
   If a user's preference choice is set to viewing PDFs in a specific page layout view, you can override the preferences by selecting the Page Layout view you believe to be the most desired view. A Single Page view displays PDF pages a single page at a time and snaps each page to the view in the Document pane.

7. **Click the down-pointing arrow adjacent to Magnification.**

8. **Choose Fit Page.**
   A Fit Page view displays the PDF page in the Document pane so the entire opening page can be viewed on each user's computer monitor. As monitors vary in size, the fit page view fills the Acrobat Document pane and might appear larger or smaller depending on the size of the user's monitor.

9. **Click OK to close the window.**
   Settings made in the Initial View Document Properties do not take effect until you save the PDF to record your changes.

10. **Choose File→Save As. Save the file as** 06_newsletter_finish.pdf **to the Tutorial06_finish folder.**

11. **Close the file.**

12. **Choose File→**06_newsletterl_finish.pdf **(Windows) or File→Open Recent File→**06_newsletter_finish.pdf.
    The file is listed in the most recently viewed files list. Selecting the file from the File/Acrobat menu opens the file with the initial view settings you made in the Document Properties window.

13. **Keep the file open to follow the steps in the next tutorial.**

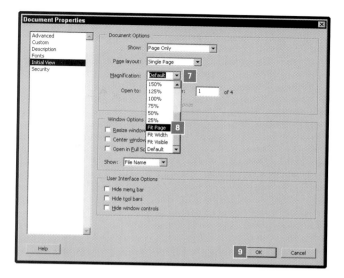

Tutorial
» Setting Page Modes

By default the page mode is set to view Page Only. When Page Only is selected in the Initial View properties, the Navigation pane is collapsed. If you want bookmarks, thumbnails, or layers displayed when the file opens, you can save the file with one of the Navigation palettes expanded. In this tutorial you learn how to display the Bookmarks panel when a user opens a PDF document.

1. **Click the Bookmarks tab.**
   The Bookmarks panel opens. Notice this file contains bookmarks. Clicking the bookmarks listed in the panel opens the pages associated with the bookmark links. If the Bookmarks panel is collapsed, users won't know that the file contains bookmarks unless they manually open the Bookmarks panel. To make it easier for the users to see at a glance that bookmarks are contained in the file, you can save the document so that the Bookmarks panel is expanded on the opening view.

2. **Choose File→Document Properties.**

3. **Choose Initial View.**
   You selected Initial View when you last visited the Document Properties dialog box. Initial View remains selected until you change categories by clicking another item in the list in the left pane. If you changed categories, be certain to click Initial View to show the Initial View options in the right pane.

4. **Click the down-pointing arrow adjacent to Page Layout to open the pull-down menu.**
   As you can see from the menu options you have choices to display a page along with the Bookmarks Panel, Pages Panel, or Layers Panel. Choosing one of the menu options other than Page Only displays the initial view with the respective panel open when a user first opens your document.

5. **Choose Bookmarks Panel and Page.**

6. **Click OK to close the window.**

7. **Choose File→Save.**

8. **Close the document.**

9. **Reopen the file.**
   Notice the file opens in a Fit Page view with the Bookmarks panel open.

10. **Keep the file open to follow the steps in the next tutorial.**

Tutorial
» Adding Document Properties

Document Properties fields are used to add information like a title, author, subject, and keywords. The Document Title can be displayed when a file opens, and all the document summary fields can be searched when you search through a collection of documents or you search an index file created with Acrobat Catalog. As a matter of practice, it's a good idea to supply document properties when you create PDF files to help you find files quickly when searching PDFs on hard drives, network servers, or CD-ROMs. In this tutorial, you learn how to supply document properties information.

1. **Choose File→Document Properties.**

2. **Choose Description.**
   The Description options include fields where you type information for the Title, Author, Subject, and Keywords. In addition you can view other important information about a file such as the creation and modification dates, the application that originally authored the document, PDF Producer, PDF version, file size, paper size, whether the file is tagged, and whether the file was saved with Fast Web View. These informational items help you understand how the PDF was created as well as other criteria that can be used to search documents.

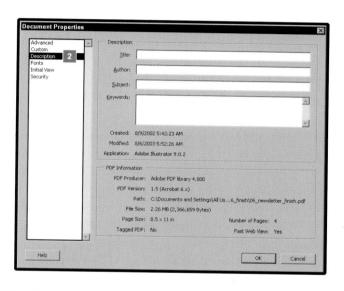

Adding Document Properties

Document Properties information can be a great advantage when searching PDFs from among large collections of files. Before adding document properties, you should give much thought in developing a schema for the kind of information you want to include. Title fields might be thought of as a root category whereas subject fields might be a subcategory. For example, a collection of human resource documents might include title names like Job Application, Maternity Leave, Employee Grievances, and so on. The subject fields might include terms like Eligibility Requirements, Procedures, Policy, and so on. When you perform a search, you might look for documents where the Title contains Maternity Leave and the Subject contains Policy to return PDF documents that contain a company's Maternity Policies.

Author fields are usually best described using department names or satellite office names rather than employee names. Employees typically change or vacate positions more often than department

or office names change. Therefore using author names like Human Resources, Manufacturing, Art Department, Administration, Accounting, and so on are much better choices than using individual employee names.

Keywords are used to add additional information to help narrow down searches. More finite descriptions as well as form numbers such as HR101, SA-204, GRE-33, and so on might be used for keywords fields.

Regardless of what information you use for populating the Document Properties fields, be certain to maintain consistency and add document information to all your PDFs at the time you create the files. You can create a matrix offering all users information on what data are used for document properties that helps your co-workers and colleagues find documents easily.

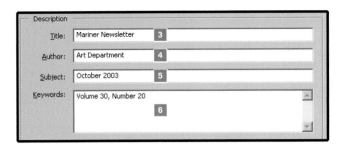

3. **Type** Mariner Newsletter **in the Title field.**

4. **Type** Art Department **in the Author field.**

5. **Type** October 2003 **in the Subject field.**

6. **Type** Volume 30, Number 20 **in the Keywords field.**
   The data you supply in these fields can be searched when you perform a search by browsing a location or searching an index file.

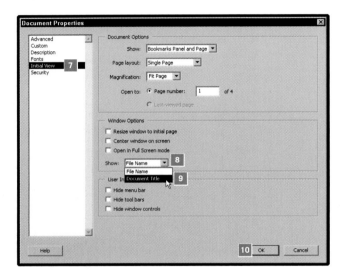

7. **Click Initial View.**
   Before exiting the Document Properties, make a change in the Initial View properties for viewing the Document Title. By default, when you open a PDF document, the PDF filename appears in the Acrobat Window Title Bar. You can change the Title Bar information to display the title you supply.

8. **Click the down-pointing arrow to open the Windows Options Show pull-down menu.**

9. **Choose Document Title.**

10. **Click OK to close the window.**

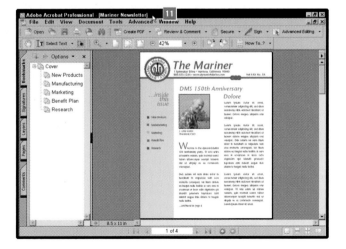

11. **Click Save.**
    Notice the Title Bar immediately reflects the change for the document title displayed in the Title Bar where [Mariner Newsletter] is shown.

12. **Keep the file open to follow the steps in the next tutorial.**

Tutorial
» Adding Page Numbers

PDF files can be created from several authoring programs and combined in a single document. If you have files where pages are converted from Microsoft Word; include diagrams created in Excel or drawing programs; or include Web pages, presentation pages, or pages from layout programs, you might want to add page numbers after all documents are combined to form a single PDF file. Acrobat 6 offers you new tools for adding text to existing documents as headers or footers. In this tutorial you learn how to add page numbers to a file using the Add Headers & Footers command.

1. **The** `06_newsletter_finish.pdf` **file should be open in the Document pane. If it is not, open the file from the Tutorial06_finish folder.**

2. **Choose Document→Add Headers & Footers.**
   The Add Headers & Footers dialog box opens. In the dialog box you have options for adding either a header or footer to a single page or range of pages. Two tabs appear at the top of the dialog box for adding either a header or footer. By default, the Header tab is selected.

3. **Type** October 2003 **in the Text field of the Insert Custom Text item.**
   Any text you type in this field can be added to the header for a page or range of pages.

4. **Click the down-pointing arrow to open the Font pull-down menu. Choose Arial Bold.**
   All fonts installed in your system appear in the pull-down menu. You can select any font for the header text from among the menu choices.

5. **Open the pull-down menu for Font Size and click 14.**

6. **Click the Insert button below the Insert Custom Text field box.**

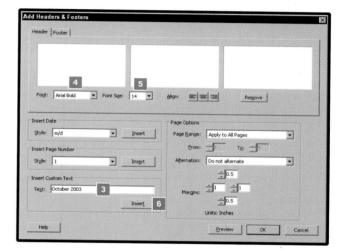

< N O T E >

You can also click in the Font Size field box and type a point size.

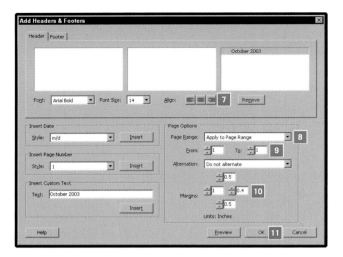

7. **Click the right-align icon (right-most icon adjacent to Align).**
   By default the text aligns to the left side of the page. By clicking the Align icons you can choose to align left, center, or right.

8. **Open the pull-down menu for Page Range and choose Apply to Page Range.**
   By default headers and footers are applied to all pages in the file. You can selectively choose the range of pages by first making the menu choice for Apply to Page Range and then entering the page range values in the From and To field boxes below the menu.

9. **Type** 1 **in the From and To field boxes.**

10. **Type** 0.4 **in the far right Margins field box.**
    The text you add for either a header or footer can be placed anywhere on the document page(s) by editing the four Margins field boxes. In this example, the default 1.0 value is too far from the right side of the page for this particular design. By adding a lower value the text moves outward toward the page edge.

11. **Click OK to close the window.**
    The text appears on the first page in the document. Page 1 in this example does not contain a page number. To number the remaining pages, you again need to return to the Add Headers & Footers dialog box. The data contained on page 1 is not disturbed as long as you apply new header information to any page or pages other than page 1.

12. **Choose Document→Add Headers & Footers.**

13. **Click October 2003 in the right column list.**

14. Click the Remove button.

Any text you add to the left, center, or right column is easily removed when you select the text and click the Remove button. In this example, we'll clear all text and add new text needed for pages 2 through 4.

15. Type Mariner Newsletter **in the Text field box under Insert Custom Text.**

16. Click the Insert button.

The text is inserted in the right column list box. Because you last selected right align, the right alignment becomes a new default during your Acrobat editing session.

17. Choose Mariner Newsletter in the list box in the top-right corner and set the font size to 12 point.

You can change point size after adding text to one of the three list boxes. Font sizes are changed either through clicking values in the Font Size pull-down menu or by typing the point size in the field box.

18. Choose 1 of n **from the Insert Page Number Style pull-down menu. Click the Insert button.**

You have several options for the style of page numbers to add as a header. Select a style and click the Insert button under the Insert Page Number heading. The new item you add to the list window appears directly below the last item added to the window.

19. Choose Click 1 of n **in the list box to select it.**

20. Change the font size to 9 point.

21. Type October 2003 **in the Insert Custom Text field box.**

22. Click the Insert button.

23. Type 2 **in the From field box and** 4 **in the To field box.**

24. Type 0.25 **in the top Margins field box.**

25. Click the Preview button.

When you click Preview, a window opens showing you the header on the first page range selected in the From field box. You can examine the position and style of the text before applying the header to the document.

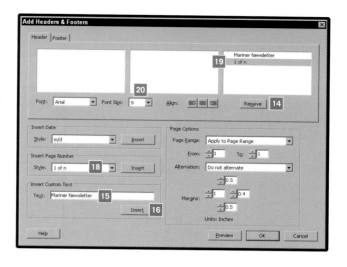

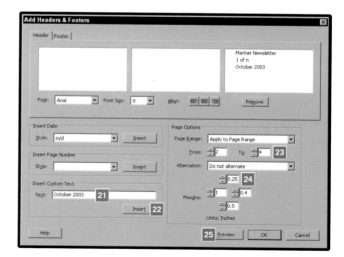

26. **Click OK in the Preview window to close it.**
    Notice the text for the header appears on page 2 in the document. After you exit the Add Headers & Footers dialog box, the text appearing in the preview window is applied to all pages in the selected page range.

27. **Click OK in the Add Headers & Footers dialog box to close it.**
    Acrobat displays a progress bar at the lower-left corner of the Acrobat window showing you the updating progress. Wait until the progress bar finishes before moving on with your edits.

28. **Click Save to update your edits.**

29. **Keep the file open to follow the steps in the next tutorial.**

< T I P >

To remove headers and footers from a document after you have added them in the Add Headers & Footers dialog box, open the dialog box and delete all items in the list windows. Click OK and Acrobat removes all the data across the page range you select in the Page Range field boxes. Essentially you are replacing the data with no data, thereby removing the header or footer.

Tutorial
» Adding a Background

Watermarks and backgrounds are added to a document in a similar fashion as adding headers and footers. A separate dialog box is used to add a watermark that appears on top of the page data or a background that appears behind page data. Backgrounds are shown in the transparent areas of the document. In this tutorial you learn how to add a background to modify the design of a PDF document.

1. **Choose Edit→Preferences (Windows) or Acrobat→Preferences (Macintosh).**
   The Preferences dialog box opens.

2. **Click Page Display.**

3. **Check the Display Transparency Grid box.**
   Before you attempt to apply a background, it's a good idea to view the PDF pages for transparent areas. A background is visible only in the transparent area when you add a background in the Add Watermark & Background dialog box. Those areas on the pages that appear opaque do not display the background data. Traditionally, when you construct pages and add text and graphics, the whitespace around the text and graphics is interpreted by Acrobat as transparent. The text and graphics on a page are opaque, hiding a background you import in Acrobat, while the transparent area shows the bacground behind the page data. When you display the transparency grid in Acrobat, the gray checkerboard display you see on the page shows the background, whereas the remaining objects ultimately hide a background.

4. **Click OK to close the window.**

5. **Examine the pages with the transparency grid in view. Click the Next Page tool to scroll through pages in the document.**
   The area on each page where you see a gray grid displays all transparent areas. In this example, all the pages contain sufficient transparency that, when adding a background, significantly changes the page design.

6. **Press Control/Command+K to reopen the Preferences dialog box.**

7. **Uncheck the box for Display Transparency Grid. Click OK to exit the Preferences dialog box.**

8. **Choose Document→Add Watermark & Background.**
   The Add Watermark & Background dialog box opens. By default, the Add a Background (Appears Behind Page) radio button is selected. You make choices for adding either a Watermark or Background by selecting the respective radio button in the top-left corner of the dialog box.

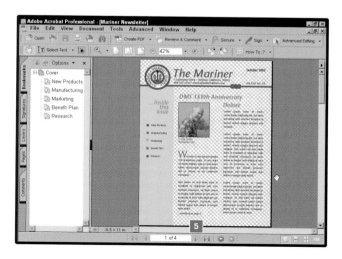

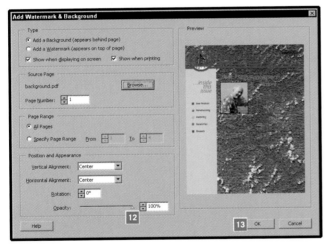

9. **Click the Browse button.**

   Be certain the radio button is selected for Add a Background (Appears Behind Page) and click the Browse button. The Open dialog box opens. In this dialog box you navigate your hard drive to find a PDF document you want to use for the background image.

10. **Navigate to the Tutorial06 folder. Click** 06_background.pdf **to select the file in the Open dialog box.**

11. **Click Open.**

   You are returned to the Add Watermark & Background dialog box. In the Preview pane you see a preview of the first page in the document with the background added to the page.

12. **Move the Opacity slider to the left until 10% appears in the field box. (Note: you can also type** 10 **in the field box to obtain a 10% opacity.)**

13. **Click OK to close the window.**

   Be certain to leave the remaining options in the dialog box at the default positions. The page range default is set to All Pages. When you click OK, the Background is added to all pages in the file.

14. **Choose File→Save As.**

   Many edits have been made to this file and you updated the file using the Save command. To optimize the file to reduce file size, use the Save As command and completely rewrite the file.

15. **Be certain you are saving to the Tutorial06_finish folder. Click Save in the Save As dialog box.**

16. **Click Yes in the Save As warning dialog box informing you that the file already exists.**

   The file is completely rewritten and optimized.

17. **Quit Acrobat.**

» Session Review

In this session you learned how to add page content in the form or headers and footers and watermarks and backgrounds. Aditionally, you learned how to save open views and change document properties. To review your work, amswer the following questions. Answers are found in the tutorial noted in parentheses.

1. Where are initial view options controlled in Acrobat? (See Tutorial: Saving an Opening View.)

2. How can you display the Bookmarks panel when a document opens? (See Tutorial: Setting Page Modes.)

3. What must you do to have a document title appear in the Acrobat window? (See Tutorial: Adding Document Properties.)

4. What are the advantages for adding document properties? (See Tutorial: Adding Document Properties.)

5. What would you use to add page numbers to the bottom of each page? (See Tutorial: Adding a Background.)

6. What would you use to create a stamp with the word "draft" appearing on each page? (See Tutorial: Adding a Background.)

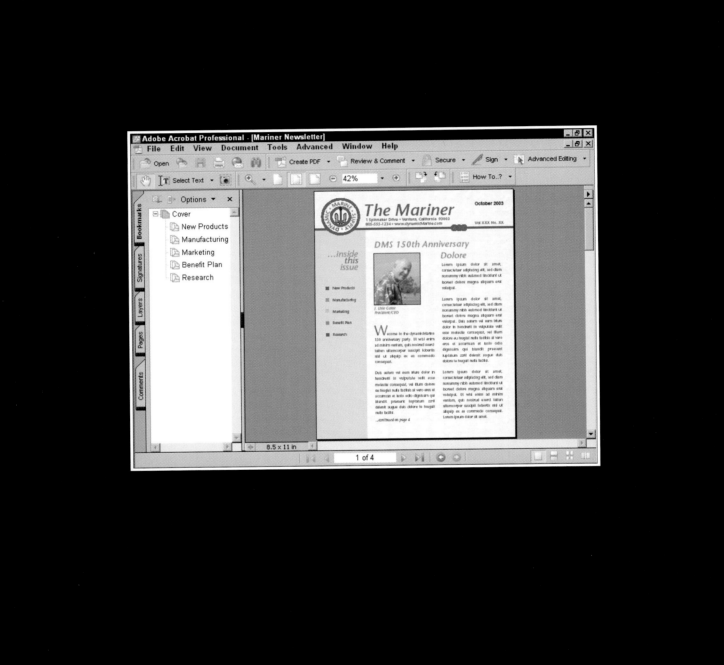

Changing Document Pages

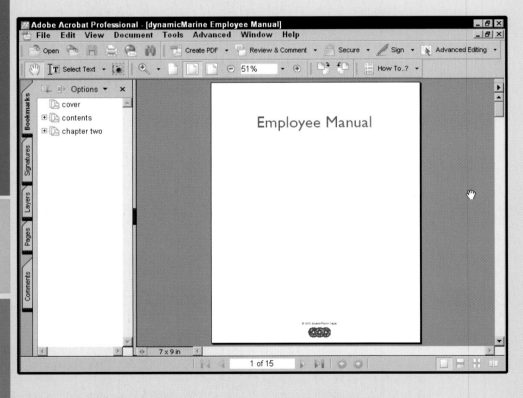

Tutorial: **Importing Multiple Pages**

Tutorial: **Inserting Pages**

Tutorial: **Replacing Pages**

Tutorial: **Ordering Pages**

Session Introduction

You may return to authoring applications to modify page content or create additional pages and need to replace existing PDF pages or insert new pages in PDFs. Rather than completely re-create new PDF documents you can modify files by adding or replacing specific pages. In this tutorial you learn how to append pages to existing documents, replace pages, and reorder pages.

TOOLS YOU'LL USE
Create PDF From Multiple Files command, Insert Pages command, Replace Pages command, Tile Vertically technique, and the Pages panel.

CD-ROM FILES NEEDED
07_acknowledgement.pdf, 07_annualReport.pdf, 07_ceoLetter.pdf, 07_employeeManual.pdf, 07_manualCover.tif, 07_sectionThree.pdf, 07_sectionThreeHead.pdf, 07_sectionTwo.pdf, and 07_sectionTwoHead.pdf (found in the Sessions/Session07/Tutorial07 folder).

TIME REQUIRED
90 minutes

Tutorial
» Importing Multiple Pages

You likely use different authoring programs to create PDF documents or acquire files from other users that need to be combined to form a single document. In this tutorial you learn how to append pages to existing PDF documents.

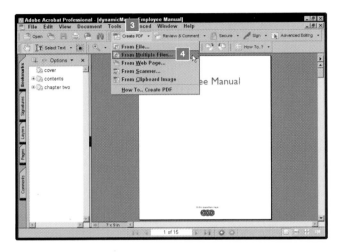

1. **Mount the CD–ROM located in the back of this book. Drag the folder Session07 from inside the Sessions folder to your desktop. Launch Acrobat by double-clicking the program icon.**

2. **Open the file** `07_employeeManual.pdf` **from the Tutorial07 folder.**
   If you remember the lessons in Session03 where you added bookmarks to the Employee Manual document, you know there are bookmark links to pages in the file. Additional pages need to be added to this file to complete the manual. Rather than create a new file and re-create the bookmarks, you can append new pages to the existing document and preserve all the exist-ing bookmarks.

3. **Click the Create PDF button.**

4. **Choose From Multiple Files.**
   The Create PDF From Multiple Documents dialog box opens.

5. **Click Browse.**
   The Open dialog box opens. Navigate to the Tutorial07 folder.

6. **Click** `07_sectionThree.pdf`.

7. **Shift-click** `07_sectionTwoHead.pdf`.
   All files between the first and last click are selected.
   These four files are appended to the open document.

8. **Click the Add button.**
   You are returned to the Create PDF from Multiple Documents dialog box.

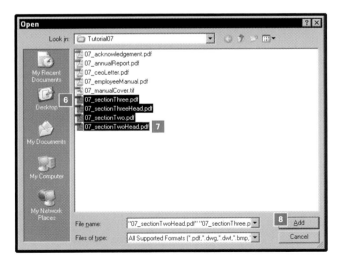

9. **Uncheck the box for Include All Open PDF Documents.**
   The open file is eliminated from the list of files to be combined into a single PDF file.

10. **Click** 07_sectionTwoHead.pdf.

11. **Click Move Up until the document appears at the top of the list.**
    The section heads need to be listed before each section content.

12. **Click** 07_sectionThreeHead.pdf **and click Move Up until the file appears third in the list.**

13. **Click OK.**
    The four files are combined into a single PDF file and appear as a new file titled Binder1.pdf. As yet the file is unsaved.

14. **Choose Window→Tile→Vertically.**
    The two open files appear in a tiled view where both files are simultaneously shown in the Document pane.

15. **Click the Pages tab.**
    The Binder1.pdf document is the active document. When you click Pages in the Navigation pane, the Pages panel opens.

16. **Click the** 07_employeeManual.pdf **document to make it the active file. Click Pages.**
    The Pages panel opens. Both files are shown in the Document pane with the Pages panel open for both files.

<NOTE>

The title shown in the Document pane for the
07_employeeManual.pdf document shows *dynamicMarine Employee Manual*. If you remember from Session06, you added a Document Description and chose to view the file by Document Title in the Initial View properties. Therefore, the Document Title appears in the Title Bar as opposed to the filename.

17. **Scroll the thumbnails to the bottom of the Pages panel so you can see page 15.**
    Drag the scroll bar or click the down-pointing arrow to scroll the page thumbnails.

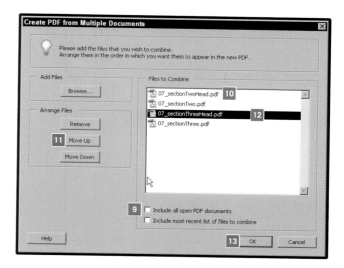

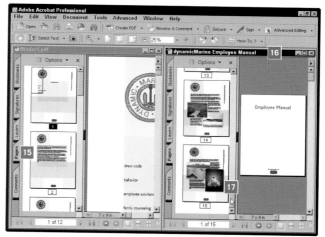

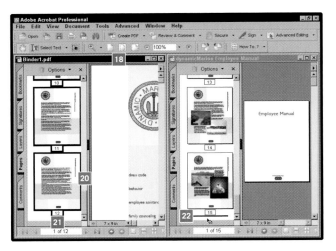

18. **Click** `Binder1.pdf` **to make it the active document.**
    Click anywhere on the document window to make the document active. When you click the document, you'll notice the title bar appears in a solid color while the inactive document title bar appears gray.

19. **Click the first page in the** `Binder1.pdf` **document.**
    Be certain the page thumbnail appears with a black keyline border. When you see the black border around the page thumbnail, you know the thumbnail is selected.

20. **Press Shift and click the last page thumbnail in the Pages panel.**
    All page thumbnails are selected in the file.

<NOTE>
You can also select all page thumbnails by clicking a page and choosing Edit➔Select All or by pressing Control/Command+A.

21. **Click and drag page 12 (or any selected page) from the** `Binder1.pdf` **document and drag it to the Pages panel in the** `07_employeeManual.pdf` **document directly below page 15.**
    Notice the cursor changes to an arrow with a tiny plus (+) symbol below the arrow. When you see the cursor change, release the mouse button and the pages are copied to the target document. Also notice a horizontal black bar appears above the cursor and below the page thumbnail. The bar shows you where the new pages are added to the target document. In this example, the pages are appended to the end of the file.

<TIP>
If you want to delete pages from one document as they are copied to another document, press the Control/Option key and then click and drag to the target document. When using the key modifier, the page is deleted from the host document while copied to the target document. You can delete all but one page from the host file. At least one page must remain in a document when deleting pages.

22. **Release the mouse button when you see the cursor change to an arrow with a plus (+) symbol below the arrow.**

23. **Close the** `Binder1.pdf` **document without saving the file.**
    Click No when prompted in a dialog box asking you if you want to save the file. The file was created as a temporary file to add the pages to the `07_employeeManual.pdf` document.

24. Click the Maximize button to expand the document window.

25. Scroll the scroll bar up in the Pages panel to page 1.

26. Choose File→Save As. Save the file to the Tutorial07_finish folder as 07_employeeManual_finish.pdf.

27. Keep the document open to follow the steps in the next tutorial.

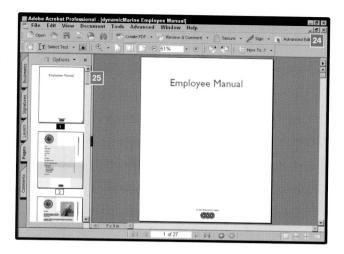

Appending Pages

When you use the Create PDF From Multiple Files command, you can combine pages in separate files along with the open document. In this tutorial you created a second file (the Binder1.pdf) and appended pages by dragging and dropping pages from the Binder1.pdf document to the target file.

If you chose to add files to the employee manual document in the Create PDF from Multiple Files dialog box, you end up with a document the same as the file you saved in step 26. Using this method, however, loses all document description information and all Initial View options you saved in the original file.

Rather than create a new PDF document where you need to add a document description and set the Initial View options, by using the existing file and appending pages you preserve all the document properties.

Acrobat also offers you an option to insert pages from a menu command where you can append pages to an existing file. However, when using the Insert Pages command, you can't order the pages. Therefore, creating a new PDF with the Create PDF From Multiple Files command tends to work best when you need to order pages first, and then append those pages through the drag-and-drop method using the Pages panel.

Tutorial
» Inserting Pages

If you have a single file to append to a document, you can use the Insert Pages command by choosing Document→Pages→ Insert. Additionally, Acrobat enables you to drag-and-drop files from your desktop to the active document. In this tutorial you learn how to insert pages in a PDF file without using the Create PDF From Multiple Files command.

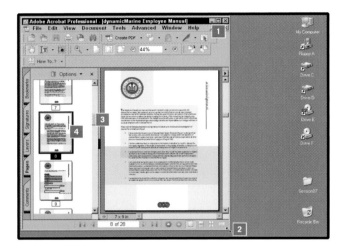

1. **Click the Minimize button in the Acrobat window (Windows). On the Macintosh, drag the far lower-right corner of the Acrobat window in toward the center of the Document pane to resize the window.**

2. **Drag the lower-right corner of the Acrobat window to resize the window to about two-thirds of your monitor view.**

3. **Drag the page thumbnails scroll bar down to view page 8 in the Pages panel.**

4. **Click the page 8 thumbnail to bring page 8 in view in the Document pane.**
   A page needs to be inserted after page 8 in the employee manual. Because only a single document is to be inserted, you don't need to use the Create PDF From Multiple files command and order pages before insertion.

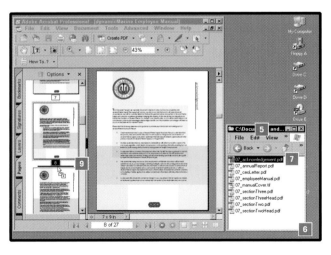

5. **Open the Tutorial07 folder on your desktop.**

6. **Size the window by dragging the lower-right corner. Position the window adjacent to the Acrobat window.**

7. **Choose** 07_acknowledgement.pdf **in the Tutorial07 folder.**

8. **Drag the file to the Pages panel below the page 8 thumbnail.**

9. **Release the mouse button when you see the cursor change to an arrow with a plus (+) symbol below the arrowhead.**
   The page is inserted after page 8 in the PDF document.

10. **Maximize the Acrobat window by clicking the Maximize button (Windows) or the plus (+) symbol in the top-left corner of the window (Macintosh).**

11. **Scroll the page thumbnails to page 1 in the Pages panel.**

12. **Click the page 1 thumbnail.**

13. **Click the Save button to update the file.**

14. **Leave the file open to follow the steps in the next tutorial.**

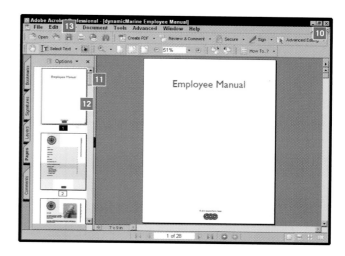

Inserting Pages

You can use a menu command to insert pages in a file. When you choose Document→Pages→Insert, the Select File To Insert dialog box opens. You select the file(s) to insert and click Select. You can also access the same menu command by opening a context menu from a page thumbnail and clicking Insert Pages. The same Select File to Insert dialog box opens when using a context menu as when using the top-level menu command.

After clicking Select, the Insert Pages dialog box opens. You make choices for inserting pages before or after a page number you type in the Page field box. Click OK and the page(s) is inserted in the file.

Using the drag-and-drop method offers you more of a visual representation for knowing exactly where a page or pages are inserted in a file. However, either method results in the same action, and pages are appended to the open file while still preserving all your document property information.

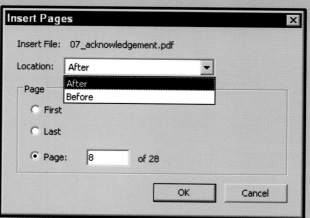

Tutorial
» Replacing Pages

Replacing pages in PDF documents is a function you'll use frequently. After you create links, form fields, comments, or other data on pages, if you delete a page, all links are broken or content is lost. If you need to modify a page in an authoring program and want to change the old page with a new page, using the Replace command replaces the page contents while preserving links, form fields, and other data added in Acrobat. In this tutorial you learn how to replace pages without disturbing links.

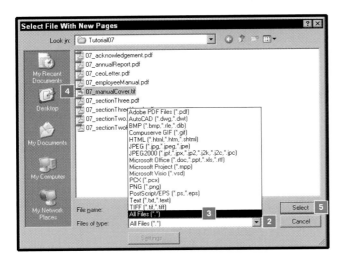

1. **Choose Document→Pages→Replace Pages.**
   The Select File with New Pages dialog box opens.

2. **Click the down-pointing arrow for Files of Type to open the pull-down menu.**

3. **Choose All Files.**

4. **Choose** `07_manualCover.tif`.
   Notice the selected file is a TIFF file. When you use either the Insert or Replace command, you can select any file type compatible with the Create PDF From File command. Pages are dynamically converted to PDF and inserted or replaced depending on the command you use.

5. **Click the Select button.**
   The Replace Pages dialog box opens.

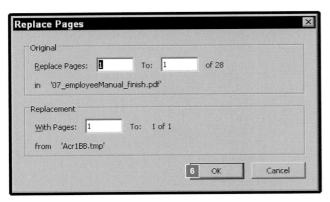

6. **Click OK.**
   By default the active page is targeted for replacement. When you selected the page 1 thumbnail in step 12 in the last tutorial, page 1 became the active page. If you notice another page listed in the Replace Pages field box, type 1 in the first field box. The Replace Pages dialog box enables you to target any page in the file for replacement. The selected file is converted to PDF and replaces the cover page (page 1 in the file).

7. **Click the Bookmarks tab.**

8. **Click the contents bookmark.**

9. **Click the cover bookmark.**
   Notice the bookmark link is operable and takes you back to the cover page. By replacing the page, your bookmarks remain intact. If you deleted page 1 in the document and inserted the new cover page, you not only need to perform two steps, but you also lose the bookmark link to the cover page.

10. **Choose File→Save As. Save the file to the Tutorial07_finish folder and rewrite the file to optimize it.**
    Click Yes when prompted to replace the file.

11. **Click the Close button to close the file.**

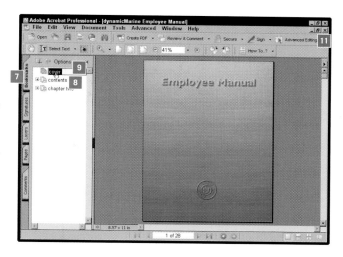

Replacing Pages Through Drag-and-Drop Methods

In order to drag a file from the desktop to the Pages panel for page insertions or replacing pages, you must drag a PDF document to the panel. Other file types cannot be dragged to the Pages panel. If you drag a document other than PDF to the Document pane, the file is converted to PDF as a new PDF document. The file type needs to be compatible with the Create PDF From File command in order to convert to PDF.

Drag-and-drop methods for replacing document pages are permitted once you have converted a document to PDF; however, you must view both documents in the Document pane. If you attempt to replace a page by dragging a PDF document from the desktop, the file is inserted in the current open file.

To replace a page between two open files, first view the documents in a tiled view by choosing Window→Tile→Vertically (or Horizontally). Open both Pages panels. Click the replacement page and drag it to the target document on top of the page to be replaced. When the target page reverses color (turns black), release the mouse button.

To get the page to reverse color indicating the page will be replaced, be certain to move the cursor directly over the page

number in the Pages panel. Placing the cursor over the page thumbnail inserts the page instead of replacing it. Release the mouse button when you see the page color reverse and the page is replaced in the target document.

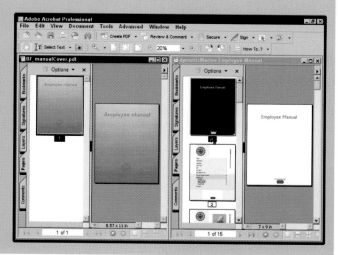

Tutorial
» Ordering Pages

Acrobat provides you with an easy method for changing page order in the Pages panel if you find that you later need to reorder your pages. In this tutorial you learn how to change thumbnail views to clearly view pages and reorder them.

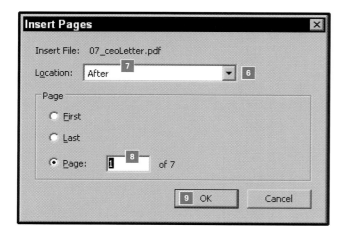

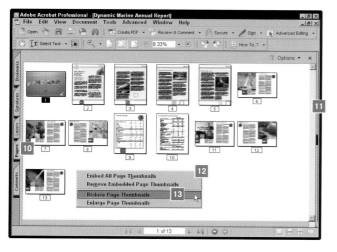

1. **Click Open.**
   Use the Open tool in the Acrobat Toolbar Well or choose File→Open.

2. **Choose** `07_annualReport.pdf` **in the Open dialog box and click Open.**

3. **Choose Document→Pages→Insert.**
   The Select File to Insert dialog box opens.

4. **Navigate to the Tutorial07 folder and click** `07_ceoLetter.pdf`.

5. **Click Select.**

6. **Click the down-pointing arrow to open the Location pull-down menu.**

7. **Choose After from the pull-down menu.**

8. **Type** `1` **in the field box.**
   Also by default you may see 1 in the field box. If another value appears, delete the value and type 1.

9. **Click OK.**
   The selected file is inserted after page 1. The inserted file contains six pages. A few pages need to be reordered in the composite document. To reorder the pages you use the Pages panel.

10. **Click the Pages tab.**
    The Pages panel opens.

11. **Drag the vertical separator bar on the right side of the Pages panel to the far right of the Document pane.**
    Dragging the vertical separator bar left or right minimizes or expands the Pages panel.

12. **Open a context menu in the Pages panel.**
    Right-click (Windows) or Control-click (Macintosh) away from any page thumbnail. A context menu opens.

13. **Choose Reduce Page Thumbnails from the pop-up context menu.**
    Notice the page thumbnails are displayed in a smaller size. Continue to reduce the page thumbnails if you can't see all the pages on your monitor. To reduce the page thumbnails, return to the context menu and select the command again. You can keep increasing or decreasing size by clicking the respective menu command for enlarging or reducing the thumbnails.

14. **Click page 10 and drag it to the position between page 1 and page 2.**

    The two financial statements (pages 9 and 10) need to be reordered to different page positions in the file. The consolidated financial statement (page 10) needs to appear after page 1, and the financial summary (page 9) needs to be relocated to the last page in the document. You can use the Pages panel much like a slide sorter and move pages around the file by clicking and dragging them to new positions.

15. **Release the mouse button when you see the vertical separator bar appear between page 1 and page 2.**

    The vertical separator bar indicates where the page is dropped. When you release the mouse button, the page is relocated between the two pages on either side of the separator bar.

16. **Click and drag page 10 and place it after page 13.**

    Once again be certain to release the mouse button when you see the vertical separator bar appear on the right side of page 13.

17. **Drag the Pages panel separator bar back to position.**

18. **Double-click page 1 in the Pages panel to view the opening page.**

19. **Choose File→Save As and save the file to the 07_Tutorial_finish folder as** 07_annualReport_finish.pdf.

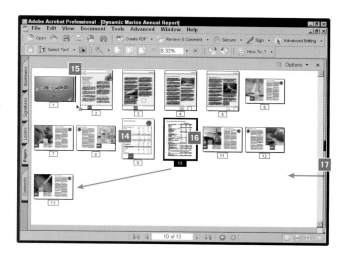

Deleting and Extracting Pages

Other page-editing commands you'll find helpful are the Delete Pages command and the Extract Pages command. Page deletions are performed by using the Document→Pages→Delete menu command or by opening a context menu in the Pages panel and clicking Delete Pages.

When you choose Document→Pages→Delete, the Delete Pages dialog box opens. Enter the page range in the From and To field boxes and click OK. By default a warning dialog box opens asking you to confirm the deletion.

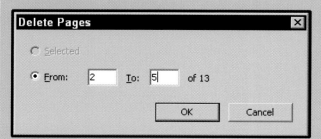

Whether a confirmation dialog box opens or not is determined in the General Preferences. When you open the Edit→Preferences (Windows) or Acrobat→Preferences (Macintosh) dialog box and click General, an option for Disable Edit Warnings appears at the bottom of the General Preference options. If you enable the check box, warning dialog boxes do not open when performing many editing tasks. This option is helpful when you need to perform the same edits many times during an editing session to avoid the extra step to click Yes each time an edit is made, but be certain to exercise care if you decide to disable the edit warnings. Some edits you make in Acrobat are not undoable, and you may need to revert your document to a last save or start over if you make mistakes.

When you open a context menu in the Pages panel, be certain to open the context menu when the cursor is placed over a page thumbnail. Context menus change depending on whether the cursor is placed over a page or whether the cursor is placed away from pages in the Pages panel.

From a context menu, click Delete Pages and the same Delete Pages dialog box opens as when using the Document→Pages→ Delete menu command. You can specify a page range and delete the pages denoted in the From and To field boxes. However, another way to mark pages for deletion is to select them in the Pages panel. Click and Shift-click to select pages in a contiguous order. You can use Control/Command-click and select pages

randomly in a non-contiguous order. Once the pages are selected, open a context menu and the Selected radio button is enabled. Click OK and all the selected pages are deleted.

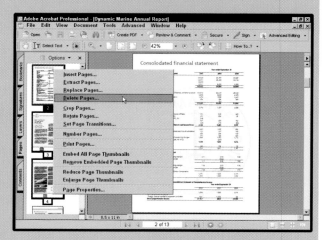

If you want to pull out a page in a PDF document and create a separate PDF file, use the Document→Pages→Extract command. A page or range of pages can be extracted from a file and you have a choice to either leave the pages in the original file or delete them after extraction. Click the check box for Delete Pages After Extracting if you want to delete pages.

If you select pages in a non-contiguous order in the Pages panel, for example page 1, 3, and 5, and select Extract from the Pages submenu or Extract Pages from a context menu, Acrobat extracts all pages between the first and last pages selected. In this case pages 1 through 5. Non-contiguous selections are not permitted when using the Extract pages command. To get around the problem, extract all pages between the first and last page in a group and then use the Delete Pages command to eliminate those pages you don't want to use.

» Session Review

In this session you learned how to save initial views, add document description, and modify PDF pages using headers and backgrounds. Answers are found in the tutorial noted in parentheses.

1. What's the advantage to appending pages to a new document over using the Create PDF From Multiple Pages command to create a new document? (See Tutorial: Importing Multiple Pages.)

2. How do you delete pages from one file when copying them to another file? (See Tutorial: Replacing Pages.)

3. What's the best method to use to change a page while preserving links? (See Tutorial: Inserting Pages.)

4. Name three ways to insert pages in a PDF document. (See Tutorial: Inserting Pages.)

5. What's the best method to append pages to a document when you need to combine several files to a host document? (See Tutorial: Importing Multiple Pages.)

6. How do you delete several pages in a non-contiguous page order? (See Tutorial: Ordering Pages.)

7. How do you change the size of page thumbnails? (See Tutorial: Ordering Pages.)

8. What is the optimum view when swapping pages between PDF documents? (See Tutorial: Replacing Pages.)

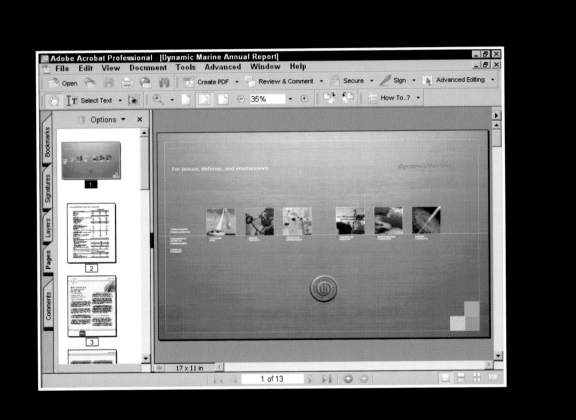

Changing Document Content

Tutorial: **Editing Text with the TouchUp Text Tool**

Tutorial: **Adding New Lines of Text**

Tutorial: **Moving, Copying, and Pasting Text**

Tutorial: **Creating Web Links from Text**

Tutorial: **Copying and Pasting Images**

Session Introduction

In the last two sessions you learned how to modify page designs and work with page-editing tasks. In addition to these editing features, you can also make minor edits to page content. In this tutorial you learn how to edit text and import images on PDF pages.

TOOLS YOU'LL USE
TouchUp Text tool, TouchUp Object tool, Select Object tool, Text Properties.

CD-ROM FILES NEEDED
08_performanceEvaluation.pdf and 08_dynamicMarineLogo.ai
(found in the Sessions/Session08/Tutorial08 folder).

TIME REQUIRED
90 minutes

Tutorial
» Editing Text with the TouchUp Text Tool

Minor text edits can be made in Acrobat Standard and Acrobat Professional with the TouchUp Text tool. Ideally, you should always return to an original authoring program to make any major changes in a document. However, for editing spelling errors, adding or deleting words to a body of text, or adding a new line of text, you can use Acrobat when you have the necessary type fonts installed in your system. In this tutorial, you learn to make some minor corrections with the TouchUp Text tool.

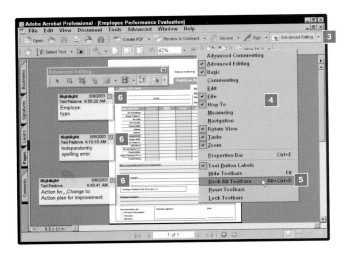

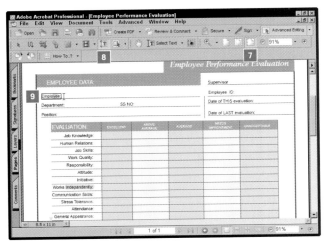

1. **Mount the CD–ROM located in the back of this book. Drag the folder Session08 from inside the Sessions folder to your desktop. Launch Acrobat by double-clicking the program icon.**

2. **Open the file 08_performanceEvaluation.pdf from the Tutorial08 folder.**
   The document contains three notes where spelling errors and text modifications are needed. In this tutorial you'll edit the text where the highlights are indicated and later delete the comment notes and highlights.

3. **Click the Advanced Editing button in the Acrobat Toolbar Well.**
   To begin an editing session where you want to change the document content, you need to access tools used for the kinds of edits you want to make. The Advanced Editing toolbar contains tools you'll use for text editing. When you click the Advanced Editing task button in the Toolbar Well, the Advanced Editing toolbar opens.

4. **Open a context menu from the Toolbar Well by right-clicking (Windows) or Control-clicking (Macintosh). You can click anywhere in the Toolbar Well to open a context menu.**

5. **Choose Dock All Toolbars.**
   The Advanced Editing toolbar is docked in the Toolbar Well.

6. **Click the close box on the note windows.**
   First take a look at the note comment to understand what edit needs to be made. Close the note window by clicking the X in the top-right corner so you can see the text clearly.

7. **Click the Fit Width tool.**
   When you click the Fit Width tool, the page zooms in the Document pane, making it easier for you to edit text.

8. **Click the TouchUp Text tool.**
   Text edits are made with the TouchUp Text tool.

9. **Click the cursor between the *y* and *e* in *Employe*. Press the *e* key on your keyboard to correct the misspelled word.**
   Acrobat pauses a moment to assess your installed fonts. Wait for the progress bar shown in the lower-left corner of the Acrobat window to finish and you'll see the new character added to the word.

<NOTE>
The Advanced Editing toolbar may open as a floating toolbar in the Acrobat window or it may expand in the Toolbar Well. If the toolbar is expanded in the Toolbar Well there is no need to dock the toolbar.

Understanding Acrobat's Text Tools

After expanding the Advanced Editing toolbar, you'll notice the appearance of two text tools in the Acrobat Toolbar Well. The tools perform different operations, and you should understand what these two tools are used for and the purposes they serve.

The TouchUp Text tool is used for editing text in PDF documents. When you click a text block, you may see a word, a line of text, or a paragraph selected. Text selections are denoted by the appearance of a keyline border around the text block when you click the text.

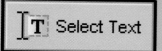

The other text tool in the Acrobat Toolbar Well is the Select Text tool. This tool is used for selecting text. However, no edits are made with the Select Text tool in regard to changing the text in a document. Whereas the TouchUp Text tool is limited to selecting individual words or lines of text, the Select Text tool can be used to select all the text on a page or all text throughout the entire document.

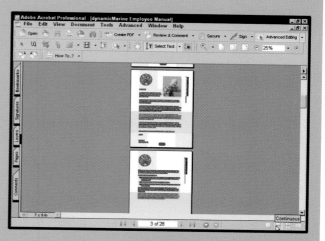

Once text is selected with the Select Text tool, the text can be copied and pasted into other applications. You can, for example, copy text with the Select Text tool and paste the text in a word processing program like Microsoft Word. In Word you can edit the text and create a new PDF document. The text from Word or any other program, however, cannot be reintroduced in the existing PDF file.

To copy text with the Select Text tool, click and drag the tool around or through the text block(s) you want to copy. Columns of text are selected by pressing the Control/Option key and dragging a marquee around the column you want to copy. To select all text on a page, navigate to the page where the text is to be copied and view the pages as a Single Page layout. Click the Select Text tool and choose Edit→Select All. To select all text in a document with two or more pages, first click the Continuous page layout tool in the Acrobat Status Bar, and then choose Edit→Select All.

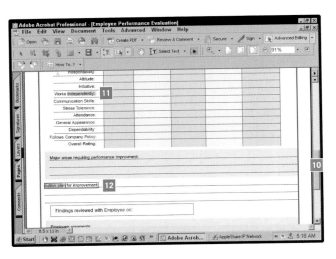

10. Scroll the document page down by clicking the down arrow or move the scroll bar so the next edits to be made are in view.

11. Click the TouchUp Text tool in the word *independantly* and correct the spelling error.

12. Click the TouchUp Text tool after *Action* and type *plan*.

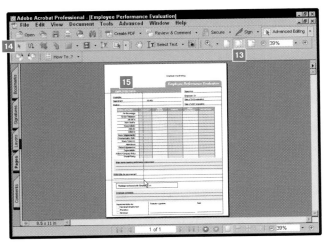

13. **Click the Fit Page tool.**

14. **Click the Select Object tool.**

15. **Click and drag a marquee around the comment highlights.**
    The three highlights are selected.

16. **Press the Backspace/Delete key or the Del key.**
    The comment highlights and respective pop-up notes are deleted.

17. **Choose File→Save As.**

18. **Save the file as** 08_evaluation.pdf **to the Tutorial08_finish folder.**

19. **Keep the file open to follow the steps in the next tutorial.**

Understanding Acrobat's Select Tools

In addition to the two types of Text tools in Acrobat, there are also two kinds of selection tools. It is equally important for you to understand the difference between these tools and the kinds of selections and edits made with each tool.

 The Select Object tool is used to select all content you create in Acrobat. The content takes the form of items like comments, links, form fields, and so on that you add with tools in Acrobat where the content does not originate in your authoring program before you convert to PDF.

When you place a marquee around an area on a page or click an object, only those elements created in Acrobat are selected. Once

selected, you can modify the content, move it, or delete it. The tool does not affect the underlying page content that you created in an authoring program.

 The TouchUp Object tool is used to select only the content on a page that was created in an authoring program. You can select text, images, and artwork on a page and move objects and delete them.

If you place a marquee atound an area or click objects, the tool does not select any content you created in Acrobat such as the comments, links, form fields, and so on mentioned previously.

Working with Fonts

One of many advantages of the Portable Document Format (PDF) is that type fonts can be embedded in the file. This feature enables you to exchange documents with different users and across different computer systems. When fonts are embedded in a PDF file, the text displays exactly the same as when you created the file in an authoring program.

The fact that fonts are most often embedded in a document requires you to unembed fonts when you edit text. The process of unembedding fonts is automatic when you click a block of text and begin your edits. To do so, however, requires you to have native fonts installed in your system. If you attempt to edit text with the TouchUp Text tool using a font that's not installed in your system, Acrobat opens a warning dialog box informing you the font cannot be found in your system and thus the line of text cannot be edited.

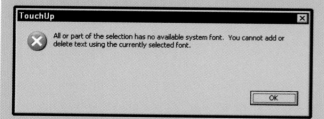

To examine document fonts and determine which fonts are used and whether they are embedded, you can view fonts and font

attributes in the Document Properties. Choose File→Document Properties and click Fonts in the left pane in the Document Properties dialog box. Fonts are listed by font name and font type; those fonts embedded in the document are described as *(Embedded Subset)*.

For more information about fonts, including the kinds of fonts that can be embedded, font restrictions for embedding, and font subsetting, see the Acrobat Help document.

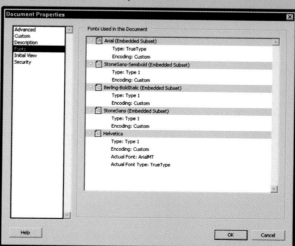

Tutorial
» Adding New Lines of Text

Occasionally, you might want to add text to a page. New lines of text can be added with the TouchUp Text tool, which eliminates the need for you to return to an authoring program for minor text additions. When you add new text to a document, you can use fonts loaded in your system and embed the fonts in the document. In this tutorial you learn how to add new text to a page and change font attributes.

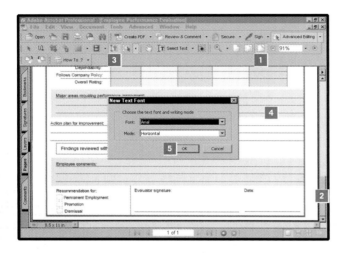

1. **Click the Fit Width button.**
   The 08_evaluation_finish.pdf document should be open in Document pane. If it is not, open the file from the Tutorial08_finish folder and click the Fit Width tool.

2. **Scroll to the bottom of the page by clicking the down arrow in the scroll bar or dragging the scroll bar to the bottom of the scroll bar.**

3. **Click the TouchUp Text tool.**

4. **Position the cursor below the third line on the right side of the page under the topic *Major areas requiring performance improvement*. Press Control (Windows) or Option (Macintosh) and click.**
   You immediately notice the New Text Font dialog box open. Before you begin typing, you can select the font you want to use from the Font pull-down menu and whether the type is added in a horizontal or vertical line from the Mode pull-down menu. Note that when the dialog box opens, you don't see a blinking cursor. You begin typing and the text is added from the position where you clicked the TouchUp Text tool while pressing the modifier key.

5. **Click OK in the New Text Font dialog box.**
   Don't be concerned about the default font or point size. By default Horizontal text is selected. Leave the defaults and click OK to see *New Text* appear where you clicked the mouse cursor. The text is selected; therefore, you can replace the text when you begin typing.

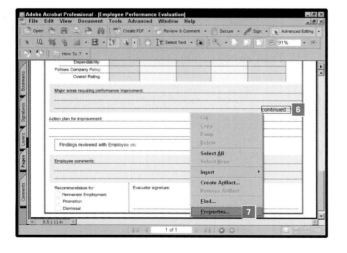

6. **Type continued...**
   This form will be used in a later tutorial where you'll add new pages for continuation of comments for the last three items on the page where you see lines for supervisor and employee comments. The word *continued* will be used to denote a link or button field that opens another page in the document. The same text needs to be added below each comment category. Before you add text, you should first change text properties.

7. **Open a context menu and choose Properties.**
   The TouchUp Properties dialog box opens.

8. **Select Arial for the font.**

   By default Arial might appear listed in the Font field box. If Arial is not shown, open the pull-down menu and choose Arial.

9. **Check the boxes for Embed and Subset.**

   To embed and subset the font, be certain to check the boxes.

10. **Open the pull-down menu for Font Size and click 9 pt.**

11. **Click the Fill color swatch and choose a dark blue color.**

    When you click the color swatch, a color palette pops up. Make any color selection from the list of swatch colors. If you want to use a custom color, click Other Color at the bottom of the color palette. Your system color palette opens where additional color selections can be made.

12. **Click the Close button.**

    Notice the text changes dynamically when you make changes to the text properties.

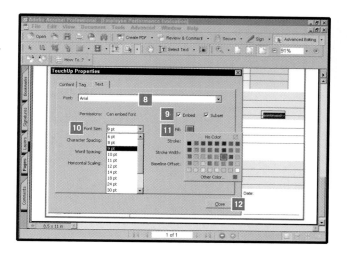

<N O T E>

If you have many text edits to make, you can leave the TouchUp Properties dialog box open while selecting other tools and menu commands. When you finish assigning text attributes, close the dialog box.

13. **Leave the file open to follow the steps in the next tutorial.**

Subsetting Fonts

Often you see the term subset when font embedding is discussed. A font subset is a percentage of characters embedded in the document usually determined by a threshold percentage. For example, if a threshold is 35% and fewer than 35% of all the characters in a font are used, the subset contains only those characters used in the document. If no subsetting is used, the entire character set for a given font is embedded regardless of how many characters in the set are used. As a matter of practice, be certain to use font subsetting when embedding fonts. The result is the creation of smaller file sizes because fewer characters are embedded in the file.

Tutorial

» Moving, Copying, and Pasting Text

Individual lines of text and text blocks can be copied and pasted in a document. In the last tutorial you created a new line of text. The same text with the same text attributes needs to be repeated twice on the form. Rather than add separate lines of text and assign attributes, you can copy, paste, and move text on a page. In this tutorial you learn how to move, copy, and paste text.

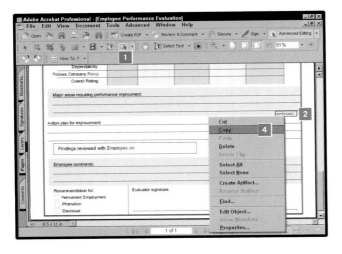

1. **Click the TouchUp Object tool.**

2. **Click the text block created in the last tutorial (the *continued...* text).**

3. **Press an arrow key on your keyboard in the direction needed to move the text along the right side of the page and below the third line in the first comment box. The text moves one point at a time. Keep pressing the arrow keys to nudge the text into position.**

<TIP>

To nudge text press the arrow keys on your keyboard in the direction you want the text to move. The text moves one point at a time. To move the text in 10-point increments, press the Control key (Windows) or the Option key (Macintosh) when you press the arrow keys.

4. **Open a context menu with the TouchUp Object tool selected and choose Copy.**

5. **Choose Edit→Paste or open a context menu and choose Paste.**
   A copy of the text is pasted on the page

6. **Click and drag the text to a position below the last line in the second comment box.**
   Press the arrow keys on your keyboard to nudge into position.

7. **Choose Edit→Paste or open a context menu and choose Paste.**

8. **Click and drag the text to a position below the last line in the third comment box.**

9. **Click the Save button.**
   Leave the file open to follow the steps in the next tutorial.

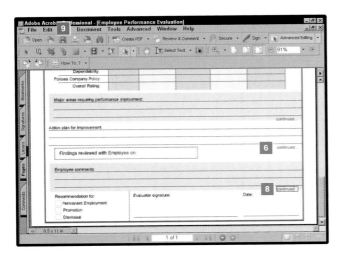

Tutorial

» Creating Web Links from Text

A handy feature in Acrobat is the capability to create URL links to Web addresses. Wherever text appears with a complete URL including http://, Acrobat can automatically create a link through a simple menu command. When the user clicks the link, the default Web browser opens and the URL address is opened in the browser's window. When you add text on a page as described in the last tutorial, you can type a URL address and create a link. In this tutorial you learn how to create Web links from URLs in a document.

1. **Scroll to the top of the page by dragging the scroll bar up to the top of the page.**

2. **Add a new line of text following steps used for creating text and assigning attributes in the last tutorial. Type** http://www. dynamicMarine.com.

3. **Nudge the text so it appears above *Employee Data*.**

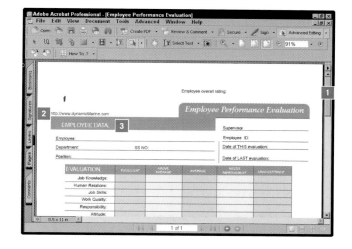

4. **Choose Advanced→Links →Create From URLs in Document.**
   The Create Web Links dialog box opens.

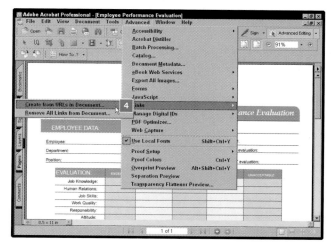

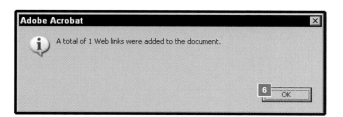

5. Click OK.

Doing so will close the Create Web Links dialog box and open an informational dialog box informing you how many Web links were added.

6. Click OK again in the informational dialog box.

7. Click the Hand tool.

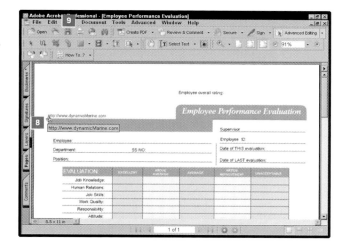

8. Move the cursor over the text you added in step 2.

Notice the cursor change to a hand with the forefinger pointing upward signifying the cursor appears over a link. The tooltip below the cursor displays the URL link. Because this URL address is fictitious, clicking the link won't open a Web page.

9. Click the Save button.

10. Leave the file open to follow the steps in the next tutorial.

Tutorial
» Copying and Pasting Images

You can copy and paste images from programs like Adobe Photoshop and artwork created in programs like Adobe Illustrator into PDF documents. The requirement for copying and pasting images or text is that the data must be in a PDF file. You must convert image files to PDF before attempting to copy the data and paste it into another PDF file. In this tutorial, you learn how to copy data from an illustration and paste it into the employee evaluation form.

1. **Choose File→Open.**

2. **Navigate to the Tutorial08 folder and open the pull-down menu for Files of type (Windows) or Show (Macintosh). Choose All Files (*.*).**
   By default, Adobe PDF files are listed in the Open dialog box. By selecting All files, you can open documents compatible with the Create PDF From File command.

3. **Click** 08_dynamicMarineLogo.ai.
   The file is an Adobe Illustrator file saved with PDF compatibility. Saving with PDF compatibility is available in the Adobe Illustrator Save dialog box. When Illustrator files are saved with PDF compatibility, they can be opened directly in Acrobat without having Adobe Illustrator installed on your computer. However, the files don't appear listed in the Open dialog box until you show all files in the Files of type/Show pull-down menu.

4. **Click the Open button.**
   The file opens in the Document pane in front of the employee evaluation form.

5. **Choose Window→Tile→Horizontally.**

6. **Click the TouchUp Object tool.**

7. **Choose Edit→Select All.**
   When you first click the TouchUp Object tool and then choose Edit→Select All, all objects are selected on the page. The logo was designed in Adobe Illustrator with many objects. To be certain all objects are selected, use the Select All command.

8. **Open a context menu and choose Copy.**
   All objects are copied to the Clipboard.

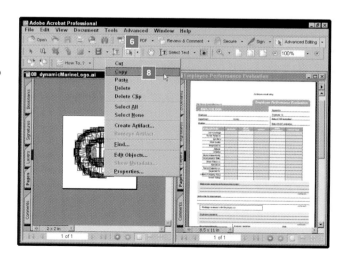

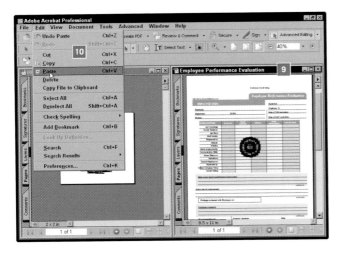

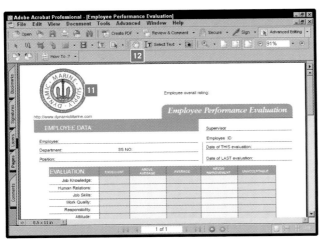

9. **Click the Employee Performance Evaluation document to make it the active window.**

10. **Choose Edit→Paste.**

    Note that there are many tiny objects in the logo. If you accidentally click outside the selected objects, the objects are deselected. If you make a mistake, you can choose Edit→Undo and the logo disappears from the evaluation form. Before closing the 08_dynamicMarineLogo.ai file, move the logo into position in the evaluation document.

11. **Press Control/Option and click the up-arrow key on your keyboard. Press Control/Option and the left arrow. Keep nudging the logo into position in the top-left corner of the document.**

    Note that using the arrow keys prevents you from inadvertently deselecting the image. To move the logo in smaller increments, release the Control/Option key and press the arrow keys.

12. **Click the Hand tool and click anywhere in the document to deselect the logo.**

13. **Choose File→Save As to rewrite the file and optimize it.**

14. **Quit Acrobat.**

< N O T E >

This session describes editing PDF content in Acrobat for minor editing tasks that can be successfully performed for PDF distribution, Web hosting, and CD-ROM archiving. If you intend to create PDF files for digital prepress and commercial printing, the types of edits described in this session might not be satisfactory for printing purposes. When sending files to commercial printers, always make your edits in the original authoring programs and create PDFs either through direct exports to PDF or by using Adobe Acrobat Distiller.

» Session Review

In this session you learned how to edit text, add new text to a document, copy and paste text and objects, and move text and objects on a page. Look over the following questions to review what you've learned in this session. Answers are found in the tutorial noted in parentheses.

1. What tool is used to edit text on a page? (See Tutorial: Editing Text with the TouchUp Text Tool.)

2. How do you select a single column of text where several columns appear on the same page? (See Tutorial: Editing Text with the TouchUp Text Tool.)

3. How can you copy all text in a PDF document? (See Tutorial: Moving, Copying, and Pasting Text.)

4. Why does Acrobat prevent you from editing text? (See Tutorial: Editing Text with the TouchUp Text Tool.)

5. How do you nudge selections more than one point at a time? (See Tutorial: Moving, Copying, and Pasting Text.)

6. Where do you change font types and sizes? (See Tutorial: Editing Text with the TouchUp Text Tool.)

7. How do you add a new line of text to a page? (See Tutorial: Adding New Lines of Text.)

8. How do you create a Web link to a URL on a page? (See Tutorial: Creating Web Links from Text.)

9. How do you add a photo to a PDF document without re-creating the PDF in your authoring program? (See Tutorial: Copying and Pasting Images.)

10. How do you select all objects on a page without selecting the data created in your authoring program? (See Tutorial: Editing Text with the TouchUp Text Tool.)

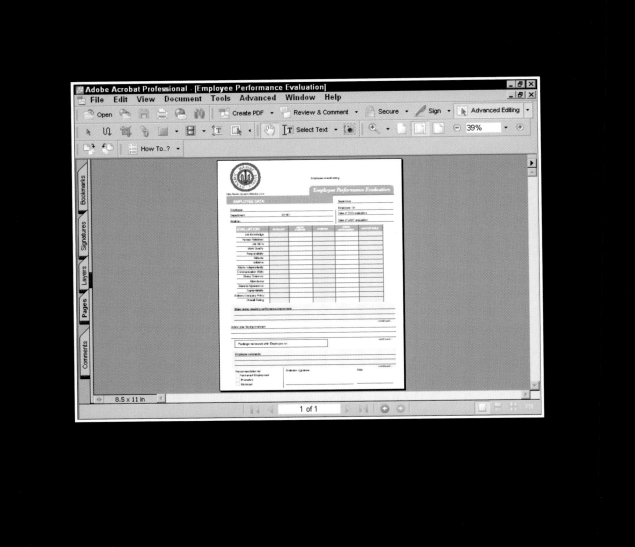

Part V
Commenting and Reviewing

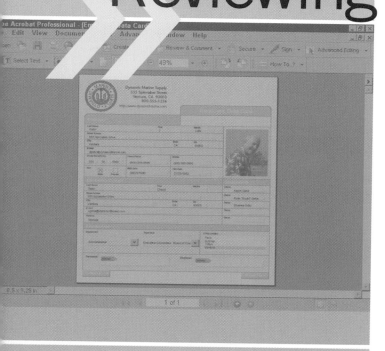

Using
Comment Tools

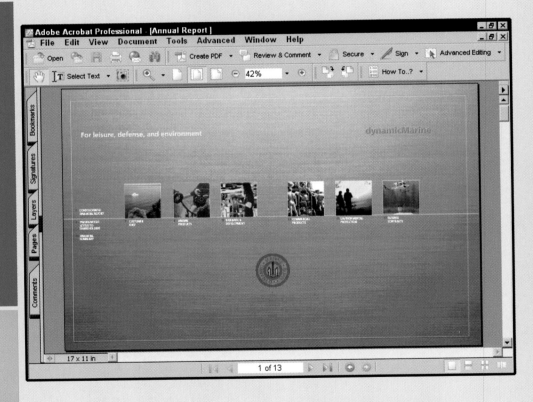

Session Introduction

Part of almost any business occupation is collaboration with colleagues and co-workers for reviewing and commenting on documents. Before files are finalized for print or distribution you might want to have them reviewed by others. Acrobat offers you many tools and features designed to facilitate the review and comment process. In this session, you learn how to create comments in PDF documents.

TOOLS YOU'LL USE
Note tool, Commenting Preferences, Highlighting tools, Drawing tools, Stamp tool, Custom stamps, Attach File tool, Paste Clipboard Image tool, and the Summarize Comments command.

CD-ROM FILES NEEDED
`09_annualReport.pdf`, `09_ceoWelcome.doc`, `09_ceoWelcome.pdf`, and `09_stamps.pdf` (found in the Sessions/Session09/Tutorial09 folder).

TIME REQUIRED
2 hours

Tutorial
» Creating Note Comments

The most frequently used comment tool is the Note tool. The Note tool is used to add notes much like sticky notes added to paper documents in office environments. Note comments have pop-up note windows where messages are typed. These pop-up note windows are also available for many other comment tools. The comment marks change according to the tool used but the note pop-ups appear the same. In this tutorial you begin a commenting session by becoming familiar with the note pop-up windows.

1. **Mount the CD–ROM located in the back of this book. Drag the folder Session09 from inside the Sessions folder to your desktop. Launch Acrobat by double-clicking the program icon.**

2. **Open the file** `09_annualReport.pdf` **from the Tutorial09 folder.**
   The document is currently in draft form. You need to review the document and add comments with a variety of comment tools. For the first comment types, you'll add some comment notes.

3. **Open a context menu on the Acrobat Toolbar Well and choose Reset Toolbars.**
   Before adding commenting toolbars, reset the toolbars back to the default position to eliminate any toolbars loaded in earlier tutorials.

4. **Click the Review and Comment task button.**
   The Commenting toolbar opens as a floating toolbar in the Acrobat window. To begin a commenting session you need to access tools used for the kinds of comments you want to make. There are two sets of toolbars used for comments and additional comment options are found in the Properties Bar and on a Comment panel. To add comments you'll want to open the toolbars and dock them in the Toolbar Well.

5. **Click the down-pointing arrow on the Review and Comment task button and click the Advanced Commenting toolbar.**
   The Advanced Commenting toolbar opens as a floating toolbar in the Acrobat window. You can access the commenting tools from the Review and Comment task button, from a context menu opened from the Toolbar Well, or by clicking View→ Toolbars and clicking the commenting toolbars listed in the submenu.

6. **Open a context menu on the Toolbar Well and choose Properties Bar.**
   In addition to the commenting tools, the Properties Bar is used to edit comment properties. Keep this toolbar open when you begin a commenting session so you can easily change comment properties.

7. **Open the context menu again from the Toolbar Well and choose Dock All Toolbars.**
   The three toolbars are docked in the Toolbar Well.

8. **Click the Note tool.**

9. **Drag a marquee in the top center area of the document with the Note tool.**

   The area where you drag the marquee defines the size of the Note pop-up window. When you release the mouse button, the note pop-up window opens with a blinking cursor enabling you to type a note comment. Also notice that when you release the mouse button, the Hand tool is selected for you.

   <TIP>

   If you want to keep a comment tool selected without reverting to the Hand tool, click the Keep Tool Selected check box in the Properties Bar.

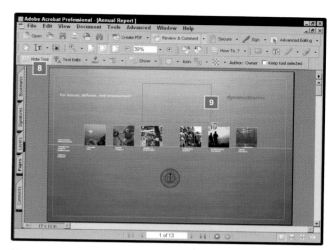

10. **Type a note comment. In this example I added the text** *These photos need to be revised.*

    Note that the title of the note window by default uses your computer login name. The identity of the note comment can be changed in the Note Properties or you can change the default in the Commenting Preferences to use your name for all subsequent comments you add to the document. In this tutorial you'll change Note Properties and in the next tutorial you learn how to change Commenting Preferences.

11. **Position the cursor in the note title bar and right-click to open a context menu.**

12. **Choose Properties from the menu options.**

    The Note Properties dialog box opens. In the Note Properties you can change the icon for the note, change the note color and opacity, change the author name, and examine the review history for comments exchanged in a review session. Some of the properties can also be changed in the Properties Bar; however, you can change the author name only from this dialog box.

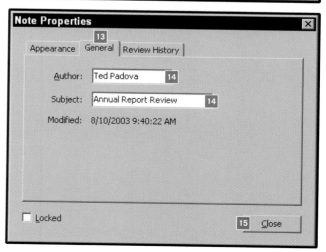

13. **Click the General tab.**

    The General Note Properties provides the options for changing the author's name.

14. **Type your name in the Author field and add a Subject by typing** Annual Report Review **in the Subject field.**

15. **Click the Close button.**

    The Note Properties dialog box closes.

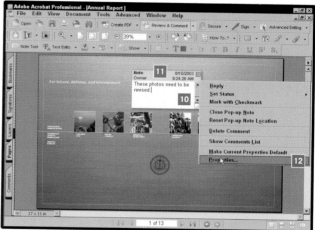

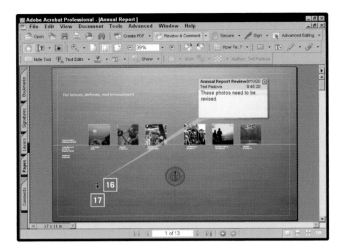

16. **Click the icon you see appear after closing the note pop-up window and drag it to the lower-left side of the page.**

    The note icon represents the comment note you created. When the pop-up window is collapsed, you can reopen the window by double-clicking the icon or using a context menu and choosing Open Pop-Up Note.

17. **Click the note icon to select it.**

    Notice the note pop-up window opens and a connector line is drawn from the note window to the note icon. The connector lines show you where the note icons are located in relation to note pop-up windows. As you draw several comments on a page, separate connector lines are drawn between each comment pop-up note window and the corresponding note icons.

    As note icons are selected, note pop-up windows open. To keep a pop-up note open when the icon is not selected, double-click the icon or click Open Pop-Up Note from a context menu.

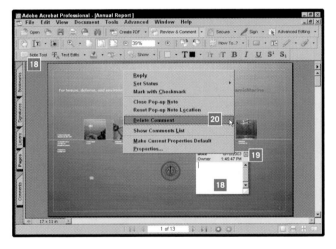

18. **Click the Note tool. Draw another rectangle on the page and release the mouse button.**

    Notice the title bar in the new note. The previous default for using your login name is added to the title bar. The last change you made to the Author field in the Note Properties does not assume a new default.

19. **Move the cursor to the note window's title bar (the yellow area at the top of the note pop-up window) and open a context menu.**

20. **Choose Delete Comment.**

    The comment icon and note pop-up window are deleted from the page. Note that you can also delete note comments by opening a context menu from the note icon and clicking delete, or by clicking the note icon to select it and pressing the Backspace/Delete key.

21. **Keep the file open to follow the steps in the next tutorial.**

Tutorial

» Setting Comment Preferences

Comments and note pop-ups attributes are assigned in the Commenting Preferences. There are an abundant number of preferences for comments, and knowing a little about some of the options helps you when creating and viewing comments. In this tutorial you learn some of the preferences for comments and how to change these preferences.

1. **Choose Edit→Preferences.**
   The Preferences dialog box opens. The first preference you'll change is related to setting new defaults for your pop-up note properties. Rather than open note properties and change the author name, you'll follow some steps to set new defaults so your name appears in the note pop-up window title bar each time you create a new comment.

2. **Click Commenting in the left pane.**

3. **Uncheck the Always Use Log-in Name for Author Name option.**
   You might see the check box disabled when you open the Commenting Preferences. If the check box is enabled, be certain to click the check box to remove the check mark from the box.

4. **Click OK.**

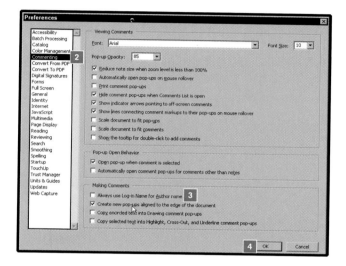

5. **Click the Note icon on the page to select it.**

6. **Click the down-pointing arrow for the color selections in the Properties Bar.**
   Some choices you have available in the Note Properties are also available in the Properties Bar. The default color for the note icon and note pop-up window title bar is yellow. You can change the color for both items by clicking a different color in the color palette that opens from a pull-down menu.

7. **Click the red color swatch.**
   Both the note icon and note pop-up window title bar change to the color you select in the color palette.

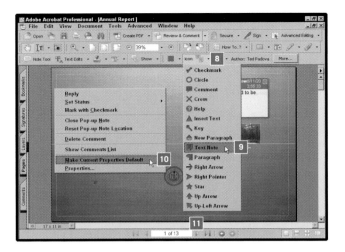

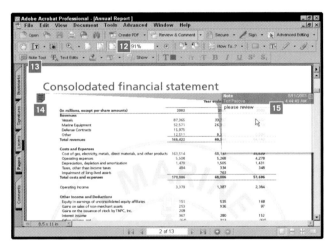

8. **Click the down-pointing arrow to open the Icon pull-down menu in the Properties Bar.**

9. **Choose Text Note.**
   The note icon changes to the shape selected in the pull-down menu.

10. **Open a context menu from either the note icon or the note pop-up window and choose Make Current Properties Default.**
    The defaults for all subsequent comments use all the attributes assigned in the Note Properties dialog box and the Properties Bar.

11. **Click the Next Page tool in the Status Bar.**

12. **Click the Fit Width button.**

13. **Click the Note Tool button.**

14. **Double-click the top of the page.**
    Note comments can also be created by double-clicking the mouse button. When you create a note by double-clicking the mouse button, a fixed size for the note pop-up window is created. Notice the note properties use all the defaults you established for Note Properties and after making the context menu selection for Make Current Properties Default.

15. **Type a comment in the note pop-up window. In this example I typed:** *please review*.

16. **Choose File→Save As. Save the file as** 09_annualReport_ finish.pdf **to the Tutorial09_finish folder.**

17. **Keep the file open to follow the steps in the next tutorial.**

Commenting Preferences

The Commenting Preferences contain many options for displaying comment notes. Here, you can affect the behavior of comments and assign different attributes. The list is long and it takes a little study and practice to become familiar with all the options. For a quick reference, mark this page and look over the following list:

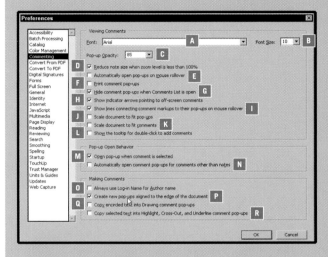

A Font: From the pull-down menu you can select any font loaded in your system to be used for the font in the comment pop-up note windows.

B Font size: The size relates to the font point size in the note comment pop-up windows. You can choose point sizes ranging from 4 points to144 points.

C Pop-up opacity: You can change note pop-up windows opacity to see a transparent view of note windows. Choices are made from the fixed sizes available in the pull-down menu or you can type a value in the field box.

D Reduce note size when zoom level is less than 100%: When a page view is reduced in the Navigation panel, comment pop-up notes are sized proportionately to the zoom view. When zooming out to smaller views, pop-up notes are difficult to read. If you want to fix the note size to a 100% view, disable the check box.

E Automatically open pop-ups on mouse rollover: Pop-up note windows can be opened or closed. Double-clicking a collapsed pop-up note window opens the window. If you want to have a pop-up note window open automatically as the cursor is placed over a comment icon, enable this check box.

F Print comment pop-ups: Enabling this check box prints the pop-up note contents for all pop-up note windows regardless of whether they are opened or collapsed.

G Hide comment pop-ups when comments list is open: The comments list is contained in the Comments panel. When you open the Comments panel, the list shows expanded comment notes with the content displayed in the panel window. To hide the pop-ups in the Document pane when the Comments panel is opened, enable the check box. If you set this item as a default, you can expand comments in the Comments panel by clicking icons to see the content of the pop-ups.

H Show indicator arrows pointing to off-screen comments: Comment icons and pop-up notes are two separate elements. They can be individually located in different places in the Document pane, either on a page or outside the page. When you scroll through a document, arrows indicate that off-screen comments are present when the check box is enabled.

I Show lines connecting comment markups to their pop-ups on mouse rollover: When you roll the mouse pointer over a comment markup (such as highlighting or a note icon), the shaded connector line between the comment and the open pop-up window appears.

J Scale document to fit pop-ups: The document page is scaled to the size of the open pop-up notes. If you have several open pop-up notes that appear off the page, the view in the Document pane is scaled to fit the page and open pop-up note windows including pop-up notes outside the page boundaries.

K Scale document to fit comments: Adjusts the page zoom so that comments outside the page boundaries fit within the current view. This option applies to all comments except pop-up note windows.

L Show the tooltip for double-click to add comments: If a comment pop-up note contains a message, the tooltip displays the message when the cursor is placed over a comment icon while a pop-up note window is collapsed. If no note message is contained in the pop-up note, moving the cursor over a comment icon produces no message and no tooltip. If you enable this check box when the pop-up note window is blank, a tooltip is displayed with the message: *Double-click to add comments.*

Commenting Preferences *(continued)*

M Open pop-up when comment is selected: You open pop-up note windows by double-clicking a comment icon. For a single click operation to open the note window, check this box.

N Automatically open comment pop-ups for comments other than notes: As you create comments with drawing tools, the Text Box tool, or Pencil tool, the pop-up note windows are collapsed by default. If you want a pop-up note window opened and ready to accept type when creating comments with these tools, check the box.

O Always use login name for author name: Uses your computer login name as opposed to the default name you can set with a context menu by selecting Make Current Properties Default. To set the defaults in a context menu, disable this check box.

P Create new pop-ups aligned to the edge of the document: By default the top-left corner of a pop-up note window is aligned to the top-left corner of the comment icon. If you enable this check box, no matter where you create the note icon, the pop-up notes are aligned to the right edge of the document.

Q Copy encircled text into drawing comment pop-ups: When proofreading a document and using the Text Edit tools, you might strike through text, highlight text, or mark it for replacement or you may use drawing tools to encircle passages of text. When you select the text to be edited or encircle text with a drawing tool, the text selection is automatically added to the note pop-up window when this option is selected. You might use this option to show the author of the PDF document how the old text appears and follow up with your recommendations to change the text. In essence, the PDF author can see a before/after comparison.

R Copy selected text into highlight, cross-out, and underline comment pop-ups: Checking this option adds the text selected with tools in the Highlighting toolbar to automatically appear in the pop-up note window.

To become familiar with all the options associated with commenting, practice changing options and view the results in the Document pane. With a little practice you can quickly learn what options work best in your workflow.

Tutorial
» Using the Highlighting Tools

The Highlighting comment tools function like highlighters and pens used with paper documents. The Highlighting toolbar contains a Highlighter tool, a Cross-Out Text tool, and an Underline Text tool. In this tutorial you learn how to use the Highlighting tools to mark up a document for a review.

1. **Click the Next Page tool in the Status Bar.**

2. **Click the Fit Width button.**

3. **Click the down-pointing arrow to open the Highlighting tools.**

4. **Choose Highlighter Tool.**
   Before you begin highlighting text, you'll change a preference setting in the Commenting Preferences.

5. **Choose Edit→Preferences (Windows) or Acrobat →Preferences (Macintosh).**

6. **Choose Commenting.**

7. **Check the last box in the Commenting Preferences. It reads as: Copy Selected Text into Highlight, Cross-Out, and Underline Comment Pop-Ups.**
   Checking this box copies the text you highlight into the pop-up note window.

8. **Click OK in the Preferences dialog box.**

9. **Drag the cursor through the text at the top-left corner of the page where you see *we continue to build a great business*.**
   Notice the text you highlight is copied to the note pop-up window. The text is placed in the note pop-up when the preference option you selected in step 7 is enabled.

10. **Open a context menu on the highlighted text and choose Open Pop-up Note.**
    To keep the note open, use the context menu selection. If you don't select the menu option, the note window closes when you move the cursor away from the highlighted text.

11. **Add the following lines of text:**

    change text to:
    dynamicMarine Supply
    continues to build a
    great business

    The text you type in the note pop-up window is a clear description for the PDF author about what text to change in the document.

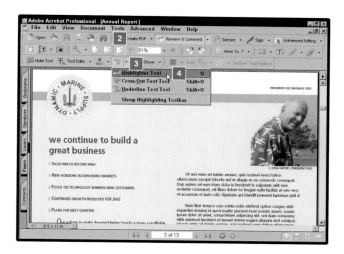

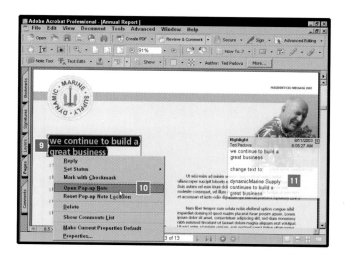

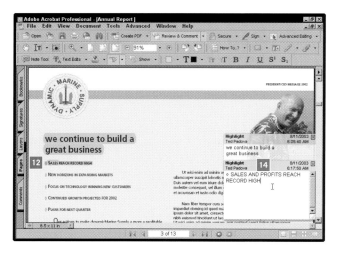

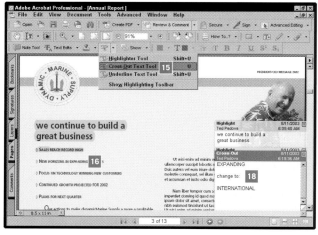

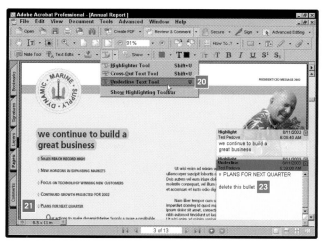

12. Drag the cursor across the first bulleted line of text.

13. Open the note pop-up window by clicking the context menu item the same as step 10.

14. Insert the cursor in the note pop-up window after SALES and type AND PROFITS.

15. Open the pull-down menu for the Highlighting tools and choose Cross-Out Text Tool.

16. Drag the cursor across *EXPANDING* in the second bulleted line. Notice the mark is a strikeout through the highlighted word.

17. Open the pop-up note window by clicking the context menu selection for opening the note.
Move the cursor over the line across the highlighted word. When the cursor changes to an arrowhead, open a context menu and make the menu choice to open the note pop-up window.

18. Type the following text in the note pop-up window:

change to:

INTERNATIONAL

19. Drag the cursor through the word *TECHNOLOGY* in the third bulleted line of text. Open the pop-up note window and type:

change to:

ENVIRONMENT

20. Open the Highlighting tools pull-down menu and choose Underline Text Tool.

21. Drag the cursor through the last bulleted line of text.

22. Open the note pop-up menu from the context menu option.

23. Type the following text in the note pop-up window: delete this bullet.
Notice each highlight appears in a different color. Default colors are used for the icon and note pop-up windows. The default preferences you changed earlier in this session are retained for the author name for the highlight comment notes, but the colors assigned to the highlight tools remain at the original defaults.

24. **Click the Comments tab to open the Comments panel.**

    Notice all the comments are stacked in the Document pane. Rather than move the comment note pop-up windows, you can review your comments easily in the Comments panel.

25. **Drag the separator bar up to open the Comments panel to a larger view.**

26. **Click the icon in the Comments panel toolbar to collapse all comments.**

27. **Click the plus icon on Page 3 to expand the comments on the current page.**

    Note all the comments you created with the Highlight tools are listed and grouped according to the type of comment added to the page. The icon at the left of the author name shows you the type of highlighted comment and to the right of the author name you see the comment text. As you can see, the Comment panel offers you an at-a-glance view of all the comments added to a given page.

28. **Close the Comments panel by clicking the Comments tab and then click the Save button.**

29. **Keep the file open to follow the steps in the next tutorial.**

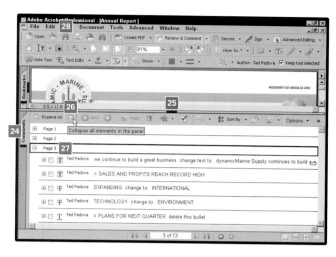

Highlighting Tools versus Text Edit Tools

As you explore the commenting tools you'll notice some similar tools in the Text Edit tools as those you have available in the Highlighting toolbar. The Text Edit tools for Highlight Selected Text, Cross Out Text for Deletion, and Underline Selected Text can be used in the same manner as the corresponding Highlighting tools.

Although you can use the tools for the same purpose, the intent for using the Text Edit tools is different than the intent for using the Highlighting tools. When you make edits with the Text Edit tools, you can export the comments to Microsoft Word. Exporting comments to Microsoft Word requires you to have Acrobat installed on Windows XP, and you must use Microsoft Office XP (Office 2002) or above. Additionally, you need the original Word document from which the PDF was created available on your hard drive in order to export the comments back to the Word document.

As the comments are exported to Word, you can accept revisions in Word, and your file is dynamically updated to reflect those comments you accept for revisions.

When marking up a PDF document with the Text Edit tools, choose Indicate Text Edits at the top of the menu. Move the cursor to the line of text to be edited and click. Return to the Text Edits menu and click the tool for the kind of edit you want to make.

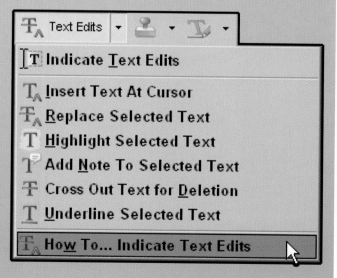

Using the Comments Panel

The Comments panel offers you many tools and menus for working with comments and review sessions. Along the top of the Comments panel, you see tools for navigating comments, replying to comments engaged in a review session, deleting comments, setting the status of comments, and sorting, searching, and printing. Where you see down-pointing arrows, pull-down menus contain commands for additional comments-management tasks.

The comments listed below the Comments Panel toolbar are stacked in a hierarchical order. Clicking the plus (+) icons expands a hierarchy while clicking the minus (-) icon collapses a group. The comment note text is editable in the Comments panel. To edit comment notes, expand a comment and click the cursor in the note comment text. You make changes to the text just like you type text in the note pop-up windows.

Some of the options in the Comment panel are discussed in Session 10. For understanding all the options you can select in the Comments panel, see the Acrobat Help file.

Tutorial

» Using the Drawing Tools

Highlighting tools used in the last tutorial work well where text needs to be marked up and correction suggestions made in regard to text passages. The drawing tools offer you many choices for marking up documents in which you want to comment on images, layout, and design. In this tutorial, you learn how to use some of the drawing tools.

1. **Click the First Page tool.**

2. **Click the Fit Page button.**

3. **Click the down-pointing arrow adjacent to the Rectangle tool in the Advanced Commenting toolbar.**

4. **Choose Show Drawing Toolbar.**
   The Drawing toolbar contains many tools for drawing geometric and irregular shapes. To easily access different tools, expand the toolbar and all tools are visible without opening pull-down menus.

5. **Drag the Drawing toolbar up to the Toolbar Well and release the mouse button when the toolbar is placed over the Toolbar Well.**
   This docks the toolbar.

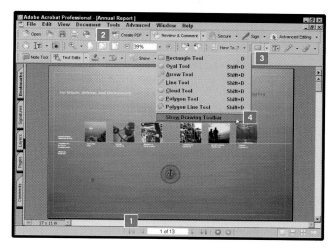

6. **Click the Rectangle tool.**

7. **Draw a rectangle around the first photo thumbnail.**
   By default, the rectangle is a line.

8. **Position the cursor over the rectangle and move to a line forming the rectangle. When you see an arrowhead appear, open a context menu and click Properties.**

9. **Click the Fill Color swatch to open the color palette pop-up menu. Click the Red swatch in the palette.**
   The rectangle fills with the selected color. The fill is opaque and hides the underling image. To add transparency to the fill, you can adjust the opacity percentage in the Appearance properties.

10. **Type 50% in the Opacity field box. (Note you can also move the opacity slider below the field box to adjust opacity percentages.)**
    The opacity does not change until you tab out of the field or close the Rectangle Properties dialog box. To see a preview of the fill with the opacity adjustment, press the Tab key.

11. **Click Close.**

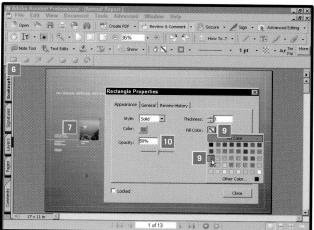

<NOTE>

Users of Acrobat Standard will notice that you have fewer drawing tools than those available in Acrobat Professional. The Arrow tool and Cloud tools are not available in Acrobat Standard. Arrowheads can be created in Acrobat Standard by using the Line tool and polygon shapes are drawn with the Polygon tool; however, additional arrowheads and a cloud polygon shape are products only found in Acrobat Professional.

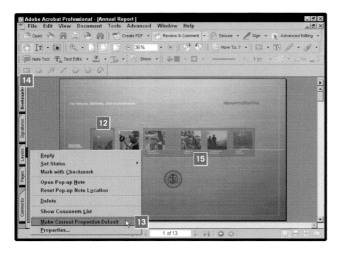

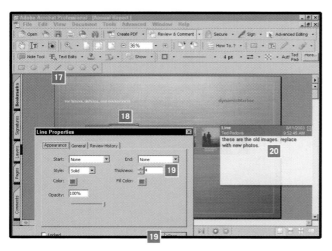

12. **Open a context menu on the Rectangle comment.**

13. **Choose Make Current Properties Default.**
    The rectangle fill becomes a new default. However, the opacity choice needs to be adjusted for each subsequent comment drawn with the Drawing tools.

14. **Click the Rectangle tool.**
    Like note comments, you are returned to the Hand tool unless you choose Keep Tool Selected in the Properties Bar. To draw a new rectangle comment, click the tool in the Drawing toolbar.

15. **Create a new rectangle around the last four photo thumbnails by dragging the Rectangle tool around them.**

16. **Open the Properties dialog box from a context menu and change the opacity to 50 percent.**

17. **Click the Line tool.**

18. **Draw a line from the top-right corner of the first rectangle comment to the top-left corner of the second rectangle comment.**

<NOTE>

If you want to constrain lines to straight lines, press the Shift key when dragging the cursor.

19. **Open a context menu and click Properties. The Line Properties dialog box opens. Type** 4 **in the Thickness field box. Click Close.**

20. **Open the note pop-up window from a context menu and type**
    these are the old images. replace with new photos.
    Notice the first two rectangle comments were not assigned text in the note pop-up window. Only a single comment is needed to instruct the PDF author what to change. By highlighting the exact images that need to be changed, the comment is clear about exactly what edits need to be made.

21. **Click the Oval tool in the Drawing toolbar.**

22. **Draw an oval around the logo.**

23. **Open a context menu and choose Properties. Change the opacity to 50 percent and click Close.**

24. **Open the note pop-up window from a context menu and type:** change this logo and replace with an embossed version.

25. **Choose File→Save As and save the file to the Tutorial09_finish folder. Overwrite the previous saved file to optimize the document.**

26. **Close the document by clicking the Close button.**

Changing Drawing Tools Properties

There are many more options for changing properties with drawing tools than have been described in this tutorial. For line comments you can add different shapes to the open and end points. You can vary line widths for all the tools, change line colors as well as fill colors, and you have opacity adjustments for all shapes.

To become familiar with the number of different options, draw different shapes using all the tools and open the Properties dialog box. Make changes and view the results. The more you practice the sooner you will become familiar with all the Drawing tools options.

Tutorial
» Commenting with Attachments

You might have a need to share a document with several users and then return to an authoring program to make changes. Some users might not have the authoring program while other users might want to see the original document. In such cases, you can send a PDF document to recipients for a review and let the users make comments. The original file can be opened from a file attachment you add to the PDF document for users who want to see the original file. Other types of file attachments include pasting Clipboard images. You can attach a pasted image to a PDF document to help you clarify comments and offer the users a visual for amplifying your meaning. In this tutorial you learn to attach files to PDF documents and paste Clipboard images.

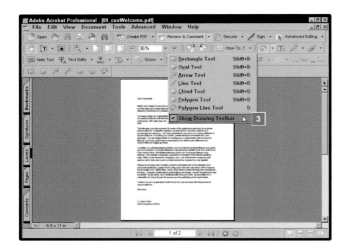

1. **Choose File→Open.**

2. **Navigate to the Tutorial09 folder and open the** 09_ceoWelcome.pdf **file.**
   The file is a draft text document created in Microsoft Word and designed for reviewers to supply feedback. In addition to sending the PDF document, the Word file is attached to the PDF so reviewers can open the Word file in Microsoft Word.

3. **Open the Drawing toolbar pull-down menu and choose Show Drawing Toolbar.**
   Notice a check mark appears adjacent to the menu command. The Drawing toolbar is no longer needed. When you click the menu command, the Drawing toolbar disappears from the Toolbar Well.

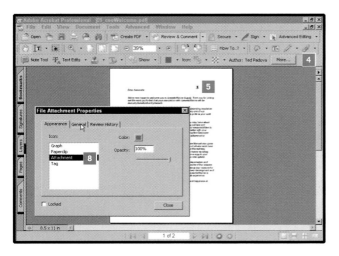

4. **Click the Attach tool.**

5. **Click the page in the top-right corner.**
   The Select File to Attach dialog box opens.

6. **Navigate to the Tutorial09 folder and click** 09_ceoWelcome.doc.
   The document is a Microsoft Word file.

7. **Click Select.**
   The File Attachment Properties dialog box opens.

8. **Choose Attachment from the Icon list.**

9. **Click the General tab. Type** CEO Draft Letter for manual **in the Description field box.**

   Reviewers who open the Properties dialog box can view the description you add here. In addition, the file description is also visible in the Comments panel and when comment summaries are created. For information on creating Comment Summaries, see the tutorial called "Summarizing Comments," later in this session.

10. **Click Close.**

    The icon appearing on the page contains a link to the attachment. When you want to extract a file attachment, select the icon, open a context menu, and then click Open File. Be aware that you need the original authoring program to open file attachments. Exceptions include files formatted as PDF or attachments that can be converted to PDF without the need for original authoring programs.

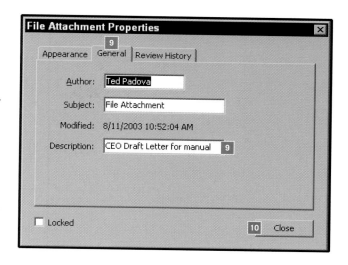

<TIP>

File attachments can be of any file you can see listed in folders or on your desktop. If you want to distribute files in a secure environment, you can use Acrobat to first attach a file and then add Acrobat Security. Users who don't have a password to open a secure PDF are prevented from accessing the file attachment. In this kind of workflow, the PDF acts as a wrapper containing other documents and provides you with an effective means for distributing documents where security cannot be applied in authoring programs. For more detail on securing PDFs, look at Sessions 16 and 17.

11. **Choose File→Save As and save the file to the Tutorial09_finish folder as** 09_ceoWelcome_finish.pdf.

12. **Open the** 09_annualReport_finish.pdf **file from the Tutorial09_finish folder.**

13. **Type** 7 **in the Status Bar and press the Enter key.**

    Page 7 opens in the Document pane. The photo on this page is different than the thumbnail image on the cover page. To make the comment clear about comparing two images on different pages, you can capture an image and make it part of a comment note. Furthermore, you can place the comment image and note on any page in the current file or another PDF document. The following steps show you how to capture the photo on this page and add it as a comment on the cover page.

14. **Click the Snapshot tool.**

15. **Draw a marquee around the photo.**

    An alert dialog box opens informing you the selection created with the Snapshot tool has been copied to the Clipboard.

16. **Click the First Page tool.**

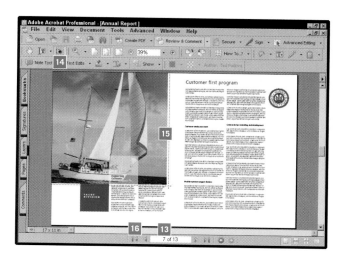

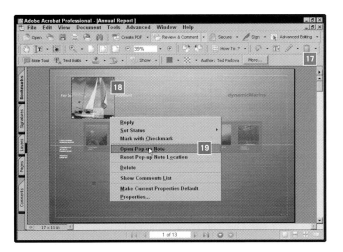

17. **Open the Attach Toolbar pull-down menu and choose Paste Clipboard Image.**

The cursor changes shape. You can click the cursor to paste the image on the page or click and drag to form a marquee defining the image size when pasted on the page.

18. **Draw a rectangle above the first photo thumbnail.**

When you release the mouse button, the contents of the Clipboard are pasted into the rectangle created with the Paste Clipboard tool.

19. **Open a context menu and click Open Pop-up Note.**

The pop-up note window opens. Because the pasted image is a comment, an associated pop-up note is available where you can add a comment in the note window.

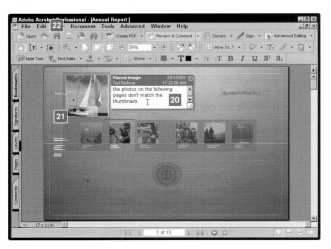

20. **Type the following in the note window:** the photos on the following pages don't match the thumbnails.

The photo icons on this page are intended to be mini views of photos found on following pages in the document. Links will later be created from the cover page to each respective page. This comment shows the PDF author the differences between the thumbnail image and the image on the corresponding page. You can add additional photos for the other four thumbnail photos, but using a single example should be clear enough to the PDF author where the problem lies.

21. **Click the rectangle comment below the pasted image. Drag a corner of the rectangle up and to the left of the top-left corner of the pasted image. Drag the right corner so the rectangle extends above and to the right of the top-right corner of the pasted image.**

Ultimately the pasted photo appears within the rectangle comment so there is no confusion as to the comparison between the photo thumbnail and the pasted photo.

22. **Click the Save button.**

23. **Keep the file open to follow the steps in the next tutorial.**

Tutorial

» Adding a Stamp Comment

Stamp comments are icons that appear similar to office stamps you use for approving, marking confidential, and reviewing paper documents. A number of preset stamp icons are available from the Stamp tool pull-down menu. Acrobat also allows you to add custom stamps using your own designs. Among the preset stamps installed with Acrobat are a range of symbols used for common office practices, as well as dynamic stamps. Dynamic stamps offer you an added benefit for dynamically including your name, date, and time to a stamp. In this tutorial you learn to use the Stamp tool and add personal information to a dynamic stamp.

1. **Click the down-pointing arrow adjacent to the Stamp tool to open the pull-down menu.**

2. **Choose Standard Business.**
   Notice the first three categories of stamps. Dynamic stamps offer you the benefit of adding your name and a date/time stamp to the stamp appearance. The second category Sign Here and the third menu option Standard Business are static and don't add your identity or a date/time stamp.

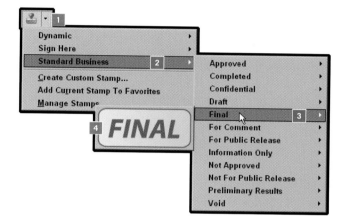

3. **Choose Final.**
   Notice the submenu opens listing a number of stamps. Each of the three menu items used for selecting stamps includes submenus where individual stamps are selected from the group.

4. **Click the Final stamp.**
   When you click a stamp in the submenu, another submenu opens where an icon is shown representing the stamp appearance. Before you make a selection for a given stamp, Acrobat shows you a mini-view of the stamp. To use the stamp you move the cursor to the thumbnail image in the last submenu to select it.

   Before moving on in this tutorial, move the cursor to each category and view the different stamps listed in the submenus. The first three menu options are used to select stamps. The last three menu options are used for other purposes that are discussed in the tutorial "Creating Custom Stamps." For now, just take a look at the different stamps contained in the first three menu items.

5. **Click away from the Stamp menu to close the menu.**

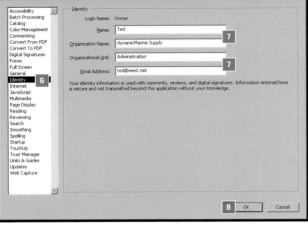

6. **Choose Edit→Preferences. Click Identity.**

   The dynamic stamps use information you add to the field boxes in the Identity Preferences. Before creating a dynamic stamp, you should fill in the identity information.

7. **Fill in the Name, Organization Name, Organization Unit, and Email Address fields.**

8. **Click OK.**

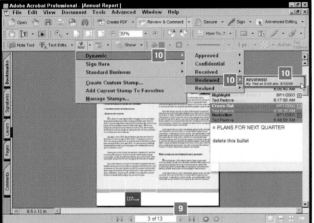

9. **Click the Next Page tool twice to navigate to page 3 in the annual report document.**

10. **Open the Stamps pull-down menu and choose Dynamic→ Reviewed→Reviewed.**

    Notice the Reviewed stamp contains your name as well as a date stamp. The name is derived from the Identity name field.

11. **Click the Fit Width button.**

12. **Move the cursor to the top of the page and draw a rectangle in the top-left corner to the right of the dynamicMarine logo.**
    Notice as you draw the rectangle the proportions are constrained to keep the stamp proportionately sized. When you release the mouse button the stamp appears within the rectangle.

13. **Open a context menu from the stamp and click Open Pop-up Note.**
    Like the other comments you added in this session, stamps also have associated note pop-up windows.

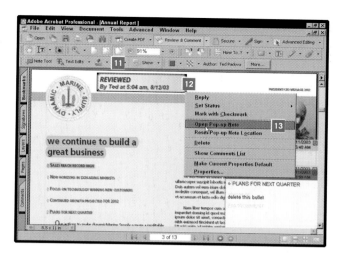

14. **Type a message in the note pop-up window. In this example I added:** please send back to art department for revisions.

15. **Click the Save button.**

16. **Keep the file open to follow the steps in the next tutorial.**

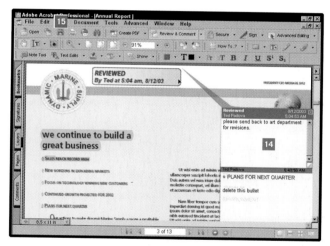

Tutorial

» Creating Custom Stamps

In addition to the preset stamps installed in Acrobat, you also have options for creating your own custom stamps from any file compatible with the Convert to PDF From File command. You can use photo images, illustrations, or icons you create in other authoring programs. The capability to use custom stamps affords you an opportunity to develop stamps customized for your workplace and individual users. In this tutorial you learn how to create custom stamps.

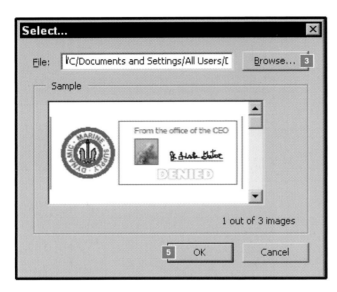

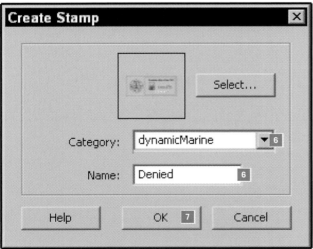

1. **Open the pull-down menu from the Stamp tool and choose Create Custom Stamp.**
   The Create Stamp dialog box opens.

2. **Choose Select.**
   The Select dialog box opens.

3. **Click Browse.**
   The Open dialog box opens. In this dialog box you navigate to the file you want to use as a custom stamp.

4. **Navigate to the Tutorial09 folder and click** 09_stamps.pdf. **Click Select in the Open dialog box.**
   You are returned to the Select dialog box. The 09_stamps. pdf file contains three pages. By default, all stamps created from multiple page PDFs show you a thumbnail view of the first page in the document.

5. **Click OK.**
   You are returned to the Create Stamp dialog box. A thumbnail view of the current selected stamp appears in the dialog box.

6. **Type** dynamicMarine **for the Category and** Denied **for the Name.**
   The Category item is the first submenu you see when you open the Stamps pull-down menu. The name you add to your custom stamp appears as a submenu choice. You can add several stamps to a category. When the Category is selected in the Stamps pull-down menu, you see all the individual stamp names you added to the category.

7. **Click OK.**
   All Stamps dialog boxes are closed and you return to the Acrobat window. To add additional custom stamps, repeat these steps.

8. **Open the Stamps pull-down menu and click Create Custom Stamp.**
   Again the Create Stamp dialog box opens.

9. **Open the Category pull-down menu by clicking the down-pointing arrow.**

10. **Choose dynamicMarine.**

    To add another stamp to the same category, select the category from the menu options. You can create several categories, and all the categories for custom stamps are selected from the pull-down menu in the Create Stamp dialog box.

11. **Click Select.**

    By default the directory path accessing the same file from the last time you added a stamp appears in the Select dialog box. In this example, it's the file 09_stamps.pdf in the Tutorial09 folder. Below the scroll bars you see the current page accessed and the total number of pages in the file.

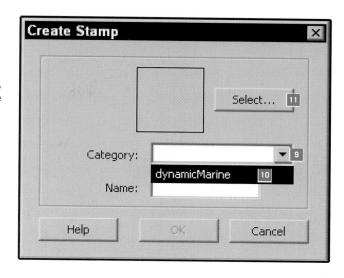

12. **Click the down arrow to scroll to page 2 in the 09_stamps.pdf file.**

    A thumbnail view of page 2 appears in the Select dialog box.

13. **Click OK.**

    Once again you return to the Create Stamp dialog box.

14. **Type Approved in the Name field.**

15. **Repeat the same steps to add a third stamp to the dynamicMarine category and add page 3 from the 09_stamps.pdf document. Name this one Pending.**

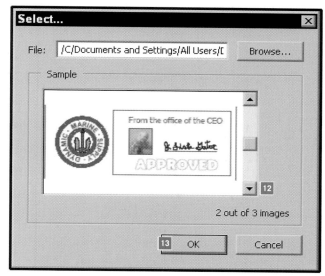

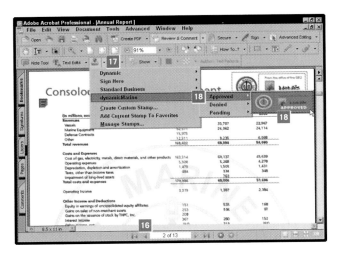

16. **Click the Previous Page tool in the Status Bar to navigate to page 2.**

17. **Open the Stamps pull-down menu.**
    Notice the new category listed in the menu options.

18. **Choose dynamicMarine→Approved→Approved (icon).**
    Notice the dynamicMarine category supports a submenu where the three stamps you added are listed and an icon for each stamp appears from a second submenu. When you click the Approved icon, the selected stamp is loaded in the Stamp tool. Dragging a rectangle on the document page places the selected stamp in the rectangle box.

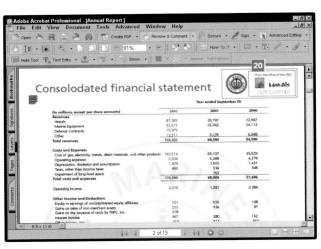

19. **Close any open pop-notes you see in the top area of the page by clicking the note pop-up close box.**

20. **Click and drag a rectangle in the top-right corner of the page.**
    After releasing the mouse button, the selected stamp appears within the rectangle. You can add a comment note by opening a context menu and selecting Open Pop-up Note or you can leave the stamp as is and let the image communicate your message. In this example, the icon is explicit enough and a note is not needed.

21. **Choose File→Save As and save the file to the Tutorial09_finish folder. Overwrite the previously saved file.**

22. **Keep the document open to follow the steps in the next tutorial.**

Adding Favorites and Managing Stamps

Below the Stamp Categories in the Stamp tool pull-down menu are menu commands for adding *favorites* to the menu and managing stamps. A favorite adds a specific stamp from a submenu as a separate menu selection. If you frequently use a stamp, you'll find it handy to add a favorite to the Stamp tool pull-down menu.

Favorites are added by first selecting the stamp you want to use as a favorite from a category submenu. Once the stamp is selected, open the pull-down menu and click Add Current Stamp to Favorites. If you want to delete a stamp from the menu, select the stamp to delete and the menu command changes to Remove Current Stamp From Favorites.

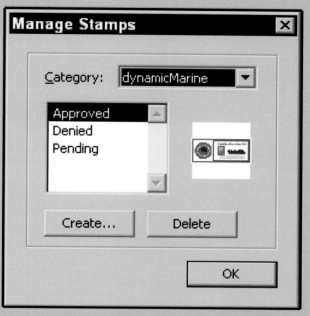

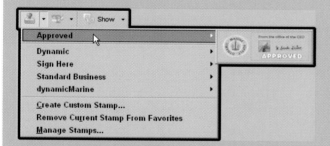

When stamps are listed as favorites, you don't need to wade through submenus to find a stamp. Clicking the stamp name opens the stamp icon you select to use the stamp.

Also in the Stamp tool pull-down menu is the command for managing stamps. Click Manage Stamps and the Manage Stamps dialog box opens.

In the Manage Stamps dialog box you can delete stamps no longer used from a category and add more custom stamps to a category. To remove a stamp from a category, select a category, select the stamp, and then click Delete. Click Create and the Create Stamp dialog box opens where you can browse to find a new stamp and add a name for it.

Tutorial
» Summarizing Comments

After commenting on a document, you can create a comment summary. When you create a summary, Acrobat creates a new PDF document containing only the pages where comments were added. In this session, you commented on three pages in a 13-page file. Therefore a comment summary created from this file yields a three-page PDF document with the comments summarized. You might want to share comment summaries with other users or you might want to use the summary when you make revisions to the original document. Acrobat provides you several options for creating summaries and how to view your comments and the pages containing the comment descriptions. In this tutorial you learn how to create comment summaries.

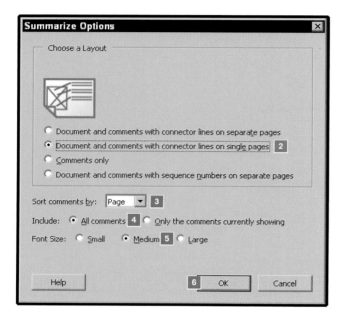

1. **Choose Document→Summarize Comments.**
   The Summarize Options dialog box opens.

2. **Click the Document and Comments with Connector Lines on Single Pages radio button.**
   You can choose from four types of comment summaries. The four radio button choices offer you different displays of comments in the PDF file generated when a summary is created. The second radio button creates comment summaries with the summary listed on the pages where the comments were created and lines from the comments to the summarized descriptions.

3. **Click Page from the Sort Comments By pull-down menu.**
   By default, Page should be selected when you open the Summarize Options dialog box. From the pull-down menu you can also choose to list comments by Author, Date, and Type of comment.

4. **Click the All Comments radio button.**
   Again, by default, the radio button should be selected. When you click All Comments, all the comments in the document are included in the summary.

5. **Click Medium for the font size.**
   The font size used to describe the summary can be adjusted for three sizes (small, medium, and large). By default, Medium is selected. Leave the default selected.

6. **Click OK.**
   Acrobat pauses momentarily as a new PDF file is created. The new file eventually appears in the Document pane in a Continuous - Facing page layout view. When the summary file is created, notice the document contains only three pages.

7. **Click the Fit Width button.**

8. **Click the Single Page button.**

   Notice the page appears on the left side of the document and the summary appears on the right. Connector lines are drawn from the summary to the comment icons on the page. This file can easily be e-mailed to other users for a final review or you can use the file to return to your authoring program and check your revisions as you make them. Comment summaries are particularly helpful for Adobe Reader users who don't have options for summarizing comments with the Adobe Reader software.

9. **Click the Save button.**

   Save the file as 09_summary_finish.pdf in the Tutorial09_finish folder.

10. **Quit Acrobat.**

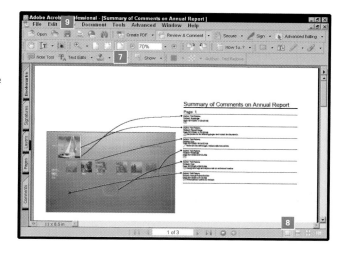

» Session Review

In this session you learned how create a number of comments using several different comment tools. You learned how to change comment preferences and how to create comment summaries. Quite a bit was covered in this session. To review the session, answer the following questions. Answers are found in the tutorial noted in parentheses.

1. How do you open note pop-up windows? (See Tutorial: Creating Note Comments.)

2. How do you change note colors? (See Tutorial: Creating Note Comments.)

3. Why doesn't your selected text appear in a note pop-up window? (See Tutorial: Setting Comment Preferences.)

4. How do you remove comments? (See Tutorial: Creating Note Comments.)

5. How do you change the comment properties to use your name for each comment you create? (See Tutorial: Setting Comment Preferences.)

6. How can you change the fill color of your drawing tool comments to see the area behind the objects you draw? (See Tutorial: Using Drawing Tools.)

7. How do you copy and paste an image you want to use for a comment note? (See Tutorial: Commenting with Attachments.)

8. How do you attach a file to a PDF? (See Tutorial: Commenting with Attachments.)

9. How do you create a custom stamp? (See Tutorial: Creating Custom Stamps.)

10. You want to access a stamp frequently. What should you do to make the stamp more accessible? (See Tutorial: Creating Custom Stamps.)

11. How do you delete custom stamps? (See Tutorial: Creating Custom Stamps.)

12. How do you create a comment summary? (See Tutorial: Summarizing Comments.)

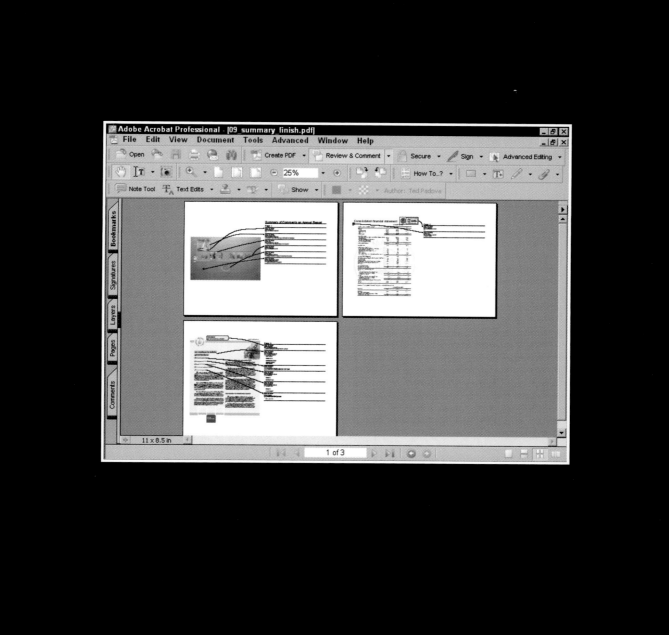

Session 10

Commenting and Reviewing

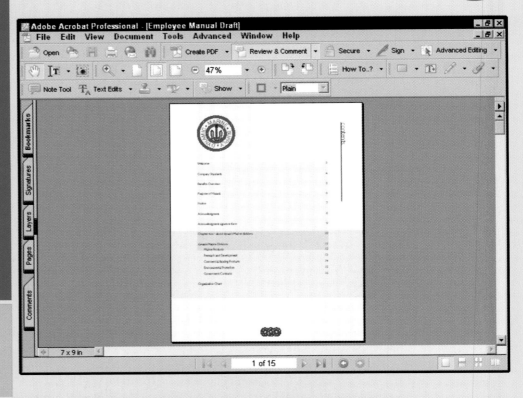

Tutorial: **Setting Up an E-mail-Based Review**

Tutorial: **Participating in a Review**

Tutorial: **Setting Comment Status**

Tutorial: **Tracking Reviews**

Session Introduction

In the last session you learned how to use commenting tools. Part of the commenting process is marking up a document for potential revisions. The second part of the process is sharing comments with other users. In this session you learn how to set up a review session and participate in e-mail-based reviews.

TOOLS YOU'LL USE
Send by Email for Review command, Review Tracker, Comments panel, Commenting toolbar, and the Advanced Commenting toolbar.

CD-ROM FILES NEEDED
10_employeeManual.pdf, 10_employeeManual.fdf, and 10_employeeManual.pdf (found in the Sessions/Session10/ Tutorial10 folder).

TIME REQUIRED
90 Minutes

Tutorial
» Setting Up an E-mail-Based Review

If you author PDF documents, you ultimately will have occasion to solicit input from other users for review and comment. Other users comment on PDF files and send their comments back to you during a review. The process begins with you sending a PDF document to other users who use the commenting tools and eventually send their comments back to you. To simplify the process, Acrobat offers you an easy method for starting a review session. In this tutorial, you learn how to create an e-mail-based review for engaging other users in reviewing and commenting on your documents.

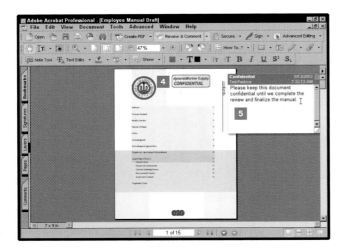

1. **Mount the CD–ROM located in the back of this book. Drag the folder Session10 from inside the Sessions folder to your desktop. Launch Acrobat by double-clicking the program icon.**

2. **Open the file** 10_employeeManual.pdf **from the Tutorial10 folder.**

   The document is currently in draft form. You need to send this document to other users for soliciting input. To do so, you'll start an e-mail-based review. The toolbars loaded in Session 9 should still be visible in the Toolbar Well. If the Commenting tools, Advanced Editing tools, and Properties Bar are not visible in the Toolbar Well, open a context menu from the Toolbar Well and open the toolbars. Dock the toolbars by using the context menu command. For a more detailed review of loading the toolbars for comment and review, turn back to Session 9.

3. **Open the Stamps pull-down menu and choose Dynamic→ Confidential→Confidential.**

   Before you begin the review session, add a confidential stamp from the Dynamic stamp category.

4. **Create a rectangle with the Stamp tool and open a pop-up note window from a context menu on the stamp.**

5. **Type in the note-pop-up window:** Please keep this document confidential until we complete the review and finalize the manual.

6. **Choose File→Save As and save the file to the Tutorial10_finish folder as** 10_employeeManual_finish.pdf.

   Before sending a file via an e-mail review, be certain to save the last edits you made.

7. **Click the down-pointing arrow on the Review & Comment task button to open a pull-down menu.**

8. **Choose Send by Email for Review.**

   The Send by Email for Review dialog box opens. In this dialog box you add recipient addresses or a mail list for all the reviewers you want to participate in the review. By default, Acrobat automatically adds a message to the reviewers instructing them on how to participate in a review as a recipient.

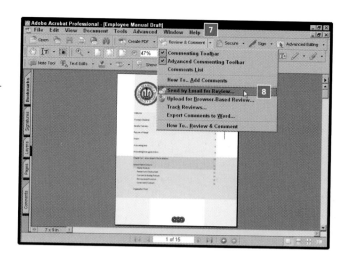

<NOTE>

All the sessions in this book are designed to instruct you on how to use Acrobat tools and features independently without participation in a workgroup. By nature, an e-mail-based review is intended for collaborating with colleagues and other users. For the most effective means to completely understand this session, you are best served by following steps in the tutorials for this session with other users who have either Acrobat Standard or Acrobat Professional installed on their computers.

If you don't have access to users who have Acrobat 6, you can follow steps by e-mailing files to yourself. It is best to use two computers. Try to find another computer loaded with Acrobat and be certain to configure your e-mail application to receive and send files from the second computer.

In this tutorial the steps are described for using your own e-mail address so all readers can clearly see the results of starting an e-mail review and participating in a review. If you work with other Acrobat users, use the e-mail addresses of users in your workgroup and ask them to comment on the tutorial document and send it back to you.

9. **Add a recipient address in the To field box. If you don't have access to another Acrobat user, enter your own e-mail address.**
   Note the subject and message boxes are automatically filled with descriptions. The Message to Reviewers box offers step-by-step instructions for other users to follow to participate in the review session.

10. **Click the Send button.**

    An alert dialog box opens. The message informs you that the PDF file has been attached to an e-mail message and given to your e-mail application. If your e-mail program is not configured to automatically send a message, you need to open your e-mail program and click the Send button to deliver the message. Acrobat supports most e-mail programs. If you use Microsoft Outlook, Outlook Express, Eudora, Apple Mail, Microsoft Entourage, or other similar e-mail programs, the program should be launched when you click the Send button in the Send by Email for Review dialog box. If you experience problems, launch your e-mail program and keep it open while you click the Send button in Acrobat.

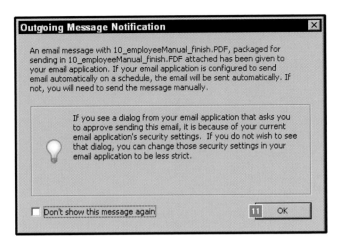

Outgoing Message Notification

An email message with 10_employeeManual_finish.PDF, packaged for sending in 10_employeeManual_finish.FDF attached has been given to your email application. If your email application is configured to send email automatically on a schedule, the email will be sent automatically. If not, you will need to send the message manually.

If you see a dialog from your email application that asks you to approve sending this email, it is because of your current email application's security settings. If you do not wish to see that dialog, you can change those security settings in your email application to be less strict.

☐ Don't show this message again   **11** OK

11. **Click OK in the Outgoing Message Notification dialog box.**

If you don't want the message to appear when sending other files for an e-mail review, check the box in the lower-left corner that reads *Don't show this message again*. The dialog box doesn't open when you start additional reviews.

12. **Close the file and keep Acrobat open.**

Your e-mail review process has begun after your e-mail program sends your message and the attached PDF document. When you start an e-mail review, the entire PDF file is sent to all recipients. The next step in the review process is for the recipients to make comments, and send their comments back to you.

Tutorial

» Participating in a Review

Users receiving files from a PDF author who starts an e-mail-based review are the recipients in the review process. A recipient opens the PDF document sent via e-mail, makes comments, and returns the comments back to the PDF author. In this tutorial you learn how to participate in an e-mail review as a participant.

1. **Open your e-mail program and retrieve your messages.**
   After sending a file to yourself or receiving files from other users, be certain to wait until the mail has had sufficient time to reach your mailbox.

2. **Double-click the file attachment.**
   The e-mail you receive from a PDF author who sends you a file from an e-mail review contains a file attachment. As you observe the attachment icon you'll notice the appearance is different than the PDF document icon. Also notice that FDF is imprinted on the icon and is used for the filename extension. In this example the filename is `10_employeeManual_finish.fdf`. FDF is used for Forms Data Format—a proprietary format developed by Adobe Systems. The file you see as the file attachment is a data file containing the comment data that acts like a wrapper sealed around the PDF document. When you double-click the FDF file, the PDF contained within opens in Acrobat and the FDF data (the comment data in this example) is imported in the PDF. The result is a file opened in the Document pane with the same appearance and data as when the file was sent to you from the PDF author.

3. **Click Close.**
   A Document Status dialog box opens informing you that the file has been sent to you for review. The description also includes help information on how to participate in an e-mail review. Notice that the Commenting toolbar opens automatically when you open the file. Additionally, another tool is added to the Commenting toolbar. The Send Comments tool appears when the toolbar is opened in a review session. After you complete your commenting, you click this tool to send comments back to the originator of the e-mail review. If you need additional help, notice the How To pane on the right side of the Acrobat window opens with help information on participating in an e-mail review.

4. **Click Save. Navigate to the Tutorial10 folder and save the file with the default name to your original tutorial folder. Be certain to not overwrite the file in theTutorial10_finish folder.**
   The first step in your recipient review process is to save the file. Be certain you save this file to a different location than the Tutorial10_finish folder.

5. **Click the Note icon on the page to select it.**

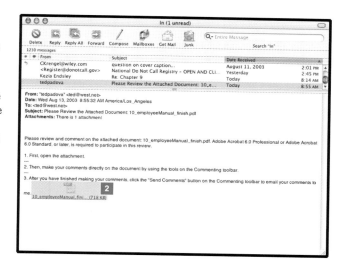

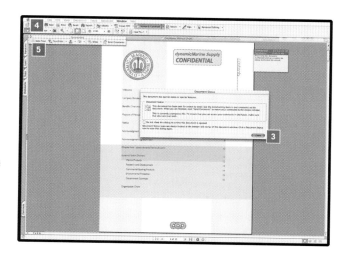

6. **Add a text note on the first page in the document and type** This file is missing the cover.

7. **Choose Document→Import Comments.**
   The Import Comments dialog box opens.

8. **Navigate to the Tutorial10 folder and click**
   `10_employeeManual.fdf`. **Click Select.**
   The file is an FDF file containing comment data. Rather than add new comments to the document, you can import comments to continue steps in the tutorial.

\<NOTE\>
You might see a dialog box open informing you that the comments are not from this document. If the dialog box opens, click Yes.

9. **Click the Save button.**
   Save the file before you submit the comments back to the PDF author.

10. **Click the Send Comments button.**
    After you complete your comment session, click the Send Comments tool on the Commenting toolbar. Your default e-mail application opens and the new comment data is attached to an e-mail message.

11. **Click Send in your e-mail application to send the e-mail and file attachment.**
    Notice your file attachment is again an FDF file. When the recipient sends comments back to the review initiator, the PDF document does not travel with the comments. The comment data is a much smaller file than the original PDF document and requires much less time and bandwidth in e-mailing the file back to the review initiator.

Exporting and Importing Comments

Comment data is saved as FDF form (Forms Data Format). The data files are always much smaller than the original PDF and makes exchanging data a much easier task than e-mailing large PDFs.

When you choose Document→Export Comments, you create an FDF data file. This file can be imported into a PDF with pages that match the original file. If you want to exchange comments with other users without starting a review session, you can export comments, attach the resulting FDF data file to an e-mail message, and send the file to other users. Other users need a copy of the PDF file from which the FDF was generated and must use the Document→Import Comments menu command to add the comments to their PDF documents.

12. Wait until your e-mail has been sent to your address and open your e-mail application and retrieve your mail. Open the file attachment by double-clicking the attachment icon (or according to the method prescribed by your e-mail program).

Notice the message contains help information now provided to the review initiator. After opening the file attachment, a dialog box informs you that the comments have successfully been placed on the file.

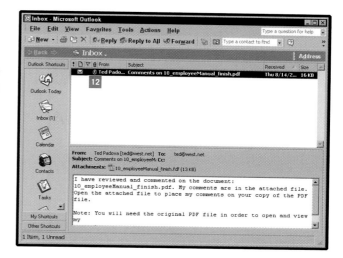

13. Click OK.

The How To pane opens informing the review initiator how to view comments and save the file.

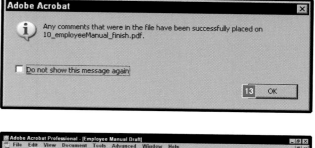

14. Click the Hide button in the How To pane to hide the help information.

15. Click the Save button.

Note comments can also be created by double-clicking the mouse button. When you create a note by double-clicking the mouse button, a fixed size for the note pop-up window is created. Notice the note properties use all the defaults you established for Note Properties and after making the context menu selection for Make Current Properties Default.

16. Keep the file open to follow the steps in the next tutorial.

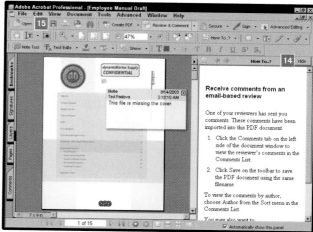

Tutorial
» Setting Comment Status

After receiving comments from other users, you can review the comments and decide whether to accept, reject, cancel, or mark comments for completion. Status marks enable you to sort and create summaries for just those comments you elect to accept from your reviewer's input. In this tutorial you learn how to mark comments for status and create a comment summary listing only the comments you accept.

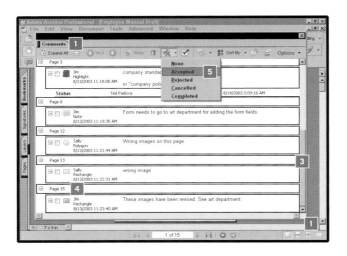

1. **Drag the Comments tab out of the Navigation pane to undock it. Expand the panel by dragging the lower-right corner to resize the panel.**

2. **Click page 1 at the top of the Comments panel.**

3. **Drag the scroll bar to the bottom of the panel window.**

4. **Press Shift and click page 15.**
   All comments are selected in the Comments panel. When you set a comment status, the status mark is applied to all selected comments.

5. **Open the Set the Comment Status pull-down menu and choose Accepted.**
   Most of the comments in this document will be accepted by the review initiator. Only a few will be rejected. Therefore, you can accept all comments and then individually change the status on the few that need to be rejected. After clicking Accepted, a check mark is placed on each comment in the Comments panel.

6. **Drag the scroll bar up to the top of the Comments panel.**

7. **Click the second comment on page 1.**

8. **Open the Set the Comment Status pull-down menu and choose Rejected.**

9. **Scroll the panel window to view page 3. Click the comment on page 3 and choose Rejected from the pull-down menu.**

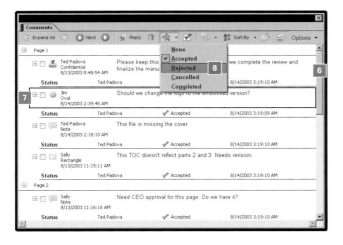

10. **Click the Filter the Comments Displayed pull-down menu.**

11. **Choose Show by Status→Accepted.**
    When you click Accepted in the menu, only those comments you marked Accepted are shown in the Comments panel.

12. **Open the Options pull-down menu by clicking the down-pointing arrow.**

13. **Choose Summarize Comments.**
    Notice the command for Summarize Comments is available from the Comments panel as well as the Document menu. After making the menu selection, the Summarize Options dialog box opens.

14. **Click the radio button for Document and Comments with Sequence Numbers on Separate Pages.**
    You'll create a different summary than the one created in Session 9. This summary creates separate pages for the document and the comments in a new PDF file.

15. **Choose Author from the Sort Comments by pull-down menu.**
    The comments are sorted by author for each page.

16. **Click the radio button for Only the Comments Currently Showing.**
    Because you filtered comments to show only those comments that were marked Accepted, the summary yields a report for only the accepted comments.

17. **Click OK.**
    The summary is created as a new PDF document and opens in the Document pane. Notice the file opens in a Continuous – Facing page layout with the original pages appearing on the left and the comment summary appearing on the right.

18. **Dock the Comments panel back in the Navigation pane by dragging the Comments tab to the far left of the Acrobat window.**

19. **Click the Save button. Save the file as** 10_commentSummary.pdf **to the Tutorial10_finish folder.**

20. **Close the file.**

21. **Leave the** 10_employeeManual_finish.pdf **file open to follow the steps in the next tutorial.**

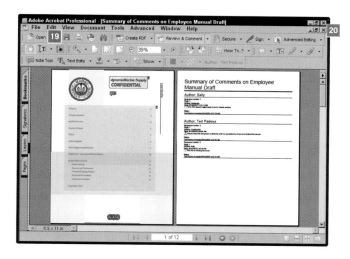

Tutorial
» Tracking Reviews

You may have several reviews in progress simultaneously. The tools for managing documents in review sessions and accessing options for reviews are found in the Review Tracker. The Review Tracker enables you to see all files you have in review as a review initiator and review participant and offers you menu commands to help manage these files. In this tutorial you learn how to access the Review Tracker and understand some of the options contained in menu selections.

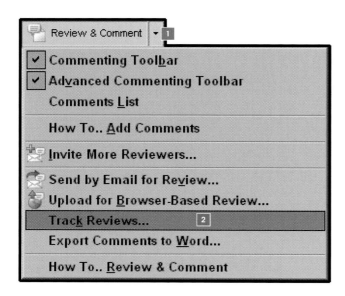

1. **Click the down-pointing arrow to open the Review & Comment pull-down menu.**

2. **Choose Track Reviews.**
   The Review Tracker opens in the How To pane.

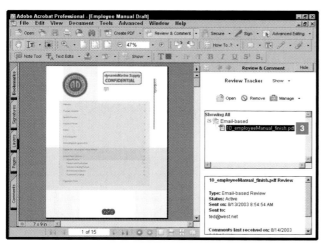

3. **Click** 10_employeeManual_finish.pdf.
   Notice the Review Tracker panel contains a list of files currently under review. If you had several files in review, all the files are listed in the Review Tracker. At the bottom of the panel is a description of the file reporting the type of review, the status, dates, and when comments were last received.

4. Click the down-pointing arrow to open the Manage pull-down menu.

Menu options are available to send an e-mail to all reviewers, remind reviewers to respond to your review solicitation, and add more reviewers to a review session. The grayed out command for Go Back Online is available only when working with another kind of review called *browser-based reviews*. The Show menu above the Manage menu offers you selections for showing Active, Completed, Sent, and Reviewed files. This menu offers sort options to display only those files within one of the categories you select from the menu.

<NOTE>

Browser-based reviews offer you an opportunity to set up a review session among a group of users where the PDF and comments are contained on a Web server. Users upload and download comments from the Web server and share their comments in a collaborative workgroup. This form of commenting takes place while viewing your comments in a Web browser and logging on to a properly configured Web server. Setting up the review session is more complex and requires configuration by your system administrator. For more information on browser-based reviews, see the Acrobat Help file.

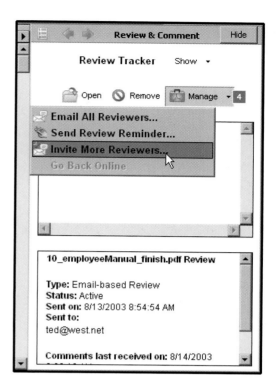

5. Click Remove.

Be certain the file is selected in the window before clicking Remove. The file is deleted from the list.

6. Close the document and quit Acrobat.

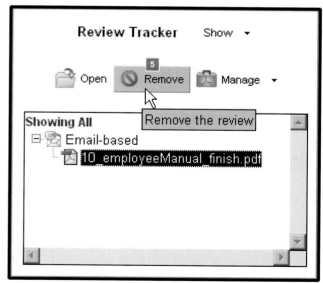

» Session Review

In this session you learned how create an e-mail-based review and participate in a review as a review initiator and a review recipient. To understand the concepts discussed in this session, answer the following questions. Answers are found in the tutorial noted in parentheses.

1. How do you start an e-mail-based review? (See Tutorial: Setting Up an E-mail-Based Review.)

2. How do you open a file you receive from a review initiator? (See Tutorial: Participating in a Review.)

3. How do you hide comments you reject during a review session? (See Tutorial: Setting Comment Status.)

4. How do you summarize only those comments you accept? (See Tutorial: Setting Comment Status.)

5. How do you invite additional reviewers to comment on a document? (See Tutorial: Tracking Reviews.)

6. How do you eliminate documents from a review list after completing a review? (See Tutorial: Tracking Reviews.)

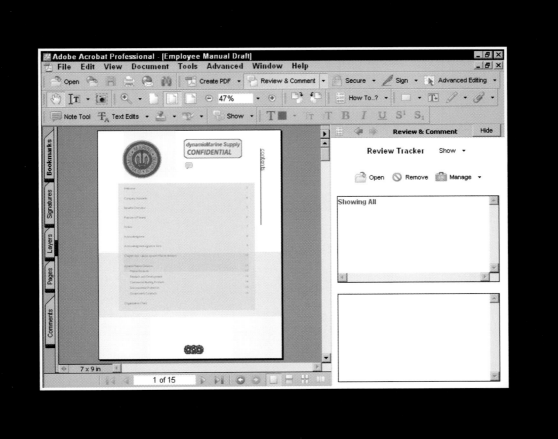

Part VI
Adding Interactivity

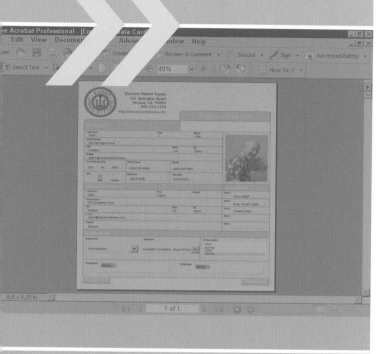

Creating Links and Buttons

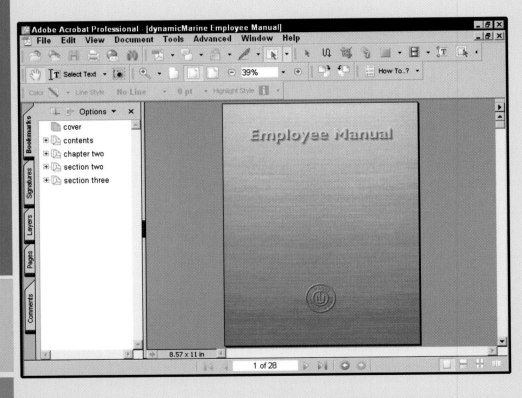

Tutorial: **Creating Links to Pages**

Tutorial: **Linking to Views**

Tutorial: **Opening Secondary Files**

Tutorial: **Opening Pages in Secondary Files**

Tutorial: **Creating Buttons (Acrobat 6 Professional Only)**

Tutorial: **Creating Button Faces (Acrobat 6 Professional Only)**

Tutorial: **Duplicating Buttons (Acrobat 6 Professional Only)**

Session Introduction

One of many advantages for using PDF documents is the ability to make your files and work-flows dynamic by adding interactive links and buttons. Through the use of link and button actions, you help users easily navigate views to pages and files. In this session you learn how to assign actions to interactive links and buttons.

TOOLS YOU'LL USE
Link tool, Button tool, Select Text tool, Link Properties, Button Properties, Custom Link, Button Properties, Snapshot tool, Advanced Editing tools, and the Properties Bar.

CD-ROM FILES NEEDED
11_arrowLt.pdf, 11_arrowLtRollover.pdf., 11_arrowRt.pdf, 11_arrowRtRollover.pdf, 11_employeeEvaluation.pdf, 11_employeeManual.pdf, and 11_orgChart.pdf (found in the Sessions/Session11/Tutorial11 folder)

TIME REQUIRED
2 hours

Tutorial
» Creating Links to Pages

In Session 3 you learned how to add bookmarks to pages for page viewing and navigation. As you move to individual pages, links from page content to other pages or other documents can be more advantageous than creating bookmarks. A table of contents is a good example where such page content might be the source for linking to other pages. As a bookmark is created to a page like a contents page, you'll find adding links from a list of content items to additional pages helpful. In this session you learn how to create links to pages within a document.

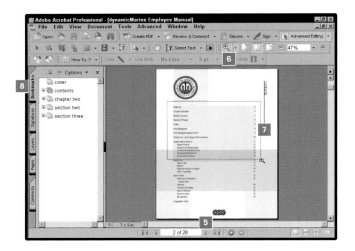

1. **Mount the CD-ROM located in the back of this book. Drag the Session11 folder from inside the Sessions folder to your desktop. Launch Acrobat by double-clicking the program icon.**

2. **Open the file** `11_employeeManual.pdf` **from the Tutorial11 folder.**
   After you complete a review session and modify your documents to meet final approval for the content, you're ready to use Acrobat for adding interactive elements. The `11_employeeManual.pdf` document is a revision after completing a review and now needs some interactive items to help users navigate the pages. You'll notice additional bookmarks have been added to the file after you appended pages in Session 7.

3. **Open a context menu on the Toolbar Well and choose Reset Toolbars.**
   If you just finished Session 10, you have the commenting tools loaded in the toolbar. These tools are not needed for the current session; therefore, resetting the toolbar eliminates the commenting tools. For adding interactive links and buttons, the Advanced Editing toolbar and Properties Bar are needed.

4. **Click the Advanced Editing task button to open the Advanced Editing toolbar. Open a context menu from the Toolbar Well and choose the Properties Bar. Return to the context menu and choose Dock All Toolbars.**

5. **Click the Next Page tool.**

6. **Click the Zoom In tool.**

7. **Click and drag a marquee around the top half of the contents items to zoom in on the page.**

8. **Click the Bookmarks tab to close the Bookmarks pane.**
   By closing the Bookmarks pane during your editing session, you can see more of the page in the Document pane.

9. **Click the Select Text tool in the Toolbar Well.**

10. **Click the Select Text tool at the beginning of the *Welcome* line of text on the page and drag to the right to highlight *3* at the end of the line.**

    As you drag the Select Text tool, be careful to select only the first line of text. You might need to move the cursor up or down a little while selecting the line to avoid selecting additional lines of text.

11. **Open a context menu with the Select Text tool still active and choose Create Link.**

    The Create Link from Selection dialog box opens.

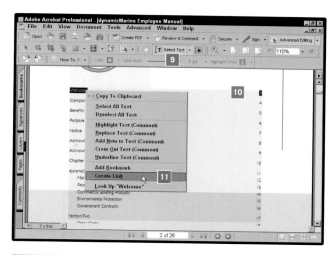

12. **Type 3 in the Page field box.**

    The Contents shows the pages where each content item is found. Enter the page number and be certain the Open a Page in this Document radio button is selected.

13. **Choose Fit Page from the Zoom pull-down menu.**

    Notice you can link to various zoom levels. While working in a zoomed view you can set the link to a different zoom level.

14. **Click OK.**

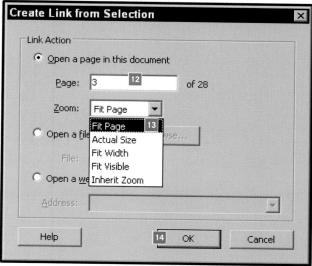

Editing Link Properties

You edit link properties by selecting a link and making changes in the Properties Bar. Additional link properties are edited in the Link Properties dialog box. To open the Link Properties dialog box, click a link with either the Select Object tool or the Link tool and click the More button in the Properties Bar. You can also double-click a link with either the Select Object tool or the Link tool to open the Link Properties dialog box or click to select the link and click Properties from a context menu.

When you open the Link Properties dialog box, you see two tabs. The Appearance Tab handles attributes for the link rectangle appearances like those attribute choices found in the Properties Bar. Click the second tab, called Actions, to edit the link destination or the action associated with the link.

Note that the Link Properties dialog box offers different options than the Create Link from Selection dialog box. Once you create a link, the Create Link from Selection dialog box is no longer available. If you make a mistake in assigning a link destination in this tutorial, follow the steps in the next tutorial to learn how to make changes in the Link Properties dialog box.

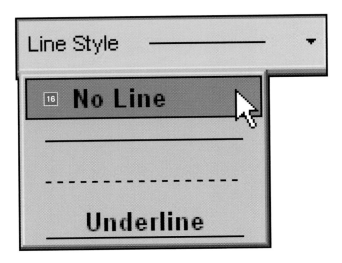

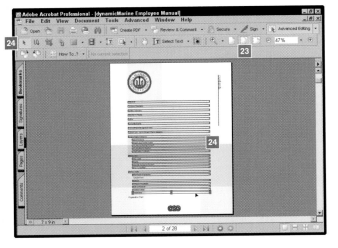

15. **Click the Link tool and click the Link to select it.**

16. **Open the Line Style pull-down menu from the Properties Bar and choose No Line.**
    By default, the link rectangle appears as a Visible Rectangle with a line. For the contents items, you'll create links without lines.

17. **Click the Link tool on the page away from the link rectangle to deselect it.**

18. **Choose No Line from the Line Style pull-down menu.**
    If you create a second link, the link properties revert back to the previous properties with the same appearance settings. To change the link property defaults, click the Link tool and be certain all links are deselected. Changes you make in the Properties Bar while links are deselected create new defaults.

19. **Click the Select Text tool.**

20. **Place the cursor in the second line of text and triple-click.**
    Notice when you triple-click the mouse button, the text is selected for the line including the page number at the right side of the line. In this case the text is selected from *Company Standards* to the end of the line where *4* appears.

21. **Open a context menu, select Create Link, and change the page number to 4.**

22. **Repeat the steps to create links and assign page numbers for the remaining lines of text where you see page numbers to the right of each line. Ignore all text where you don't see a page number on the right side of the page.**

23. **Click the Fit Page tool.**

24. **Click the Select Object tool.**
    Notice the link rectangles are shown and can be selected with the Select Object tool. For selecting multiple links, the Select Object tool can be used to draw marquees around the links you want to select. If, when using the Link tool you need to click a link, press the Shift key and click additional links for multiple link selections.

< T I P >
You can also select all links on a page by clicking the Link tool and choosing Edit→Select All.

25. **Choose File→Save As and save the file as** `11_employeeManual_finish.pdf` **to the Tutorial11_finish folder.**

26. **Keep the file open to follow the steps in the next tutorial.**

Tutorial
» Linking to Views

When you create a link, the Create Link from Selection dialog box offers several options for linking to a view from the choices listed in the Zoom pull-down menu. The choices are fixed zoom levels. If you want to zoom to a different view, you need to use another method for linking to the desired view. Among the methods available to you is using a Snapshot and linking to a Snapshot view. In this tutorial you learn how to create snapshots and link to snapshot views.

1. **Click the Hand tool. Click the link you created for page 9.**
   Page 9 opens in the Document pane.

2. **Click the Snapshot tool.**

3. **Drag a marquee around the form fields and release the mouse button.**
   After releasing the mouse button, a dialog box opens informing you that the selected area has been copied to the Clipboard.

4. **Click OK in the alert dialog box.**

5. **Click the Previous View button.**
   The last view from the contents page opens in the Document pane.

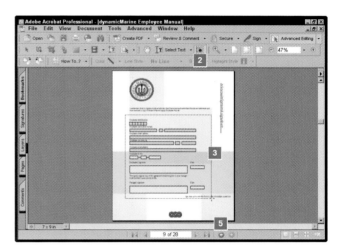

6. **Click the Fit Width tool.**

7. **Click the Select Object tool.**

8. **Click the link for: *Acknowledgement signature form.***

9. **Click the More button in the Properties Bar.**
   The Link Properties dialog box opens.

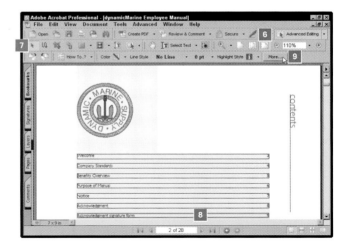

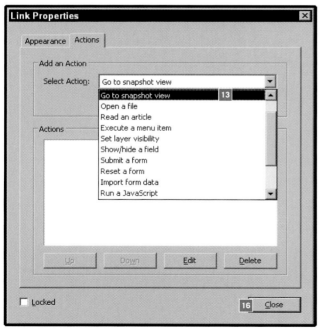

10. **Click the Actions tab.**

Notice the dialog box appears much different than the Create Link from Selection dialog box. You have two tabs in the Link Properties for assigning or changing properties. The Appearance tab provides options for changing the link rectangle appearances much like the choices available in the Properties Bar. The Actions tab handles the link actions. The link you created needs to be edited to change the action from linking to a page in a Fit Page view to linking to a snapshot view. To change the action, you first delete the old action and then add a new action.

11. **Click *Go to a page in this document* in the list window to select it.**

12. **Click the Delete button.**

The last action assigned to the link is deleted.

13. **Open the Select Action pull-down menu and choose Go to Snapshot View.**

14. **Click Add.**

The Create View From Snapshot dialog box opens informing you the snapshot on the Clipboard is now converted to a Go to page destination and added to the list of actions.

15. **Click OK in the Create View From Snapshot dialog box.**

Once you select an action in the Select Action pull-down menu, you need to add the action to the Action list window. A single action or multiple actions can be added to the Action list window. When the link is clicked with the Hand tool, all actions are invoked in the same order as they appear in the Actions list window.

16. **Click the Close button.**

< T I P >

If you have several links to create and edit link actions or you want to test links after creating them, you can leave the Link Properties dialog box open. All your menu commands and tools are accessible while the dialog box is in view.

17. **Test the link. Click the Hand tool and move the cursor over the link. When the Hand tool changes the icon shape to a hand with the forefinger pointing upward, click the mouse button.**

The link destination opens in the Document pane.

18. **Choose Save and keep the file open to follow the steps in the next tutorial.**

Link Actions

When you open the pull-down menu for Select Action, a scrollable list offers you a number of link actions that can be assigned to links, form fields, bookmarks, and page actions. The action types are the same for all items in Acrobat that can be assigned an action.

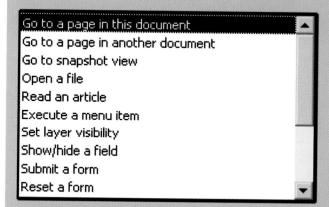

To view all the actions, drag the scroll bar on the right side of the Select Action pull-down menu.

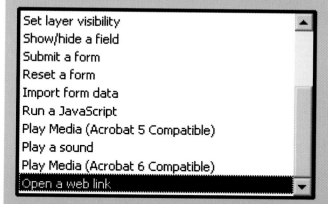

For those actions that link to views, the process for creating a link to a view is the same. You first view the destination, and then you add the action by selecting it in the pull-down menu and click the Add button. Therefore, linking to a view to a layer visibility, to a snapshot, to another page, or to a page in another document, is all performed by following the same steps. Be certain you first navigate to the desired view, and then add the action.

As you work with different interactive items in Acrobat, you'll frequently return to the Select Action pull-down menu. To understand the different action items, review the following item descriptions and mark this page for future reference.

» **Go to a page in this document.** Opens a page in the current document.

» **Go to a page in another document.** Navigates to a specific page in another document.

» **Go to snapshot view.** First take a snapshot, and then link to the snapshot view. Snapshots can be taken in the current active file or another file. When linking to a snapshot view, the snapshot is converted to a link destination.

» **Open a file.** Opens another PDF document at the default page number in the Initial View properties. Most often Initial Views are set to the first page in a file.

» **Read an article.** Article threads must be present in a file. If you have several article threads, you specify which article is to be read. When the link is selected, the view changes to the top of the first column in the article thread.

» **Execute a menu item.** This feature is very powerful. You can execute almost all the commands found in the top-level menus. When you create a link to execute a menu command a dialog box opens where the menu commands are selected. On Windows menu item selections are made in the Menu Item Selection dialog box. On the Macintosh, menu selections are made from the Acrobat menus.

» **Set layer visibility.** When you have PDF files with Adobe PDF layers, you can create links to different layer views. The links work similarly to linking to page views.

» **Show/hide a field.** Fields can only be created in Acrobat Professional; however, once fields appear on a page, the Show/hide action is used to show and hide fields. Users of either Acrobat Standard or Acrobat Professional can create links that show and hide fields. When you use the action, a dialog box opens where you choose to either show or hide fields. All fields in a file are listed in the dialog box.

» **Submit a form.** Forms and form data can be submitted via e-mail and to Web servers. This action is used to create submit buttons.

Link Actions *(continued)*

» Reset a form. Clears all or selected data fields on an Acrobat PDF form.

» Import form data. Like importing comments you learned in Session 10, form data can also be imported and exported. The action opens a dialog box where you browse your hard drive to locate a data file to import.

» Run a JavaScript. JavaScript adds almost infinite opportunities for you to make your documents more dynamic, add interactivity, and process form data. The action opens the JavaScript Editor where custom JavaScripts are edited and debugged.

» Play Media (Acrobat 5 Compatible). The link actions play media files linked to the PDF document.

» Play a sound. Sound files are embedded in a PDF with Acrobat 5 compatibility. When a sound is available, the action plays the sound.

» Play Media (Acrobat 6 Compatible). Acrobat 6 media can be linked or embedded in a file. The link action plays media with Acrobat 6 compatibility.

» Open a Web link. The link action is assigned a URL. When the link action is executed, your default Web browser opens the URL destination.

Setting Cross-Document Linking Preferences

The Specify Open Preference dialog box offers you options for controlling opening views for cross-document links or allowing users to open links according to their individual preference settings. For consistent viewing among many users, your best option is to set cross-document linking to either New Window or Existing Window. Using these settings overrides a user's preferences and you are assured that all users see the same number of documents open in the Document pane when clicking links on your files. When New Window is used, a document link opens without closing the document containing the link. Using Existing Window closes the document containing the link as the new file opens.

If you receive files from other users that default to the user preference, the linked documents open according your individual preference settings. To set your own preferences, choose Edit→ Preferences (Windows) or Acrobat→Preferences (Macintosh). Choose General in the left pane. The check box for Open Cross-Document Links in Same Window controls how the linked files open.

If the check box is enabled, the result is the same as using the Existing Window option in the Specify Open Preference dialog box. That is, the new file opens as the host document closes. Disabling the check box opens cross-document links in new windows while keeping host files open.

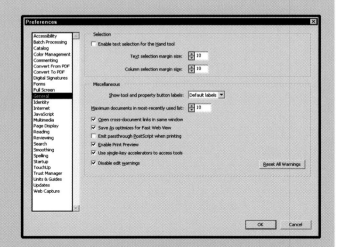

As a PDF author, you'll want to override these preferences in the Specify Open Preferences dialog box for users because some users will have the preference option checked and others will not. Setting the options you want for the document link views in the Specify Open Preferences dialog box allows you to create consistent views among all users.

Tutorial

» Opening Secondary Files

Link actions enable you to link to secondary files. Any file on your computer can be a link destination. If you link to PDF documents, the document opens in the Document pane. If you link to native files from authoring programs, the files open in their respective native application. When you create links to secondary PDF documents, you have options for how the cross-document links are handled. In this tutorial you learn how to link to PDF files and set the cross-document view options.

1. **Enter** 2 **in the Status Bar and press Enter/Return to return to the contents page. Click the Fit Width tool.**

2. **Click the Select Text tool.**

3. **Triple-click the text:** *Sample Form.*
   The Sample Form item on the contents page refers to a separate PDF document. The link to be created is a link to open another file.

4. **Open a context menu and choose Create Link.**
   The Create Link from Selection dialog box opens.

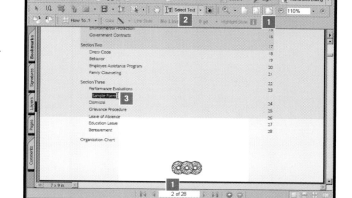

5. **Click the Open a File radio button.**

6. **Click the Browse button.**
   The Select Destination Document dialog box opens.

7. **Navigate to the Tutorial11 folder and click**
   `11_employeeEvaluation.pdf.` **Click Select.**
   The Specify Open Preference dialog box opens.

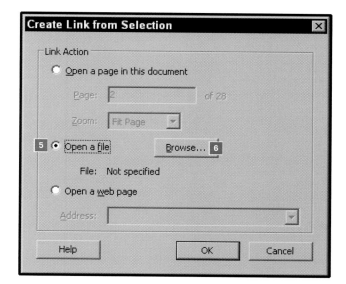

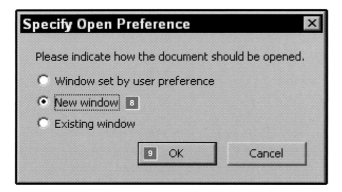

8. **Click the New Window radio button.**
   The Specify Open Preference dialog box offers you three
   options for how the target document opens. The first choice is
   determined from the user's cross-document linking preference
   setting in the General Preferences dialog box. The second
   option opens a file in a new window while the host document
   containing the link remains open behind the new document.
   The third option closes the host document while the new document opens.

9. **Click the OK button.**
   You are returned to the Create Link from Selection dialog box.

10. **Click OK to return to the Document pane.**

11. **Select the Hand tool. Click the link you just created.**
   The link destination opens in the Document pane.

12. **Choose Window to open the Window menu.**
   Notice that the employee manual document and the new link
   destination are both open.

13. **Close the employee evaluation file by clicking the Close button.**
   The contents page should still appear in a Fit Width view.

14. **Keep the employee manual document open to follow the steps in
   the next tutorial.**

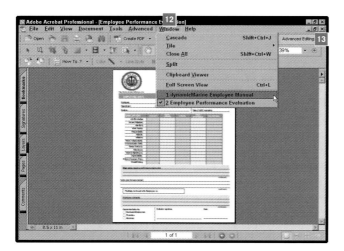

Tutorial

» Opening Pages in Secondary Files

The Open a File action setting should always be used when you want to open PDF documents on the first page or when you want to open a file other than a PDF document in an authoring program. However, you may have files where you want to create links to pages other than the first page in a PDF document. In the employee manual you create links from the contents page. If you link to a file from the contents page, you may want the user to be able to return to the contents page after viewing a linked document. Because the contents page is page two in the employee manual, the Open a file action won't send the user back to page two. Fortunately Acrobat offers another action where you can assign opening views to specific pages. In this tutorial you learn how to link to pages in secondary files.

1. **Click Open.**

2. **Open the** `11_orgChart.pdf` **file from the Tutorial11 folder. Save the file as** `11_orgChart_finish.pdf` **to the Tutorial11_finish folder.**
   You should now have two files open — the employee manual document and the organization chart. You saved the file to the finish folder so you can link to and from the employee manual finish file and the organization finish file.

3. **Click the Fit Window tool.**

4. **Click the Snapshot tool.**

5. **Drag a marquee around the boxes and below the last row to include the text:** *return.*
   When you release the mouse button, a dialog box informs you that the selected area has been copied to the Clipboard.

6. **Click OK in the dialog box informing you that the snapshot has been copied to the Clipboard.**
   The snapshot has been taken on the organization chart file. Now you can link to the snapshot from the employee manual file. Rather than use the Open a file action, you use the Go to snapshot view action.

7. **Choose Window→dynamicMarine Employee Manual.**

8. **Click the Link tool.**
   In order to link to a snapshot, you need to use a Custom Link. Selecting the text and creating a link from the selection doesn't provide you with access to the custom link settings. In order to gain access to the list of actions, you need to use the Link tool and open the link Actions properties.

9. **Draw a link rectangle around the text** *Organization Chart* **at the bottom of the contents page.**
   The Create Link dialog box opens after you release the mouse button. Click Custom Link in the Create Link dialog box and the Link Properties dialog box opens.

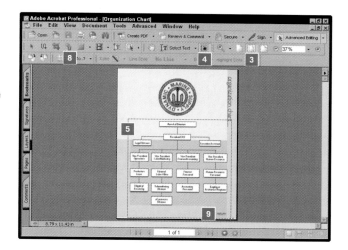

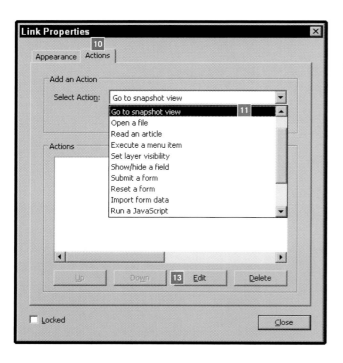

10. **Click the Actions tab in the Link Properties dialog box.**

11. **Choose Go to Snapshot View in the Select Action pull-down menu.**

12. **Click Add. Click OK in the Create View from Snapshot dialog box.**

13. **Click Edit.**

    The action has been added to link to the snapshot view. To specify the open preferences, you need to click the Edit button and make your choices in the Go to a Page in Another Document dialog box. Notice when you click Edit, the link is treated as a link to a page in another file as evidenced by the Go to a Page in Another Document dialog box.

14. **Choose New Window from the Open in pull-down menu.**

    The link is designed to open the organization chart as a new window while the employee manual document remains open. If you choose Existing Window instead, the file opens at a default view and does not open in the snapshot view. Be certain you use New Window when linking to snapshots in secondary files.

15. **Click the OK button.**

16. **Click Close in the Link Properties dialog box.**

17. **Click the Hand tool and click the link to the organization chart.**

    The file opens in the foreground. Click Window and you can see that both files are open in the Document pane.

18. **Click the Link tool.**

19. **Drag a marquee around the word *return* at the bottom of the page.**
    The Create Link dialog box opens. Notice that you didn't use
    the Select Text tool and create a link from a context menu.
    When you create links from text selections, you don't have an
    option to create custom links. You need to use the Link tool to
    create a custom link.

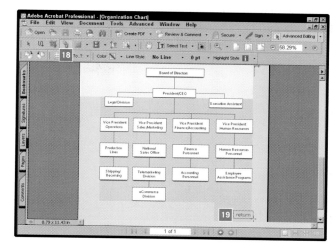

20. **Click Custom link.**

21. **Click OK.**
    The Link Properties dialog box opens.

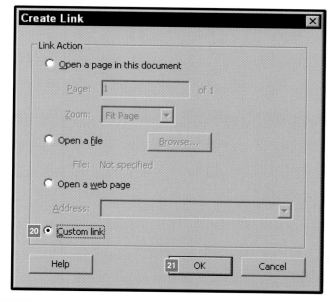

Linking and Directory Paths

When you created links in this tutorial, you linked from the
11_orgChart_finish.pdf file in the Tutorial11_finish folder
to the 11_employeeManual_finish.pdf document, which
is also in the Tutorial11_finish folder. The directory paths for links
are absolute and they must be preserved when copying files on
your hard drives, network servers, or CD-ROMs. Therefore, you can
copy the Tutorial_finish folder to another location on a hard drive,
network server, or CD-ROM as long as you leave both files in the
Tutorial_finish folder or place them both together in another

folder. The important thing is the files need to reside in the same
folder.

If you want to reorganize files where the files are located in different folders, you need to reestablish the links. Before you engage
in Acrobat sessions for creating links, try to organize files in the
folders in which you want them to appear. Be certain of the file
locations, folder names, and how you want your organization
schema to work before creating links.

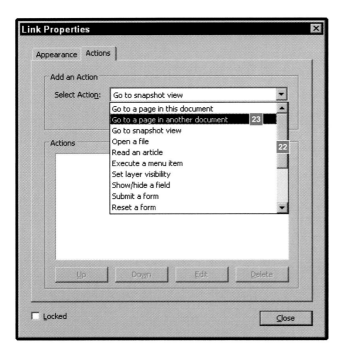

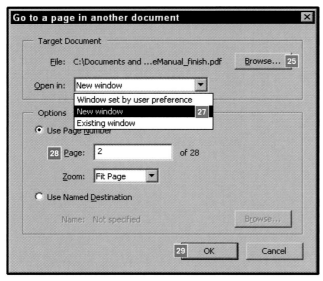

22. **Scroll the scroll bar up in the Select Action pull-down menu.**

23. **Choose Go to a Page in Another Document.**

24. **Click Add.**
    This link is designed to return the user to page 2 in the employee manual. Therefore, you cannot use the Open a file action. When you click Add, the Go to a Page in Another Document dialog box opens where you browse for the file to link to and set the options.

25. **Click the Browse button.**

26. **Navigate to the Tutorial11_finish folder and click**
    `11_employeeManual_finish.pdf`. **Click Select in the Select Destination dialog box.**

27. **Choose New Window from the Open in pull-down menu.**
    Notice that Existing Window is not selected in the Go to a Page in Another Document dialog box. As of the first release of Acrobat 6, creating a link to another page in a secondary document does not work properly if you use Existing Window. This might be a bug in the initial release. If you find a maintenance upgrade resolves the problem, you can use Existing Window if the bug is fixed in newer releases.

28. **Type** 2 **in the Page field box.**
    Notice to the right of the field box you see a number indicating the total number of pages in the document. You can open any page by entering a value in the field box up to the number shown at the right of the field box. If you attempt to enter a value higher than the total number of pages and click OK, Acrobat opens a dialog box informing you the page does not exist.

29. **Click OK.**

30. **Click Close in the Link Properties dialog box.**

31. **Choose Save to update your edits.**

32. **Click the link you just created.**
    The employee manual finish document opens in a Fit Page view and the Bookmarks pane is opened. The contents page opens in the Document pane.

33. **Choose Window➜Organization Chart.**

34. **Close the file. Leave the employee manual document open to follow the steps in the next tutorial.**

Tutorial
» Creating Buttons (Acrobat 6 Professional Only)

Links have some disadvantages when compared to using buttons. Buttons are part of the form tools in Acrobat Professional, and these tools are not available in Acrobat Standard. Using links as compared to buttons provides some disadvantages, including the inability to use icon appearances for the link rectangles and no provision for copying and pasting links across pages in a document. In this tutorial, you learn how to create navigation buttons, apply button faces for changing appearances, and duplicate buttons across pages.

1. **Click the Fit Width tool.**

2. **Scroll to the bottom of page 2 in the employee manual by clicking the down arrow in the scroll bar.**

3. **Click the Button tool in the Advanced Editing toolbar.**

4. **Drag a marquee in the lower-right corner of page 2.**
   When you release the mouse button, the Button Properties dialog box opens.

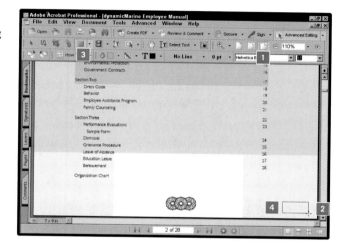

5. **Click the General tab in the Button Properties dialog box.**

6. **Type** goNext **in the Name field box.**
   By default, Acrobat names your fields automatically as each field is created. Button fields begin with Button1 and continue with Button2, Button3, and so on. When creating form fields, you'll find it much easier to manage your documents by adding more descriptive names for your fields.

7. **Click the Appearance tab to open the Appearance properties.**
   Appearance properties offer you similar options as you find with link rectangles. Also notice you can use the Properties Bar to change the Button rectangle appearances. In this tutorial, you'll change the contents of the rectangle and set the rectangle to no color for the border and fill.

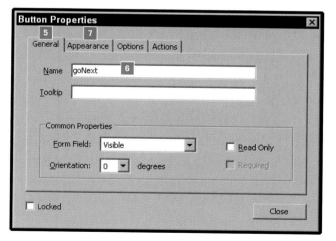

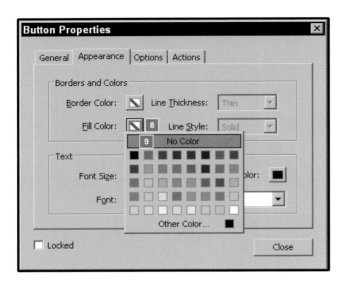

8. **Click the Fill Color color swatch.**
   A pop-up color palette opens where you select colors for the rectangle fill.

9. **Click No Color in the color palette.**
   Notice as you change appearances in the Button Properties the appearance settings are reflected dynamically in the Document pane. If the dialog box is not hiding the button field, you can see the attributes applied for options choices you make in the Button Properties. By default, the Border Color is set to No Color. Notice the No Color item is represented by a square with a diagonal red line. If your Border Color is set to any other color, change it by clicking the color swatch and clicking No Color.

10. **Leave the file open and the Button Properties dialog box in view to follow steps in the next tutorial.**

Tutorial

» Creating Button Faces (Acrobat 6 Professional Only)

Buttons offer you an option to add images to the button rectangles you can import from different file types such as PDF, TIFF, and JPEG. In addition to importing images, you can also create rollover effects like often seen in Web pages. In this tutorial, you learn how to add images for button faces and create rollover effects.

1. Click the Options tab.
The Button Properties dialog box should still be open and the Button created in the last tutorial should still be selected. The Options properties tab opens. Options for Button fields enable you to apply fills to the fields in the form of images and icons.

2. Choose Icon Only from the Layout pull-down menu.

3. Choose Push from the Behavior pull-down menu.
Notice when you choose Push, you see the State options for Up, Down, and Rollover. A Rollover effect is similar to the kinds of rollover displays you see for buttons and icons on Web pages. When the cursor is positioned over a button, the image changes to another image. The Push option is the only Behavior state that supports rollovers. In this tutorial you'll create a rollover effect for the button face.

4. Click the Choose Icon button.
The Select Icon dialog box opens.

5. Click Browse in the Select Icon dialog box.
The Open dialog box opens. In this dialog box you navigate your hard drive to locate the button face you want to use. The file types compatible for importing as button faces are the same file types you have available when creating PDFs from files. Therefore, you can import a variety of image formats as well as PDF documents.

6. Navigate to the Tutorial11 folder.

7. Click 11_arrowRt.pdf.

8. Click the Select button.
After clicking Select, you return to the Select Icon dialog box. A thumbnail image for the file you select is shown in the dialog box.

9. Click OK to close the Select Icon dialog box to return to the Button Properties dialog box.

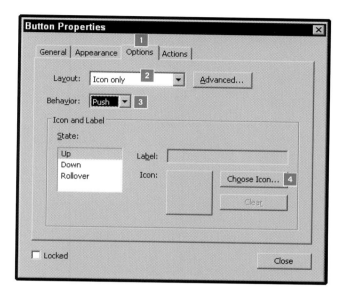

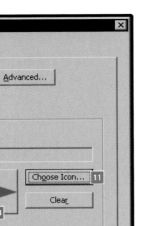

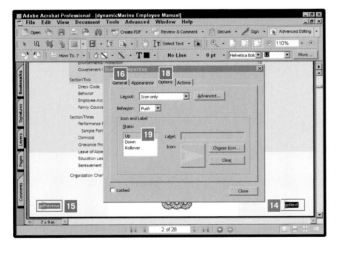

10. **Choose Rollover in the State list.**

11. **Click the Choose Icon button.**

12. **Click Browse in the Select Icon dialog box. Click** 11_arrowRtRollover.pdf **in the Open dialog box. Click Select and click OK when you return to the Select Icon dialog box.**

13. **Notice the icon you select is visible as a thumbnail image in the Options properties.**
    If you make a mistake and want to remove the image from a button, click the Clear button. To follow the remaining steps in this tutorial, be certain to avoid clicking Clear.

14. **Leave the Button Properties dialog box open and click the goNext button. Keep the mouse button pressed and press Control (Windows) or Option (Macintosh).**

15. **Press the Shift key and drag to the left side of the document page.**
    When you press Control/Option and drag, you duplicate the button. When you add the Shift key, you constrain the movement. As you drag left, the vertical movement is locked while the Shift key is pressed and you drag horizontally. When you release the mouse button, the button field is duplicated. All the attributes assigned to the button remain as an exact copy of the original button. To change the icon images you need to edit the Options properties.

16. **Click the General tab.**

17. **Change the button field name to** goPrevious **in the Name field.**

18. **Click the Options tab.**

19. **Choose Up for the state and then click the Choose Icon button. Follow the same steps to select an icon by clicking Browse in the Select Icon dialog box.**

20. **Click** 11_arrowLt.pdf **in the Open dialog box and click Select. Click OK in the Select Icon dialog box. Follow the same steps for the rollover image. Be certain to click Rollover for the State and use the** 11_arrowLtRollover.pdf **file.**

21. **Click Actions.**
    The Actions properties are the same as those you have available for links. Actions are selected from the Select Action pull-down menu. Note that the button for goPrevious is selected. Keep the button selected as you follow the steps ahead.

22. Open the Select Action pull-down menu and choose Execute a Menu Item. Click Add.

On Windows the Menu Item Selection dialog box opens. This dialog box contains all the same options you have in the top-level menu bar. On the Macintosh, the Menu Item dialog box opens but you make your menu choices in the top-level menu bar.

23. Choose View→Go To→Previous Page.

For Windows users you select the menu option in the Menu Item Selection dialog box. Macintosh users make the same selection from the View menu at the top of the Acrobat Window.

24. Click OK in the Menu Item Selection (Windows) or Menu Item (Macintosh) dialog box.

25. Click the button on the right side of the page.

26. Follow the same steps by selecting Execute a Menu Item and use the View→Go To→Next Page menu command. Click OK in the Menu Item Selection/Menu Item dialog box.

Keep the file open to follow the steps in the next tutorial.

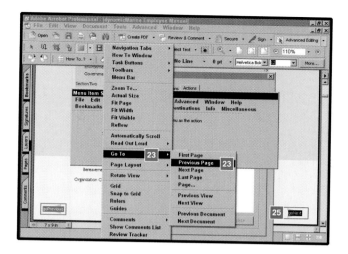

Button Labels

The Layout pull-down menu offers you seven ways to display button labels. When you click an option for showing a *label* or showing a label with an icon, the label is typed in the Label field box. The font attributes are derived from choices you make in the Appearance tab for Font Size, Font, and Color. The different layout options are shown here.

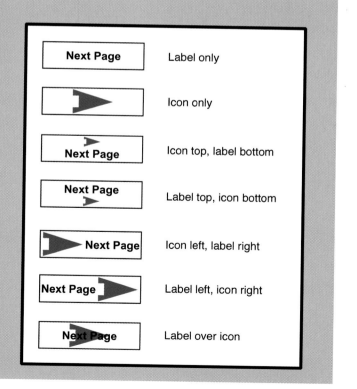

Tutorial

» Duplicating Buttons (Acrobat 6 Professional Only)

One of the best advantages for using buttons over links is the ability to duplicate buttons across a range of pages. If you create navigation buttons, you need only create individual buttons for a single page and assign all the properites to the buttons one time. When you duplicate buttons, the properties and appearances are duplicated. In this tutorial you learn how to duplicate button fields.

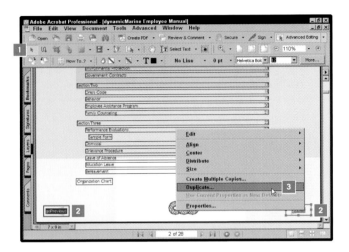

1. **Click the Select Object tool.**

2. **Drag the cursor through both button fields.**
   When you marquee a group of fields to select them, be certain to drag with the Select Object tool. If you use the Button tool, Acrobat assumes you want to create another button field.

3. **Open a context menu and choose Duplicate.**
   The Duplicate Field dialog box opens. In this dialog box you can select the page range for duplicating buttons. When you click OK, the buttons and the attributes assigned to them are duplicated across the pages identified in the From and To field boxes. The Duplicate menu item is not available for links. Links can only be copied and pasted on individual pages.

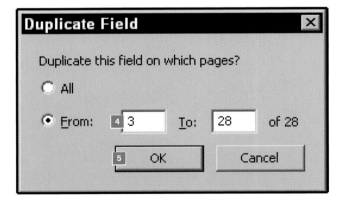

4. **Enter 3 in the From field box. By default you should see 28 appear in the To field box.**
   Because you have buttons on page 2, there is no need to create duplicates for page 2. Enter 3 for the first page to receive the duplicates and be certain 28 appears in the To field box.

5. **Click OK.**
   The buttons are duplicated across all pages.

6. **Click Fit Page.**

7. **Click the Hand tool.**

8. **Position the Hand tool on the goNext button on page 2 and click.**
   You should see page 3 open in the Document pane. Click several buttons moving back and forth through the pages.

9. **Click File Save As and save the file to the Tutorial11_finish folder, overwriting the previous file to optimize it.**

10. **Quit Acrobat.**

» Session Review

In this session you learned how create interactive links and buttons. There are many attributes you can assign to links and buttons, and it can seem a little overwhelming when you first start adding interactive features to your documents. To help you become more familiar with adding actions to links and buttons, look over the following questions. Answers are found in the tutorial noted in parentheses.

1. How do you create links from text in PDF documents? (See Tutorial: Creating Links to Pages.)

2. How do you create a custom link from selected text? (See Tutorial: Linking to Views.)

3. How do you link to a snapshot? (See Tutorial: Linking to Views.)

4. Where can you change link appearances? (See Tutorial: Linking to Views.)

5. How do you link to another file? (See Tutorial: Opening Secondary Files.)

6. How do you link to a page other than the opening page in another file? (See Tutorial: Opening Secondary Files.)

7. How do you close a file when you link to other files? (See Tutorial: Opening Secondary Files.)

8. How can you tell whether you have several files open after clicking links? (See Tutorial: Opening Secondary Files.)

9. How do you add an icon to a Button field? (See Tutorial: Creating Buttons (Acrobat 6 Professional Only).)

10. How do you set a link to go to the next page view? (See Tutorial: Creating Buttons (Acrobat 6 Professional Only).)

11. How do you add an image to a button rectangle? ? (See Tutorial: Creating Button Faces (Acrobat 6 Professional Only).)

12. How do you duplicate buttons? (See Tutorial: Duplicating Buttons (Acrobat 6 Professional Only).)

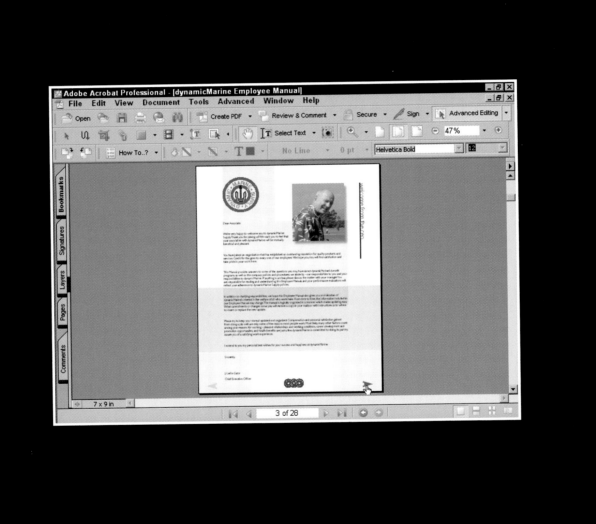

Working with Multimedia

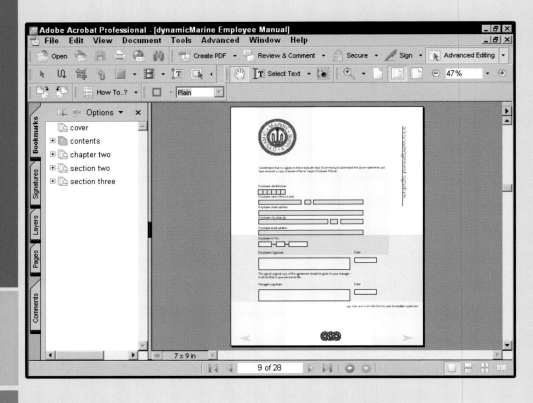

Tutorial: **Adding Sounds**

Tutorial: **Playing Sounds with Page Actions (Acrobat Professional Only)**

Tutorial: **Importing Acrobat 5 Compatible Media (Acrobat Professional Only)**

Tutorial: **Creating Play Buttons**

Tutorial: **Importing Acrobat 6 Compatible Media (Acrobat Professional Only)**

Tutorial: **Creating Acrobat 6 Compatible Media Play Buttons**

Session Introduction

Nothing contributes more to creating interactive documents than sounds and movie clips. With many new additions for media support, Acrobat 6 enables you to import a variety of sound and movie files to further enhance interactivity. In this session you learn how to import sound and movie files.

TOOLS YOU'LL USE
Movie tool, Sound tool, Pages panel, Page Actions, Select Object tool, Link tool, Link Properties, Advanced Editing toolbar, and the Properties Bar.

CD-ROM FILES NEEDED
12_acroEmailReview.pdf, 12_acroIntro.pdf.,
12_acroIntro_final.pdf, 12_digitalIDinfo.wav,
12_employeeManual.pdf, 12_employeeManualFinal.pdf,
12_moviePoster.pdf, 12_videoBookmarks.mov,
12_videoComments.mov, 12_videoEmailReview.mov,
12_videoForms.mov, 12_videoViews.mov, and
12_videoPageEditing.mov (found in the
Sessions/Session12/Tutorial12 folder).

<NOTE>
The files 12_acroIntro_final.pdf and 12_employeeManual_final.pdf are not placed in the Tutorial12_finals folder in order to preserve links to files in the Tutorial12 folder. Use these files to compare your results after completing the tutorials in this session.

TIME REQUIRED
90 minutes

Tutorial
» Adding Sounds

Acrobat has a Sound Comment tool that enables you to record and add sounds in the form of comments. However, sound comments cannot be saved as separate files and used like sound files where sounds can be played with buttons, links, and actions. For creating and importing sounds, you need a sound-editing program capable of saving sounds as separate files. Once you create sound files in a sound-editing program, you can import the sounds in PDF documents and create buttons and actions to play the sounds. In this tutorial you learn how to import sound files and play sounds from actions.

1. **Mount the CD-ROM located in the back of this book. Drag the folder Session12 from inside the Sessions folder to your desktop. Launch Acrobat by double-clicking the program icon.**

2. **Open the file 12_employeeManual.pdf from the Tutorial12 folder. Turn to page 9.**
   You should have the Advanced Editing tools and the Properties Bar docked in the Toolbar Well. If you changed your editing environment, reset the toolbars and load the Advanced Editing tools and the Properties Bar.

3. **Click the down-pointing arrow adjacent to the Movie tool to open a pull-down menu.**

4. **Choose Expand This Button.**
   The Advanced Editing toolbar is expanded to show the Sound tool.

5. **Click the Bookmarks tab to collapse the Bookmarks panel.**

6. **Click the Fit Width tool and scroll to the bottom of the page.**

7. **Click the Sound tool in the Advanced Editing toolbar.**

8. **Drag a marquee around the icon at the bottom center of the page.**
   When you release the mouse, the Add Sound dialog box opens.

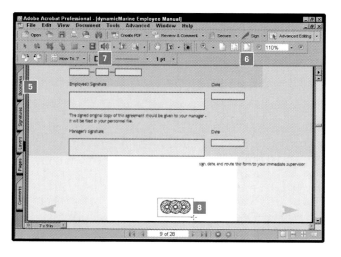

9. **Choose the Acrobat 5 (and Earlier) Compatible Media option.**
   The Add Sound dialog box changes, offering you fewer options for sound file attributes than those displayed when Acrobat 6 Compatible Media is selected.

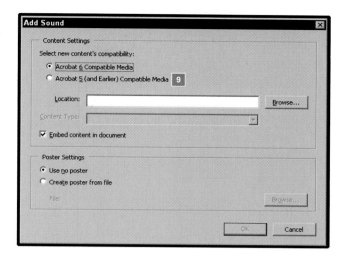

10. **Click Browse.**
    The Select Sound dialog box opens. The dialog box works similarly to the Open dialog box where you navigate your hard drive, select a file, and click the Select button to import the sound.

11. **Navigate to the Tutorial12 folder and click** `12_digitalIDinfo.wav`. **Click Select in the dialog box.**
    Acrobat pauses a moment as the sound is imported in the open document.

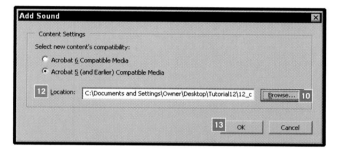

12. **Notice the Location field box displays the directory path and file-name of the imported sound file.**

13. **Click OK.**

Acrobat Sound Compatibility

When you open the Add Sound dialog box, you have a choice for determining which compatibility is to be used with the sound import. The options are choices you make for using either Acrobat 6 or Acrobat 5 compatibility. Depending on which compatibility you intend to use, you have different attributes you can assign to the sound import.

Acrobat 6 compatibility provides options for embedding the sound file or linking to the sound file. When a sound is embedded, the file size grows to accommodate the sound import. If you choose to not embed a sound, the file is linked to the PDF. Linked files need to be transported along with PDF documents in order to play the sounds.

Acrobat 6 compatibility also provides options for using a poster. Posters are like button faces you used in Session 11. A poster can be retrieved from a file and appears inside the sound frame. You can import any file compatible with the Create PDF from File command for a poster appearance. If you save PDFs with Acrobat 6 compatibility, users of earlier versions of Acrobat might have problems playing sounds. Use the Acrobat 6 compatibility setting when you know your files are distributed to users with Acrobat 6 viewers or greater.

Acrobat 5 compatibility provides no options for linking sounds to PDF documents and no options for creating posters. When you import a sound with Acrobat 5 compatibility, the sound is always embedded in the PDF document.

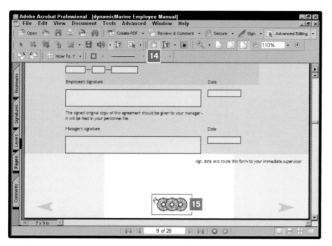

14. **Click the Hand tool.**

15. **Place the cursor inside the sound import frame and click.**
By default you should see a border around the rectangle drawn with the sound tool. When you click the mouse button on the sound frame, the sound plays. This method of importing a sound requires a user to manually click to play a sound. You can use Acrobat 6 compatibility and add a poster informing a user to click to play a sound. However, if you want to play sounds when users open pages, you can use other methods for sound imports. In particular, playing sounds when pages open are best established with Page Actions, as you learn in the next tutorial.

16. **Choose File→Save As. Save the file to the Tutorial12 folder as** `12_employeeManual_finish.pdf.`
Note the file is saved to the Tutorial12 folder. The sound file is linked to the PDF document and the directory path is absolute. Acrobat looks to the same folder for the sound file as where the PDF document resides. If you save to another folder, a warning dialog box opens when you click the sound informing you that the sound cannot be found.

17. **Keep the file open to follow the steps in the next tutorial.**

<NOTE>
You can also import sounds when assigning actions by clicking the Play a Sound action. This option does not require you to use the Sound or Movie tool. When you open a Page action (bookmark, link, or field) and click Play a Sound from the Select Action pull-down menu and click Add, the Select Sound File dialog box opens. Navigate your hard drive and open the sound file you want to import. The sound is imported and the sound plays when the action is invoked.

Tutorial
» Playing Sounds with Page Actions (Acrobat Professional Only)

Sounds can be played when PDFs open, when new pages are viewed, and when play actions are assigned to interactive elements such as bookmarks, links, buttons, and so on. The sound frame on the page in the employee manual acts as a button to play the sound but requires a user to manually click the button to hear the sound. By assigning a Page action, you can have the sound play automatically without user intervention each time a page opens. In this tutorial you learn to adjust sound properties and assign Page actions to play sounds.

1. **Click the Sound tool.**

2. **Open a context menu from the sound frame on page 9.**

3. **Choose Properties.**
   By default, the sound frame contains a black border. Using a border or a poster is necessary when users need to find a sound and know where to click the sound button. However, if you elect to play a sound when opening a page, the border is no longer needed. At any time you can change an appearance for sounds by opening the Movie Properties dialog box.

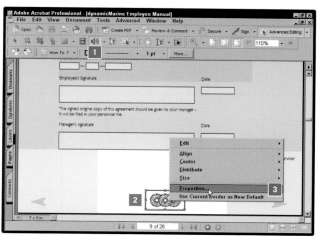

4. **Click the Appearance tab.**

5. **Choose Invisible Rectangle from the Type pull-down menu.**

6. **Click Close.**
   Notice the sound frame now appears without a border.

<TIP>
You can also change appearances for sound frames by selecting the rectangle with either the Sound tool or the Select Object tool and making appearance choices in the Properties Bar. Click the Line pull-down menu and click No Line from the menu to remove a border.

<NOTE>
Sounds can be added to page actions in Acrobat Standard by using the Play a Sound action. However, the Sound and Movie tools are available only in Acrobat Professional.

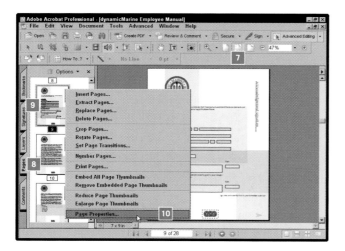

7. **Click the Fit Page tool.**

8. **Click the Pages tab to open the Pages panel.**

9. **Open a context menu on page 9 in the Pages panel.**
   Be certain to click the page 9 thumbnail before opening a context menu. If you click outside the page thumbnail, a different context menu opens.

10. **Choose Page Properties.**
    The Page Properties dialog box opens.

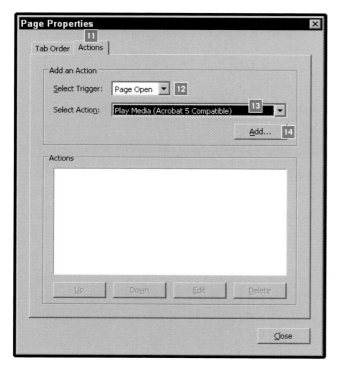

11. **Click the Actions tab.**
    Notice the Select Action pull-down menu contains the same actions you discovered in Session 11 when creating links and buttons. Appling actions to pages are handled the same way as when adding actions to bookmarks, links, and buttons.

12. **Choose Page Open from the Select Trigger pull-down menu.**
    By default, Page Open is the trigger. The trigger is the condition for when a Page action is invoked. You have choices for using a Page Open or a Page Close trigger. Therefore, you can choose to play a sound or invoke any other action when a page opens or when a page closes.

13. **Open the Select Action pull-down menu and choose Play Media (Acrobat 5 Compatible).**
    When you import a sound file, you determine the compatibility in the Add Sound dialog box. If you add a sound with Acrobat 5 compatibility, you must use the Play Media (Acrobat 5 Compatible) action. If you click Play Media (Acrobat 6 Compatible) in the Select Action pull-down menu, Acrobat opens a dialog box informing you that an Acrobat 6 compatible file is not contained in the current document. Before you can play a sound file with an action, you first need to import the sound using the Sound tool or the Movie tool and use actions consistent with the file compatibility.

14. **Click the Add button.**
    The Play Media (Acrobat 5 Compatible) dialog box opens.

15. **Click OK.**

    By default, the sound file is automatically placed in the Select Media field box. If you have several sound files in a document, the pull-down menu for Select Media enables you to select the sound file you want to play with the Page action. Also by default, the Play option is selected from the Select Operation pull-down menu. You also have choices from this menu for Stop, Pause, and Resume. If a sound is playing, one of the other pull-down menu items invokes an action to interrupt the play.

16. **Choose File→Save As.**

17. **Save the file to the Tutorial12 folder and overwrite the previous version to optimize the file.**

18. **Click the Hand tool.**

    When you have the Sound tool selected as your current tool, Acrobat interprets your document mode as an authoring mode. If you attempt to scroll pages and return to the page containing the action to play the sound, a warning dialog box opens informing you that the media cannot play while in authoring mode. Therefore, you need to click the Hand tool to move from authoring mode to viewing mode and the sound plays when you open the page containing the action.

19. **Click the Next Page tool to advance one page.**

20. **Click the Previous Page tool to move back to page 9.**

    The sound plays when the page opens.

21. **Close the file and keep Acrobat open to follow the steps in the next tutorial.**

Play Options

In the Movie Properties dialog box you have options for playing video clips. The default play option is set to play the movie within the movie frame. You can change the default in the Movie Properties dialog box to play a video in a floating window. When you click the Hand tool on a movie frame or via a play button, the movie frame remains fixed at the current poster view while a floating window opens and plays the movie. After completion, the floating window closes.

Acrobat 6 compatible media offers additional playback options found in the Playback Location in the Rendition Settings (see the sidebar called "Using Renditions" later in this session). You can choose to play back videos in the document in a floating window or in Full Screen mode (for information on Full Screen mode, see Session 13).

Both Acrobat 5 and Acrobat 6 compatible media offer you options for showing player controls. When you elect to use this feature, a player control bar opens where buttons for playing, pausing, and stopping a video are selected.

Tutorial

» Importing Acrobat 5 Compatible Media (Acrobat Professional Only)

Importing movie clips also involves choices for importing either an Acrobat 5 compatible media file or an Acrobat 6 compatible file. Like sound imports, there are many distinctions between using one compatibility version versus another. In this tutorial you learn how to import and work with Acrobat 5 compatible movie clips.

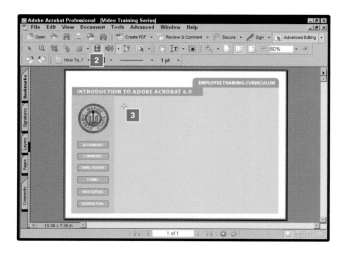

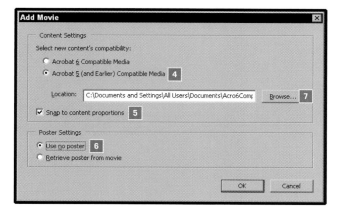

1. **Click Open. Navigate to the Tutorial12 folder and open the file 12_acroIntro.pdf.**
   Note this file is set to open in a Fit Page view. The zoom size is optimum for screen resolutions at 800×600 or less. If you work on a monitor with a larger screen size, click the Actual Size tool to zoom to a 100% view. You should see the page fit completely in the Document pane. A 100% view is an optimum size for viewing video files without distortion.

   <NOTE>
   The video files used in this session are clips from a complete training program on Acrobat 6 produced by Total Training. Review all the files for step-by-step instructions on how to perform a variety of tasks in Acrobat 6.

2. **Click the Movie tool.**

3. **Move the cursor to the top-left corner of the empty space where you see the background color and double-click the mouse button.**
   The Add Movie dialog box opens.

4. **Click Acrobat 5 (and Earlier) Compatible Media.**

5. **Be certain the Snap to Content Proportions check box is enabled.**
   By default the check box is enabled. When the box is checked, sizing the movie frame keeps the movie proportionately sized, thus preventing any distortion if you resize the frames.

6. **Click Use No Poster.**
   Movie posters can be created from the first frame in a movie clip. If you don't want the first video frame to appear in the movie frame, select this option.

7. **Click the Browse button.**
   The Select Movie File dialog box opens.

8. **Navigate to the Tutorial12 folder and click
   12_videoBookmarks.mov.**

9. **Click the Select button.**

   The movie clip is assigned a link from the frame to the file on
   your hard drive. When using Acrobat 5 compatibility, movies
   are linked to PDF documents.

10. **Double-click the Movie tool in the document window in the same
    approximate location as when you first double-clicked the tool in
    step 3.**

    The Add Movie dialog box opens again. Use the same choices.

11. **Use the same attribute choices for the Movie Properties as in
    steps 4 through 6 and click the Browse button.**

12. **Choose** 12_videoComments.mov **in the Select Movie File
    dialog box and click Select.**

    Don't be concerned where the movie frames appear on the
    page. You'll adjust the position and sizes after importing all
    the files.

13. **Repeat the same steps and import the following files:**
    12_videoForms.mov, 12_videoEmailReview.mov,
    12_videoViews.mov, **and** 12_videoPageEditing.mov.
    All movie files are used in this tutorial.

14. **Click the top foreground frame.**

15. **Drag the lower-right corner to size the rectangle to fit within the
    space in the colored background without interfering with the title
    or left column.**

<NOTE>

You can move the frame by moving the cursor inside the frame and
drag it around the page.

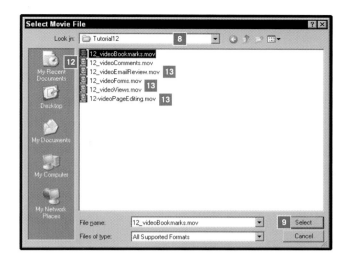

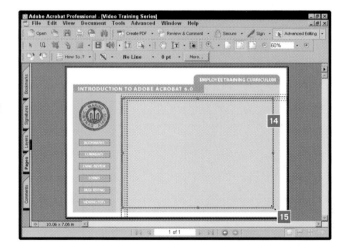

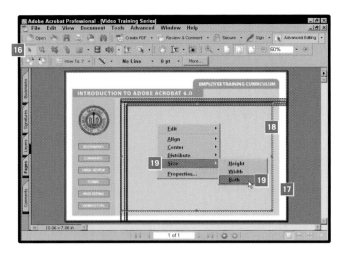

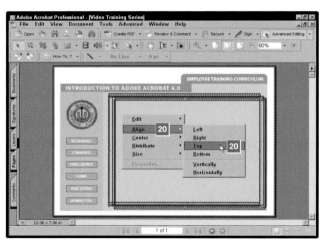

16. **Click the Select Object tool.**

17. **Drag through the frames to select them. Note: you can also choose Edit→Select All or press Control/Command+A.**

18. **Press Shift and click the Select Object tool on the foreground frame (the rectangle you sized in step 15).**
    When you press the Shift key, you keep the selection active. Clicking the foreground frame changes the highlight color to red while the other frame highlights remain blue. The red frame is a target for which all other frames can be sized and aligned.

19. **Open a context menu and choose Size→Both.**
    All frames are sized to the same size as the target frame.

20. **Be certain the selection is still active and the foreground frame is the target, and open a context menu again. Choose Align→Top.**

21. **Open a context menu again and choose Align→Left.**
    All frames are sized and aligned to the target frame. If you need to nudge the frames to center them in the open space on the page, press the arrow keys in the direction you want to move the group.

22. **Choose File→Document Properties.**

23. **Click Description.**

24. **Observe the file size.**
    Notice the file size is 1.35MB. The video files occupy approximately 40MB of hard disk space. Because you used Acrobat 5 compatibility the files are linked to the PDF document. The movies can play as long as you transport the movie files along with the PDF document and keep all links within the same directory path. Also, by using Acrobat 5 compatibility you are assured all users with earlier versions of Acrobat can see the movies when exercising play options.

25. **Choose File→Save As and save the file as** 12_acroIntro_ finish.pdf **to the Tutorial12 folder.**
    Note that the file is saved to the Tutorial12 folder and not the Tutorial12_finish folder. The links you made to the movie files are absolute, and the PDF file needs to remain within the same path as the linked movie files.

26. **Keep the file open to follow the steps in the next tutorial.**

Tutorial

» Creating Play Buttons

Because several movies are stacked in the same document you created in the last tutorial, you need some method for selecting a file you want to play. Only the top file can be played by using the Hand tool and clicking the movie frame. To make movie selections and play possible, you can create play buttons. In this tutorial you learn to use links for play buttons to play movie files.

1. **Click the Fit Width tool.**

2. **Scroll to the bottom of the page by dragging the scroll bar down.**

3. **Click the Link tool.**

4. **Draw a rectangle around the Bookmarks button.**
   When you release the mouse button, the Create Link dialog box opens.

<NOTE>

Users of Acrobat Professional can use either Links or Button fields for play buttons.

5. **Click Custom Link.**

6. **Click OK.**
   The Link Properties dialog box opens.

7. **Select the Actions tab. Click Play Media (Acrobat 5 Compatible) from the Select Action pull-down menu.**

8. **Click Add.**
   The Play Media (Acrobat 5 Compatible) dialog box opens.

9. **Open the Select Media pull-down menu and click Annotation from 12_videoBookmarks.mov.**
   Notice all the files you imported are listed in the Play Media (Acrobat 5 Compatible) dialog box.

10. **Click OK in the Play Media (Acrobat 5 Compatible Media) dialog box.**
    Leave the Link Properties dialog box open.

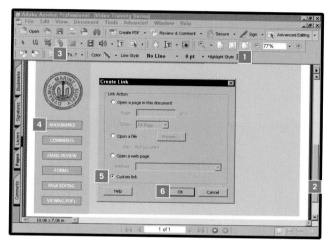

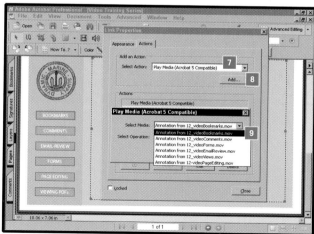

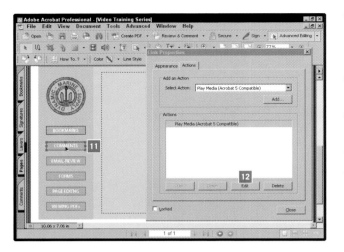

11. **Press Control/Option and click the link rectangle. Keep the keys pressed and drag down to the next box.**
When you press Control/Option and click and drag, the rectangle is duplicated.

12. **Click Edit in the Link Properties dialog box.**
The Play Media (Acrobat 5 Compatible) dialog box opens.

13. **Open the Select Media pull-down menu and click Annotation from 12_videoComments.mov.**

14. **Click OK.**

15. **Repeat the same steps to duplicate links and edit the properties. The movie filenames are self-descriptive and relate to the names contained in the boxes on the page.**

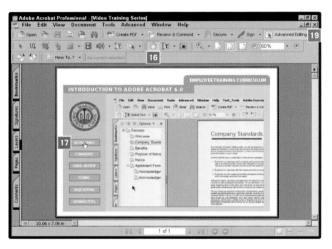

16. **Click the Hand tool.**

17. **Click the first link button.**
The video plays. Click each subsequent link to test them and be certain you have all the video files linked to the document.

18. **Choose File→Save As and overwrite the file in the Tutorial12 folder to optimize it.**

19. **Click the Close button.**

Tutorial

» Importing Acrobat 6 Compatible Media (Acrobat Professional Only)

Acrobat 6 compatible media imports offer you many more options than linking to Acrobat 5 compatible media. Acrobat 6 compatibility supports many different media formats, enables you to embed media in PDFs, supports retrieving movie posters from files, and offers you a host of options for creating different renditions. In this tutorial you learn some of the advantages for importing Acrobat 6 compatible media.

1. **Click the Open button.**

2. **Open the** `12_acroEmailReview.pdf` **file from the Tutorial12 folder. Adjust the page view as described in step 1 of the previous tutorial.**

3. **Click the Movie tool.**

4. **Double-click the page with the Movie tool.**
   The Add Movie dialog box opens.

5. **Be sure the radio button for Acrobat 6 Compatible Media is selected.**
   By default, the radio button should be selected.

6. **Click Browse.**

7. **Open the Tutorial12 folder and click** `12_videoEmailReview.mov`. **Click Select.**
   The directory path and file is described in the Location field box in the Add Movie dialog box.

8. **Click the down-pointing arrow to open the Content Type pull-down menu.**
   By default, Acrobat recognizes the format for the file type you target for importing. In this example, an Apple QuickTime movie is selected as evidenced by the Content Type field box showing video/quicktime. From the pull-down menu you can view all the formats supported when you select Acrobat 6 Compatible Media. Take a moment to review the file formats compatible with Acrobat 6.

9. **Release the down-pointing arrow to collapse the menu.**

10. **Click the Retrieve Poster from Movie radio button.**
    The first frame in the movie is used as the poster image.

11. **Click OK.**
    Acrobat pauses a moment as the movie file is embedded in the document. Wait until you see the Status Bar showing the import progression finish before moving on.

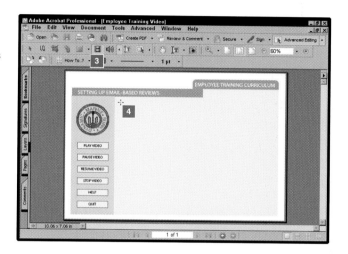

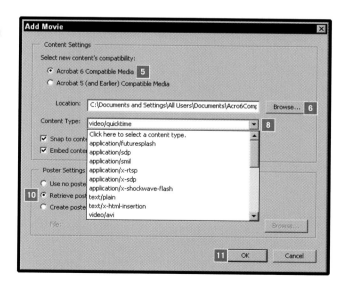

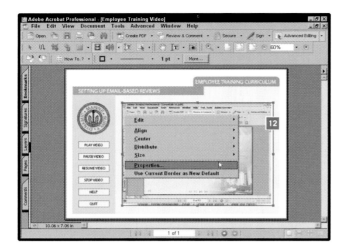

12. **Click and drag the movie frame to size and center in the Document pane. Open a context menu and choose Properties.**
The Multimedia Properties dialog box opens. In this dialog box you have options for various Settings, Appearance, and Actions. The Settings tab provides options for adding and editing renditions, and the Actions tab offers options the same as those found when creating actions for bookmarks, links, fields, and page actions.

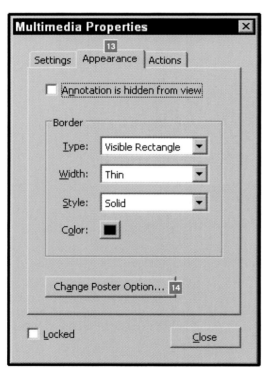

13. **Click the Appearance tab.**
The Appearance tab offers you choices for setting the movie frame appearances and poster options. With Acrobat 6 compatible media you have the same options for using no poster or retrieving a poster from a file like Acrobat 5 compatible media poster options. In addition, you have an option for creating a poster from a file.

14. **Click Change Poster Option.**
The Change Poster Option dialog box opens where you see options for using no poster, retrieving a poster from a file, and creating a poster from a file.

15. **Click Create Poster from File. Click Browse to open the Select Poster File dialog box. Navigate to the Tutorial12 folder and click** `12_moviePoster.pdf` **file. Click Select.**
In the Select Poster File dialog box you navigate your hard drive to find a poster you want to use to file the movie frame. The file types can be any file compatible with Create PDF from File. Click the file to import and click Select. You return to the Change Poster Option dialog box.

16. **Click OK when you return to the Change Poster Option dialog box.**
You return to the Multimedia Properties dialog box. In the background you see the poster image fill the movie frame.

17. **Click Close in the Multimedia Properties dialog box.**

18. **Leave the file open to follow the steps in the next tutorial.**

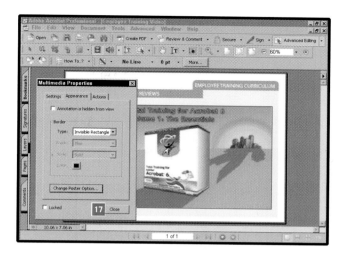

Using Renditions

When you import a sound or video, the rendition of the clip is assigned to a Mouse Up trigger and plays according to the properties you enable for the play options. By default imported sounds and videos have a single default rendition. When using Acrobat 6 compatible media, you have an opportunity to add different renditions

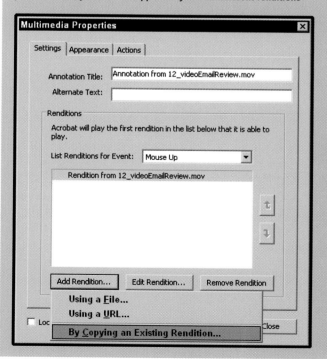

to the same media clip or multiple media clips. For example, you might have a rendition that plays a large media clip and you might want to add an alternative clip of a duplicate movie with a smaller file. When hosting the media on a Web site, you can assign what media clip is downloaded to a user's computer based on the user's connection speed. The movie frame remains the same but the attributes contain two different renditions of the same frame.

You have options for editing existing renditions after importing a media clip or you can add new renditions to an imported file. When you add new renditions, they are listed in the Settings tab in the Multimedia Properties dialog box.

By default a rendition is listed in the lower window in the Settings properties. To add a rendition, click the Add Rendition button. A pull-down menu opens where you make choices for one of the following:

» Using a File: For local files select Using a File. The Select Multimedia File dialog box opens where you navigate your hard drive and select the file to use. This option might be used to select a duplicate file smaller or larger in size than the original rendition.

» Using a URL: If you want files downloaded from Web sites, select Using a URL. The Add a New Rendition Using a URL dialog box opens where you add the URL address for where the file is located. When you add the URL, a pull-down menu opens where you can select the content type for the media format.

Using Renditions *(continued)*

» **By Copying an Existing Rendition:** If you want to use the same rendition as one listed in the Settings list window for the purpose of duplicating the rendition and providing alternate attributes, select By Copying an Existing Rendition. The Copy Rendition dialog box opens where you select the rendition to copy from a pull-down menu.

Select any one of the three options and click the Edit button to open the Rendition Settings dialog box.

You can choose to edit an existing rendition or edit the new rendition added to the media file. If you want to edit a rendition, select Edit Rendition from the Settings properties. If you add a new rendition, the Rendition is added to the list window. Select a Rendition and click the Edit button and the Renditions Settings dialog box opens.

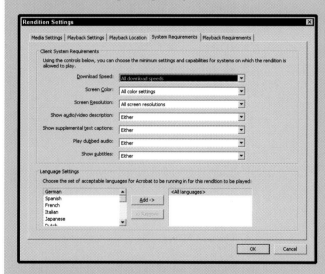

A considerable number of options are available in the various tabs of the Rendition Settings dialog box. By default the dialog box opens at the Media Settings tab. The various tabs and choices you have include:

» **Media Settings:** Make choices from the Media Settings tab for the rendition name, the media location and content type,

and the rendition for alternate text, and choose from the Allow Temp File pull-down menu for various options related to accessibility. If the media is to be made accessible to JavaScript, be certain to check the box for enabling JavaScript.

» **Playback Settings:** Click the Playback Settings to make choices for the player window visibility, volume settings, showing player controls, continuous looping, or times played. In the list at the bottom of the Playback Settings, click the Add button to add the type of media players you want users to use for playing the media. You have an option for enabling all players and a setting for the preferred player.

» **Playback Location:** Make choices for where the media is played such as in the document, floating window, or full screen. If floating window is selected, you have many choices for document size and position.

» **System Requirements:** From a pull-down menu you have choices for connection speeds. If you want a particular rendition to be downloaded for all users with 384Kbps connections or greater, you can make the choice in this dialog box. In addition you have choices for screen displays, captions, subtitles, and language choices.

» **Playback Requirements:** Based on options you selected in the other settings tabs, a list is displayed in the last settings tab. Each item has a check box for enabling a required condition. Check all the boxes for those items you want to make a required function.

Click OK in the Rendition Settings dialog box when you are finished setting the options in the various tabs. If you need to add another rendition with some alternative options to the last rendition you edited, copy the rendition and make the necessary edits. You can list as many renditions as you like to provide much flexibility for your viewer audience and the systems they use.

The number of options for setting attributes in the Renditions Settings dialog box are extraordinary. To completely understand all the settings and what they do for you, look over the Acrobat Help file.

Tutorial

» Creating Acrobat 6 Compatible Media Play Buttons

Playing Acrobat 6-compatible media occurs by clicking a movie frame. When it's intuitive for a user to know when a movie clip is added to a PDF document, you don't need to add any buttons or descriptions for informing users that a movie clip exists on a page. In other circumstances, you'll want to add a play button. In this tutorial you learn how to add a play button for an Acrobat 6 compatible movie clip.

1. **Click the Fit Width tool and scroll to the bottom of the page by dragging the scroll bar down.**

2. **Click the Link tool and drag a marquee around the Play Video Box. When you release the mouse button the Create Link dialog box opens.**

3. **Click Custom Link and click OK in the Create Link dialog box.**
   The Link Properties dialog box opens.

4. **Open the Select Action pull-down menu and click Play Media (Acrobat 6 Compatible). Click Add.**
   The Play Media (Acrobat 6 Compatible) dialog box opens. By default Play is selected from the Operation to Perform pull-down menu.

5. **Click Annotation from** `12_videoEmailReview.mov`.
   The OK button is grayed out in the Play Media (Acrobat 6 Compatible) dialog box. To make the OK button active, click the media clip name in the Associated Annotation window. After clicking the filename, the OK button becomes active. By default, Play is selected and you are not required to click OK in this dialog box. If you click Cancel, the default Play action is used. However to make changes in the Operation to Perform pull-down menu, you need to select the filename and click OK.

6. **Click OK.**

7. **Leave the Link Properties dialog box open and click the link with the Link tool. Press Control (Windows) or Option (Macintosh) and then press Shift and drag down to the Pause Video box.**
   The link is duplicated.

8. **Choose Play Media in the Actions list in the Link Properties dialog box and click Edit.**
   Once again the Play Media (Acrobat 6 Compatible) dialog box opens.

9. **Choose Pause from the Operation to Perform pull-down menu and click OK.**
   The Link action is assigned to pause the movie.

10. **Repeat the same steps for duplicating the link and editing the action. Use the Resume and Stop menu commands for the two boxes below the Pause Video box.**

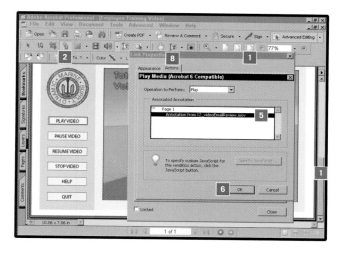

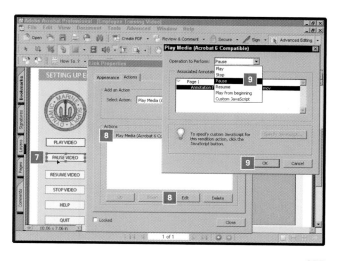

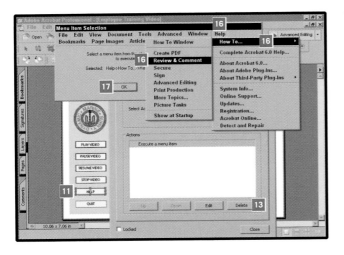

11. **Duplicate the last link and Control/Option+Shift and drag down to the Help box.**

12. **Choose Play Media (Acrobat 6 Compatible) in the Actions list window.**

13. **Click Delete.**

14. **Choose Execute a Menu Item from the Select Action pull-down menu.**

15. **Click Add.**
    In Windows, the Edit Menu Item Selection dialog box opens where all menu items are selected from the dialog box. On the Macintosh the Menu Item dialog box opens where menu items are selected from the top-level menu bar.

16. **Choose Help→How To→Review & Comment.**

17. **Click OK in the Menu Item Selection/Menu Item dialog box.**
    The link action you assign to the help link opens the How To pane displaying the help information for review and comment. Users unfamiliar with Acrobat can easily click the button and gain immediate access to help information.

18. **Duplicate the help link and move the duplicate to the Quit box.**

19. **Use the same steps to add another Execute a Menu Item action. Click Edit to open the Menu Item Selection/Menu Item dialog box. Choose File→Close in the Menu Item Selection dialog box (top-level menu bar on the Macintosh) and click OK. Click Close in the Link Properties dialog box.**

20. **Choose File→Save As and save the file to the Tutorial12_finish folder as** 12_acroEmailReview_finish.pdf.

21. **Choose File→Document Properties. Click Description in the left pane.**
    Notice the file size for this document is over 10MB. Because you embedded the video in the PDF document, the file size grows to accommodate the added media clip. The advantage you have with embedding content is only the PDF document needs to be transported to other sources. Once the media is embedded, the source video clip is no longer needed by Acrobat.

22. **Click the links to be certain all link actions apply to the individual boxes where you created the links.**

23. **Quit Acrobat.**

» Session Review

In this session you learned how to import sounds and videos. With the many options for using either Acrobat 5 or Acrobat 6 compatible media, there is much to remember. Answer the following questions to help you recall the steps to import video and sounds and change attributes. Answers are found in the tutorial noted in parentheses.

1. How do you import sound files? (See Tutorial: Adding Sounds.)

2. Why wouldn't a sound file play when you click a link designed to play the sound? (See Tutorial: Playing Sounds with Page Actions (Acrobat Professional Only).)

3. How do you change the border appearances for sound frames? (See Tutorial: Playing Sounds with Page Actions (Acrobat Professional Only).)

4. What are the differences between importing Acrobat 5 and Acrobat 6 media? (See Tutorial: Importing Acrobat 5 Compatible Media (Acrobat Professional Only).)

5. How do you add an image to a movie clip? (See Tutorial: Importing Acrobat 6 Compatible Media (Acrobat Professional Only).)

6. What kinds of play controls can you establish for your media clips? (See Tutorial: Creating Play Buttons.)

7. How do you duplicate links? (See Tutorial: Creating Play Buttons.)

8. Why do these PDF documents become so large in file size? (See Tutorial: Importing Acrobat 6 Compatible Media (Acrobat Professional Only).)

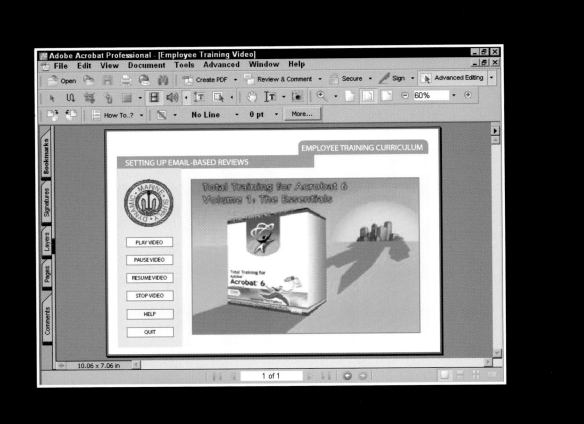

Session 13

Creating Presentations

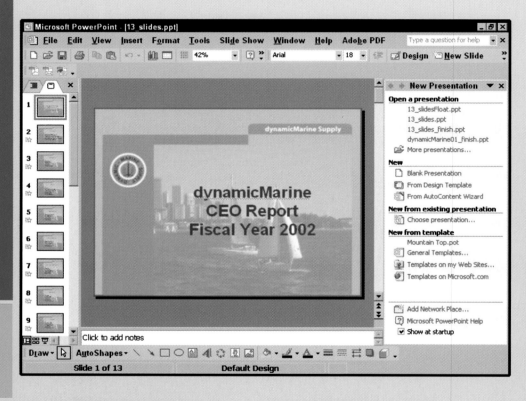

Tutorial: **Adding Animation in PowerPoint**

Tutorial: **Converting PowerPoint Files to PDF**

Tutorial: **Using Full Screen Views**

Tutorial: **Adding Links to Slides**

Session Introduction

Acrobat is an ideal presentation tool when you want to link to PDF documents and add interactivity. With new multimedia support for animation created in programs such as Microsoft
PowerPoint, you can easily convert slide presentations to PDF, complete with animation effects.
In this tutorial you learn how to convert Microsoft PowerPoint files to PDF and view documents
in Full Screen Views.

TOOLS YOU'LL USE
Microsoft PowerPoint, Full Screen preferences, Full Screen View,
Advanced Editing toolbar, Select Text tool, Link Properties command.

CD-ROM FILES NEEDED
13_slides.ppt, 13_financialHighlights.pdf,
13_financialStatement.pdf, and 13_slides_finish.pdf
(found in the Sessions/Session13/Tutorial13 folder).

TIME REQUIRED
60 minutes

Tutorial
» Adding Animation in PowerPoint

Microsoft PowerPoint is the de facto standard for creating slide presentations. In PowerPoint you can add transitions and animation effects to communicate your message with flair and interest. Once the effects have been created in PowerPoint, you can export the PowerPoint file with the PDFMaker macro you learned how to use in Session 4. When PDFMaker is used, the effects from PowerPoint are preserved in the resultant PDF document. Before you convert to PDF, you need to add the animation effects in PowerPoint. In this tutorial you learn some simple steps for adding animation in PowerPoint files.

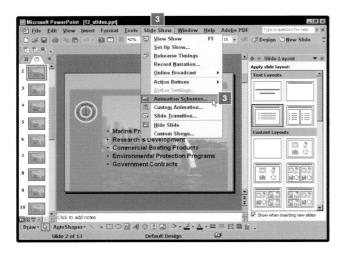

1. **Mount the CD-ROM located in the back of this book. Drag the folder Session13 from inside the Sessions folder to your desktop. Launch Microsoft PowerPoint by double-clicking the program icon.**
   If you don't have Microsoft Office installed on your computer, you can look over the steps in the first tutorials. The last two tutorials involve working in Acrobat. Open the file `13_slides_finish.pdf` from the Tutorial13 folder to follow the steps in the last two tutorials.

2. **Open the file `13_slides.ppt` from the Tutorial13 folder.**
   A slide presentation has been created for you. Creating slide presentations in PowerPoint is not part of this discussion. If you want to learn more about creating PowerPoint presentations, see the Microsoft Office User Manuals and look over the help options found in the Help Menu in PowerPoint. When you open the `13_slides.ppt` file, the slides are shown in the Slides pane.

3. **Choose Slide Show→Animation Schemes.**

4. **Click slide 2 in the Slides panel.**

5. **Scroll the Slides panel down to view slide 13. Press Shift and click slide 13.**
   All slides from 2 through 13 are selected. When you apply an animation effect, the effect is applied to the selected slides.

6. **Scroll the Apply to Selected Slides Window down to the bottom.**

7. **Click Float.**
   There are a number of animation schemes listed in the scrollable window in the Slide Design panel. You can test the different effects by clicking an effect and clicking the Play button at the bottom of the panel. In this example, Float is used. Feel free to add any effect you want.

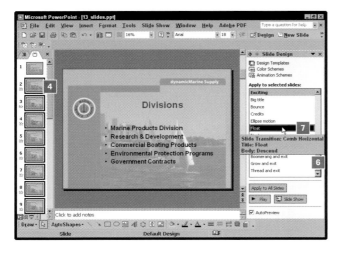

8. **Choose Slide Show→View Show or click the Slide Show button at the bottom of the Slide Design panel.**
   Click the View Show menu command to preview the slide show. Slides are automatically cycled through the presentation showing you the animation effects. At the end of the slide show, PowerPoint halts with a blank slide.

9. **Press Esc to exit the slide show.**

10. **Choose File→Properties.**
    The Properties dialog box opens. In this dialog box you can add summary information that is retained in the resultant PDF document as a document summary.

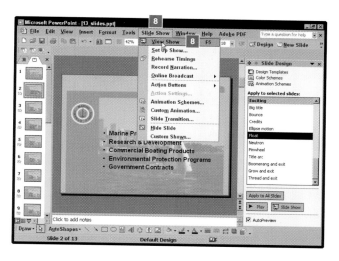

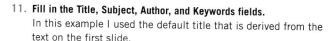

11. **Fill in the Title, Subject, Author, and Keywords fields.**
    In this example I used the default title that is derived from the text on the first slide.

12. **Click OK.**

13. **Choose File→Save As. Save the file to the Tutorial13_finish folder as** 13_slides_finish.pdf.

14. **Keep the file open to follow the steps in the next tutorial.**

<NOTE>

Microsoft PowerPoint has many transition and slide effects that can be applied to individual slides, a selected group of slides, or to the entire slide presentation. You can add different effects to separate lines of text on each slide and you can apply effects to master pages. If you want to explore some of the options available for displaying slides, try practicing applying effects and view the slide shows by clicking the Slide Show button in the Slide Design panel. Save different versions of a slide show as separate files and convert the files to PDF. At times the results in Acrobat may be different than the effects you see in the PowerPoint slide show previews. View results in Acrobat to be certain the slides view as you expect.

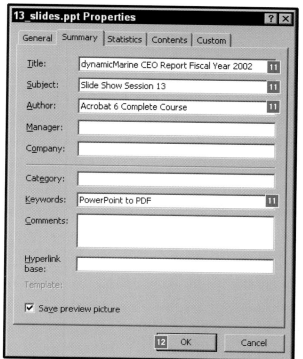

Tutorial
» Converting PowerPoint Files to PDF

After you complete your edits in Microsoft PowerPoint, it's time to convert the slide show to a PDF document. You can use the PDFMaker macro in Microsoft PowerPoint to convert to PDF or convert the PowerPoint file to PDF within Acrobat. In this tutorial you learn how to convert a PowerPoint file to PDF by using PDFMaker within PowerPoint.

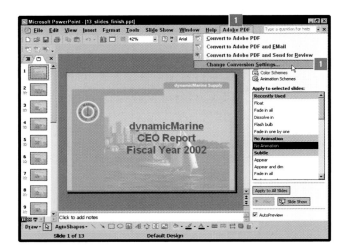

1. Choose Adobe PDF→Change Conversion Settings.

The Adobe menu and the Acrobat tools in the Microsoft PowerPoint toolbar contain the PDFMaker menu commands and tools. When you install Acrobat, be certain Microsoft Office is installed first, and install Acrobat after the Office installation. If you install Acrobat before installing Microsoft Office, the PDFMaker tools won't appear in the Office applications. When you click Change Conversion Settings, the Adobe PDFMaker dialog box opens.

2. **Click the first three check boxes on the Settings tab.**
View Adobe PDF Result opens the resultant PDF document in Acrobat. If Acrobat is not open, the PDFMaker macro launches Acrobat and opens the PDF. Prompt for Adobe PDF File Name opens the Save Adobe PDF File As dialog box where you can navigate your hard drive and target a folder for the saved document as well as edit the filename. This option helps prevent accidentally overwriting existing files. Convert Document Information converts the summary information you added in the last tutorial to the Acrobat document summary.

3. **Click Add Bookmarks to Adobe PDF.**
Bookmarks are not necessary for slide presentations when you view the PDF document as a presentation. However, if you want to edit slides in Acrobat, they can be helpful and you can always delete them when not needed. When you click the Add Bookmarks check box, each slide is bookmarked and the bookmarks link to the respective slides.

4. **Click Enable Accessibility and Reflow with Tagged PDF.**
As a matter of practice, it's a good idea to enable accessibility and reflow even if your slides are not intended for use with screen readers. In the event you want to port your slides to handheld devices and reflow text or extract text for use in other programs, adding structure to the document is helpful.

5. **Click Save Slide Transitions in Adobe PDF.**
Transitions are separate items from animation schemes you added in PowerPoint. Although this item has no effect on the presentation in this tutorial, you can keep the check box enabled as a default in the event you return to PowerPoint and want to convert any transitions and convert to another PDF document.

6. **Click Convert Multimedia to PDF Multimedia.**
This item also has no effect on the slide presentation used in this tutorial. Keep it checked as a default in the event you add multimedia in PowerPoint and want to convert the media to Adobe PDF multimedia.

7. **Click PDF Layout Based on PowerPoint Printer Settings.**
The Page Setup dialog box offers options for determining page size. In this tutorial file the page size is a custom page size assigned in PowerPoint. To retain the custom page size in the resultant PDF document, be certain to enable this check box.

8. **Click OK.**
The attributes for the PDF conversion setting are established when you click OK. From this point you move on to converting the slide show to PDF.

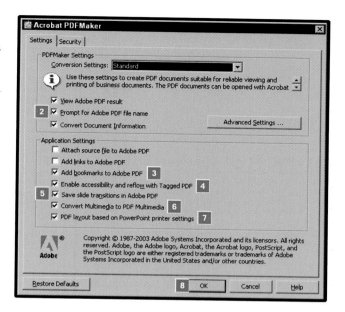

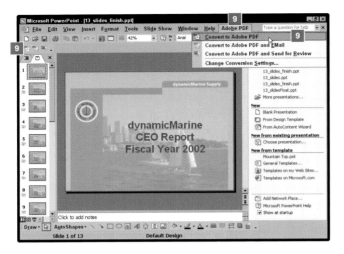

9. **Choose Adobe PDF→Convert to Adobe PDF or click the Convert to PDF tool in the Microsoft PowerPoint toolbar.**
   When you click the menu command or the tool, the Save Adobe PDF File As dialog box opens.

10. **Navigate to the Tutorial13_finish folder and click Save.**
    By default, the filename changes from `13_slides_finish.ppt` to the same filename with a PDF extension. Keep the default name and save the file. The PDFMaker works away converting the PowerPoint document to a PDF file. When the PDFMaker finishes the file conversion, the document opens in Acrobat.

    <NOTE>
    If you do not have Microsoft PowerPoint installed on your computer, begin at the next step in this session. Open the file `13_slides_finish.pdf` to continue.

11. **Choose File→Document Properties.**
    The Document Properties dialog box opens.

12. **Click Description.**
    If you added the document summary information in Microsoft PowerPoint and enabled the check box for converting document summary information in the Adobe PDFMaker dialog box, the document summary information appears in the Description field boxes.

13. **Click OK.**

14. **Leave the file open to follow the steps in the next tutorial.**

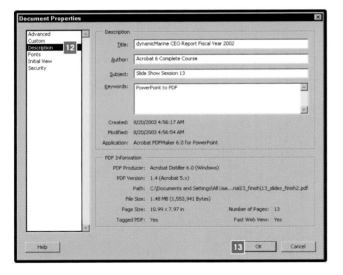

Tutorial
» Using Full Screen Views

When you view your presentation in Acrobat, you'll notice no animation effects are viewed on the document pages as you move through the slides. Animation effects are only visible in another viewing mode. In this tutorial you learn how to view PDFs in Full Screen View.

1. **Click the Fit Page tool.**

2. **Click the Next Page button.**
   Keep clicking the next page button to scroll through the pages. Notice the effects from PowerPoint are not visible as you move through the pages.

3. **Click the First Page button to return to the opening page.**

4. **Choose Edit→Preferences (Windows) or Acrobat→Preferences (Macintosh).**
   The Preferences dialog box opens.

5. **Click Full Screen in the left pane.**
   The Full Screen preference options are shown in the right pane. Among the options are all settings you apply to viewing PDFs in Full Screen View.

6. **Ensure that Escape Key Exits is enabled.**
   By default the check box is enabled. Be certain you keep this check box enabled to easily release the Full Screen mode and return to the normal viewing mode. If you disable the check box, you need to use the keyboard shortcuts (Control/Command+L) to toggle between normal viewing mode and Full Screen mode.

7. **Click Left Click to Go Forward One Page; Right Click to Go Back One Page.**
   This option enables you to use the left and right mouse buttons to move forward and back in your slide presentation.

8. **Choose Blinds Horizontal from the Default Transition pull-down menu.**
   Transitions can be added in Acrobat. If you create transitions in PowerPoint, be certain to check No Transition in the pull-down menu so the PowerPoint transitions are used. In this example, you use a transition from Acrobat as there are no transitions in the file you exported to PDF. Be aware that the animation effects added in PowerPoint are different than transitions.

9. **Click OK.**

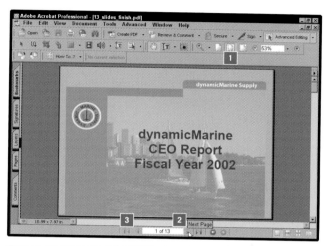

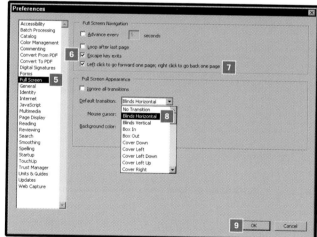

<TIP>
You can purchase USB adapters to plug into a USB port on a laptop or desktop computer for remote control slide viewing. These adaptors can be purchased for less than $100 US and usually have two buttons that are used for moving back and forth through the pages. If you're using an adaptor for remote control operation, be certain to enable the Left Click to Go Forward One Page; Right Click to Go Back One Page check box in the Preferences dialog box.

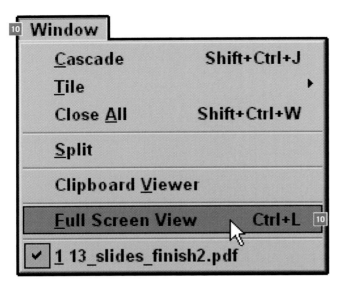

10. **Choose Window→Full Screen View.**
Notice the keyboard shortcut in the menu (Ctrl+L)
(Command+L on Macintosh). When toggling between Full
Screen View and normal view, you can quickly change viewing
modes by using the keyboard shortcuts. When you click the
menu command or use the keyboard shortcut, the view
changes to full screen.

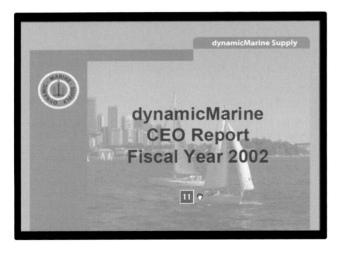

11. **Click the mouse button.**
The cursor appears momentarily and then disappears as you
view slides in Full Screen View. When you click (left-click) the
mouse button, the text appears on the first page. Click again
and you move to page 2. Each subsequent mouse click shows
the text move into the page according to the animation effect
added in Microsoft PowerPoint.

12. **Repeat mouse clicks and move through the slides.**

<NOTE>
You can also use the Page Down and Page Up keys on your keyboard to move forward and backward through slides or press the
right- and left-arrow keys for page navigation.

13. **Press Esc.**
Pressing the Escape key returns you to normal viewing mode.

14. **Choose File→Document Properties.**
    The Document Properties dialog box opens.

15. **Click Initial View in the left pane.**
    PDF files can be saved to open automatically in Full Screen
    View. To change the view options, make your selections in the
    Initial View properties.

16. **Click Single Page from the Page Layout pull-down menu. Click Fit
    Page from the Magnification pull-down menu.**
    These settings don't have an effect on full-screen viewing, but
    when you return to a normal viewing mode, you might want to
    view pages in a Fit Page View and scroll pages in a Single
    Page layout.

17. **Click Open in Full Screen mode.**
    This option controls the full-screen viewing when you open
    the file. When the check box is enabled, the file opens in
    Full Screen View.

18. **Choose Document Title from the Show pull-down menu.**
    Again, this option has no effect in full-screen viewing. When
    you return to Edit mode, you can see the Document Title
    derived from the document summary information appear in
    the Acrobat title bar.

19. **Click OK.**
    All the initial view attributes are assigned; now you need to
    save the file to update your edits.

20. **Click the Save button in the Toolbar Well.**

21. **Close the document. Reopen the file.**
    The file opens in Full Screen View. Move through the pages
    to again view the animation effects and the transitions you
    applied in Acrobat.

22. **Press Esc. Click the First Page tool to return to the opening page.**
    You return to normal viewing mode and navigate to the first
    page in the file.

23. **Keep the file open to follow the steps in the next tutorial.**

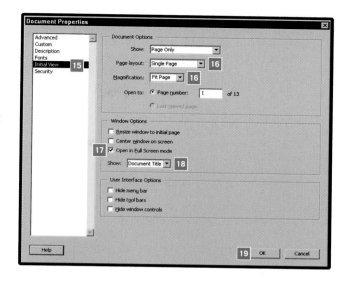

Tutorial
» Adding Links to Slides

While viewing slides in Full Screen View, you can link to other files and open them, all the while remaining in a Full Screen View. The interactivity you add with links, buttons, page actions, and media imports are all available while viewing PDFs in Full Screen View. In this tutorial you learn how to link to other documents from links and view the linked destinations while viewing your slide presentation in Full Screen View.

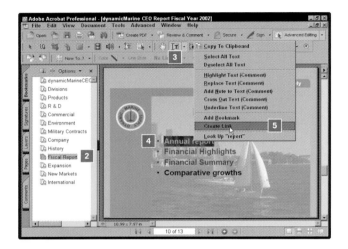

1. **Click the Bookmarks tab to open the Bookmarks pane.**
   Notice the PDF contains bookmarks from the PowerPoint Presentation. When you set the Adobe PDF Settings to Add Bookmarks to Adobe PDF, each slide in PowerPoint was bookmarked.

2. **Click the Fiscal Report bookmark in the Bookmarks pane.**
   Page 10 (the bookmark destination) opens in the Document pane.

3. **Click the Select Text tool.**

4. **Triple-click to select the line of text: *Annual Report*.**

5. **Open a context menu and choose Create Link.**
   The Create Link from Selection dialog box opens.

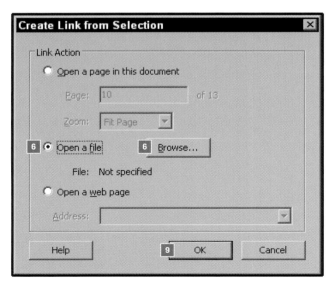

6. **Click Open a File. Click Browse.**
   The Select Destination Document dialog box opens.

7. **Navigate to the Tutorial13 folder and click `13_financialStatement.pdf`. Click Select.**
   The Specify Open Preferences dialog box opens.

8. **Click New Window and click OK.**
   The target document is set to open while the slide presentation remains open in the background.

9. **Click OK in the Create Link from Selection dialog box.**

10. **Follow the same steps using the Select Text tool to select the next line of text (*Financial Highlights*). Create a link in the same manner as described in steps 5 through 9. Link it to the `13_financialHighlights.pdf` document.**

11. **Press Control/Command+L.**

    Your view changes to Full Screen View and page 10 is shown. When you activate Full Screen View, the current active page in the Document pane is viewed in the Full Screen window.

12. **Click the first link on the page.**

    Because your view is Full Screen View, the document you open—either from a link or by pressing Control/Command+O and clicking a file in the Open dialog box—remains in Full Screen View. You can open and close files without changing the view by using links, buttons, page actions, and keyboard shortcuts.

13. **Click the Close button.**

    This file has a button that executes the File➜Close menu item. You can also close the file by using the keyboard short-cut Control/Command+W.

14. **Press Esc.**

15. **Choose File➜Save As and overwrite the file in the Tutorial13_finish folder to optimize it.**

16. **Quit Acrobat.**

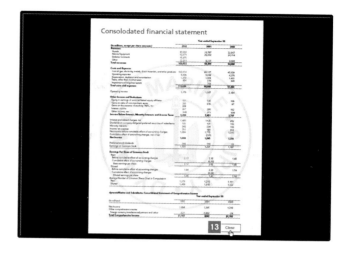

» Session Review

In this session you learned how to add animation effects in PowerPoint and convert the PowerPoint file to PDF. You also learned how to set Full Screen View properties and view the PowerPoint animations while in Full Screen View. Additionally, you learned how to link to files and view the links in Full Screen Views. To review this session, answer the following questions. Answers are found in the tutorial noted in parentheses.

1. How do you add animation effects in PowerPoint? (See Tutorial: Adding Animation in PowerPoint.)

2. How do you create bookmarks from PowerPoint files? (See Tutorial: Converting PowerPoint Files to PDF.)

3. How do you add document information to a PDF file from PowerPoint files? (See Tutorial: Converting PowerPoint Files to PDF.)

4. Where do you change attributes for the way PowerPoint files are converted to PDF? (See Tutorial: Converting PowerPoint Files to PDF.)

5. Why can't you see the animation effects created in PowerPoint in a PDF file? (See Tutorial: Using Full Screen Views.)

6. How do you set up a document to open in Full Screen View? (See Tutorial: Using Full Screen Views.)

7. How do you move forward and backward through slides in Full Screen View? (See Tutorial: Using Full Screen Views.)

8. How to you exit Full Screen View? (See Tutorial: Using Full Screen Views.)

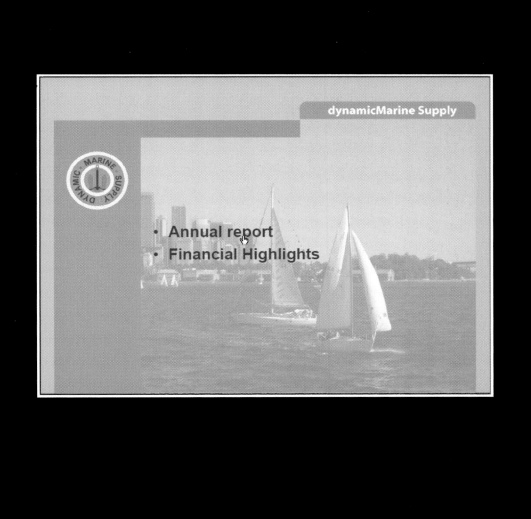

Part VII
Creating Acrobat PDF Forms

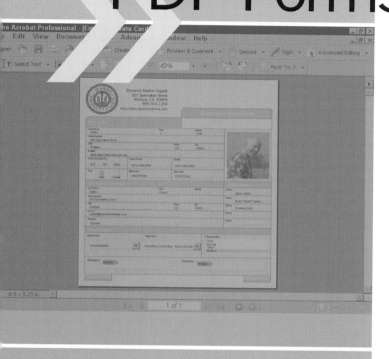

Editing and Filling In Forms

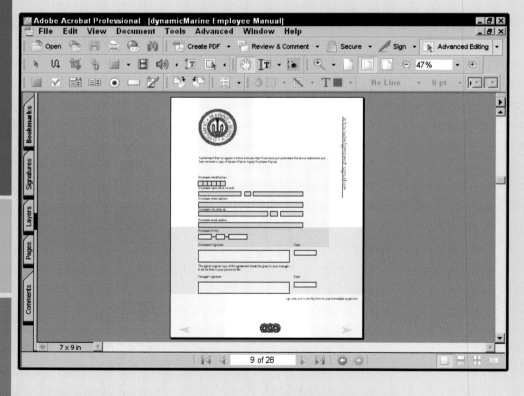

Tutorial: **Setting Field Tab Order**

Tutorial: **Resetting Forms**

Tutorial: **Creating Submit Buttons**

Tutorial: **Filling In Forms**

Session Introduction

One of the most common uses for PDF documents is creating Acrobat PDF forms. As Adobe Reader, Acrobat Standard, and Acrobat Professional users, you can fill in forms. Creating forms and accessing form field tools are available only in Acrobat Professional. In this session, you learn how to perform various editing tasks on forms that can be accomplished in either Acrobat Standard or Acrobat Professional, and you learn how to fill in forms, which can be performed in any Acrobat viewer.

TOOLS YOU'LL USE
Text Field tool, Link tool, Advanced Editing toolbar, Select Object tool, and the Properties Bar.

CD-ROM FILES NEEDED
14_application.pdf and 14_employeeManual.pdf (found in the Sessions/Session14/Tutorial14 folder).

TIME REQUIRED
60 minutes

<NOTE>
The tutorials in this session demonstrate editing tasks you can make using either Acrobat Standard or Acrobat Professional. For more detail on creating form fields using the Acrobat Professional software, a bonus chapter is available on the CD-ROM. Open the Session 14A folder and review the session's PDF document to learn how to create form fields using Acrobat Professional.

Tutorial
» Setting Field Tab Order

Users navigate through fields on a page by clicking with the Hand tool in field boxes to add data or by pressing the Tab key to advance through the fields. The field tab order is determined from the order in which you create fields. If you create fields in a random order, you can reorder the tab sequence so a user tabs through fields in a logical order. You can reset the tab order in either Acrobat Standard or Acrobat Professional. In this tutorial you learn how to reset field tab orders.

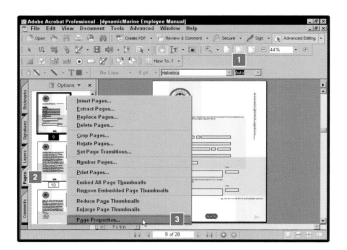

1. **Mount the CD-ROM located in the back of this book. Drag the folder Session14 from inside the Sessions folder to your desktop. Launch Acrobat by double-clicking the program icon. Open the file 14_employeeManual.pdf from the Tutorial14 folder. Click the Fit Page tool.**

2. **Click the Pages tab to open the Pages panel.**

3. **Click Page 9 in the Pages panel and open a context menu. Click Page Properties from the menu.**
   The Page Properties dialog box opens. From Session 12 you'll remember that page actions are addressed in the Page Properties dialog box. The first tab in the Page Properties is the Tab Order settings. By default, this tab is in view when you open the Page Properties dialog box.

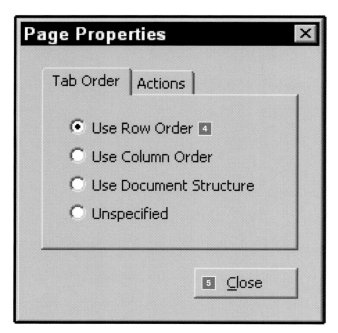

4. **Click Use Row Order to enable the radio button.**
   The Tab Order properties offer you options for tabbing according to the Row Order, the Column Order, and the Document Structure; and when no tab order is selected, the default is the Unspecified Order. When you select Use Row Order, the tab order uses the first row and each tab advances to the next column in the same row. After the first row, the next tab order is the fields across the second row, and so forth.

5. **Click Close.**

6. **Click the Hand tool.**

7. **Press the Tab key.**

   The first field is selected and the cursor blinks inside the first field.

8. **Press Tab and continue tabbing through the fields.**

   Notice the cursor jumps to the next field in the first row. With each subsequent tab, the cursor moves across the row. As you tab from the last field in a row, the cursor moves to the first field in the next row.

9. **Choose File➔Save As and save the file to the Tutorial14_finish folder, overwriting the last save.**

10. **Close the document.**

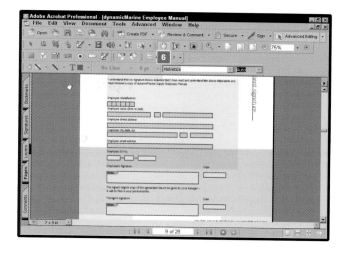

Tutorial
» Resetting Forms

If users want to clear a form and start over filling in form fields, they need to navigate to each field and clear the data. To help users who complete your forms clear all data fields or a selected group of data fields, you can add a button to reset a form. Acrobat Standard users can also create reset buttons by using the Link tool. In this tutorial you learn how to create a reset button to clear data from form fields. If you use Acrobat Standard, use the Link tool in place of the Button tool to complete the steps.

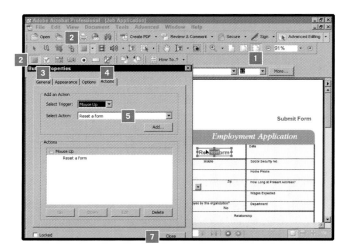

1. **Open the file** `14_application.pdf` **from the Tutorial 14 folder. Click the Fit Width tool and drag the scroll bar to the top of the page.**

2. **Click the Button tool and drag a rectangle marquee around the words** *Reset Form*. **Acrobat Standard users, click the Link tool and drag a rectangle around the same text.**
   The Button/Link Properties dialog box opens. If using the Link tool, click Custom Link and click OK.

3. **Click the General tab and name the field** Reset a form. **Click the Appearance tab and change the Border Color and Fill Color to No Color. If using the Link tool, click Appearance and set the appearance properties to the same values for no border and no fill.**

4. **Click the Actions tab.**

5. **Choose Reset a Form from the Select Action pull-down menu. Click Add to add the action to the Actions list.**
   Acrobat Standard users have the same action available when using a link. If you use Acrobat Standard, create a custom link and click Actions. Click Reset a Form from the Select Action pull-down menu and click Add. Using either a button field or a link and selecting Reset a Form opens the Reset a Form dialog box. In this dialog box you make choices for which fields are cleared when a user clicks the button/link. By default all fields are targeted for clearing the data.

6. **Click OK in the Reset a Form dialog box.**
   The default is accepted and all fields are marked for clearing data.

7. **Click Close.**

8. **Click the Hand tool. Click in a field and type text in the first few text fields on the form.**

9. **Click the Reset Form button/link.**
   Notice the data is cleared and all list and combo box fields are reset to defaults.

10. **Click Save and keep the file open to follow the steps in the next tutorial.**

Tutorial
» Creating Submit Buttons

One of the advantages of using Acrobat viewers to complete forms is that data resides in electronic form and it eliminates the need for keying in data fields to retain or manipulate the data. Once users finish completing a form you'll want a mechanism for sending data to you and collecting the data for use in Acrobat or for exporting to databases. PDFs and data can be submitted electronically to Web servers and e-mail addresses. The advantage of creating buttons to submit data is that Adobe Reader users can click the submit buttons and submit data to you without having to purchase Acrobat Standard or Acrobat Professional. Because Adobe Reader users cannot save data introduced on PDF forms, a submit button is necessary for Adobe Reader users to route either the PDF form or the form data to you. In this tutorial you learn how to create a submit button for this purpose. If you use Acrobat Standard, you can use a link in place of the button field.

1. **Click the Button Field tool (Acrobat Standard users click the Link tool).**

2. **Drag a rectangle marquee around the words** *Submit Form*.

3. **Name the form field** submit. **Set the appearance properties in the Appearance tab to no border and no fill. Click Actions.**

4. **Click Submit a form from the Select Action pull-down menu.**

5. **Click Add.**
   The Submit Form Selections dialog box opens.

6. **Type** mailto:*<your e-mail address>* **in the URL field.**
   The *mailto* statement instructs Acrobat to send the results to an e-mail address. In this line, enter your own e-mail address so you can test the results.

7. **Click the FDF Include radio button.**
   The Export Format options offer you different choices for the data format to export and send to the address specified in the Enter a URL for This Link box. When clicking FDF Include, only the form data are submitted to the address you supply in the field box. When users receive the FDF (Forms Data Format) data, they can import the data in PDFs where the form fields match the field names and attributes from the exported form. FDF files are much smaller in file size than PDF documents, which enables users to e-mail data in much shorter transmission times.

8. **Click OK.**

9. **Click Pages to open the Pages panel. Open a context menu and click Page Properties. Choose Use Row Order to change the field tab order.**
   As you learned in the tutorial "Setting Field Tab Order" earlier in this session, the tab order is changed in the Page Properties dialog box.

10. **Choose File→Save As and save the file to the Tutorial14_finish folder, thus overwriting the previous file.**

11. **Keep the file open to follow the steps in the next tutorial.**

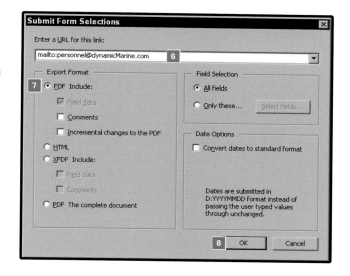

<NOTE>
You can test the submit button by completing the form in Adobe Reader and clicking the submit button. When the e-mail is sent to your own address, an FDF file is attached to the message. Note the location of the file attachment and open your form in Acrobat Standard or Acrobat Professional. Click the Reset Form button and choose Advanced→Forms→Import Forms Data to open the Select File Containing Form Data dialog box. Navigate your hard drive and locate the FDF file. Click the file and click Select in the Select File Containing Form Data dialog box. The data is imported after clicking the Select button.

Tutorial
» Filling In Forms

Users of all Acrobat viewers can complete a fill-in form. As a recipient of a form, you'll want to know where form fields are positioned and clearly see the fields. Using the employee application form you can see that the form design does not clearly show the form field boundaries, which makes the fill-in difficult. In this tutorial you learn how to complete forms and change your appearance settings to help locate all fields on a form.

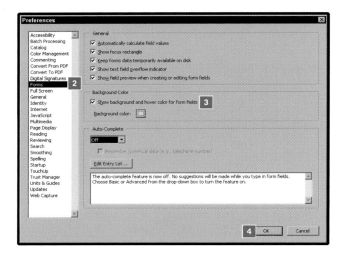

1. **Choose Edit➔Preferences (Windows) or Acrobat Preferences (Macintosh).**

2. **Click Forms in the left pane.**

3. **Click Show Background and Hover Color for Form Fields.**
   This option in the Forms preferences displays a nonprinting background color for form fields. You change colors by clicking the color swatch and selecting colors from the pop-up color palette. By default, the color is blue.

<NOTE>
Also found in the Forms preferences is an option for auto-completion. When auto-complete is turned on, Acrobat remembers your field entries and automatically supplies data from an entry list. To turn auto-completion on, open the Auto-Complete pull-down menu and click Basic or Advanced. A description of the setting you select appears in the window below the Edit Entry List button. As data is added to your entry list, you can edit the options by clicking the Edit Entry List button and remove items from the list. When you click OK in the Forms Preferences dialog box and begin filling in a form, Acrobat starts recording your entries. As you tab to fields, a recommendation is added to a field with a pull-down menu where you can choose other items from the entry list. To turn the auto-complete feature off, return to the Forms preferences and click Off in the Auto-Complete pull-down menu.

4. **Click OK.**

5. **Press Tab.**
   The cursor moves to the first field in the tab row order. On this form, the first field is a date field.

6. **Type a date and press Tab. Continue tabbing through the fields and complete the form.**

7. **Test all the fields. After completing the form, click Reset Form to clear the data.**

8. **Close the file without saving and quit Acrobat.**

» Session Review

In this session you learned how to create Acrobat PDF forms by adding form fields using the seven form field tools. You learned how to change field properties and you learned how to fill in forms. To review this session, answer the following questions. Answers are found in the tutorial noted in parentheses. (Don't forget to review Session 14A on the CD if you have Acrobat Professional and want to learn more about creating form fields.)

1. How do you change the field tab order? (See Tutorial: Setting Field Tab Order.)

2. How do you clear data on a form? (See Tutorial: Resetting Forms.)

3. How do you send data to an e-mail address? (See Tutorial: Creating Submit Buttons.)

4. Which file format is used to send data when you want to keep the file size small? (See Tutorial: Creating Submit Buttons.)

5. How do you see the form fields on a page when you fill in a form? (See Tutorial: Filling In Forms.)

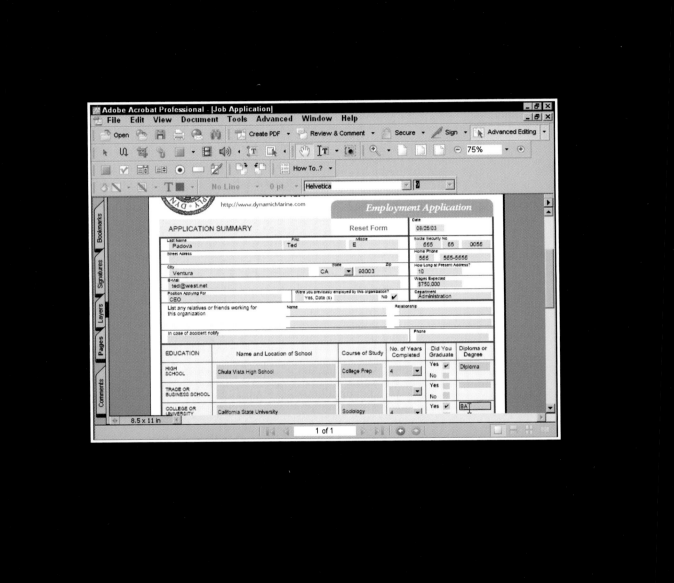

Creating
JavaScripts

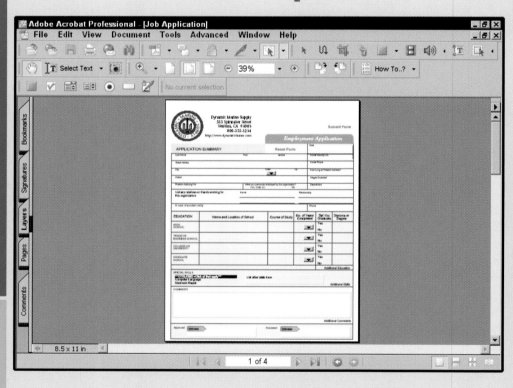

Tutorial: **Creating Page Templates**
(Acrobat Professional Only)

Tutorial: **Creating JavaScripts**

Session Introduction

The Acrobat implementation of JavaScript enables you to extend Acrobat PDF documents to an infinite number of possibilities for designing forms and adding interactivity to documents. In this session, you learn how to create page templates and add new pages from templates with JavaScripts.

TOOLS YOU'LL USE
Forms toolbar, Button tool, JavaScript editor

CD-ROM FILES NEEDED
15_application.pdf (found in the Sessions/Session15/Tutorial15 folder).

TIME REQUIRED
1 hour

Tutorial

» Creating Page Templates (Acrobat Professional Only)

Page templates are added to PDF documents for the purpose of duplicating the pages and appending them to a document. You can create page templates with form fields, spawn the template as a new page, and fill in new fields on the duplicated pages. Page templates are created in Acrobat Professional only; however, if a PDF file contains a page template and you open the document in Acrobat Standard, templates can be spawned as new pages in either Acrobat Standard or Acrobat Professional. In this tutorial, you learn how to create a page template in Acrobat Professional.

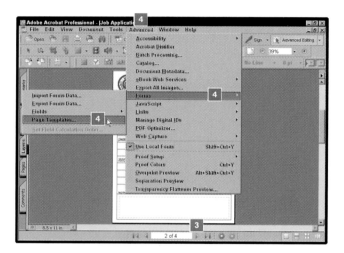

1. **Mount the CD-ROM located in the back of this book. Drag the Session15 folder from inside the Sessions folder to your desktop. Launch Acrobat by double-clicking the program icon.**
   If you are an Acrobat Standard user, open the file in the Tutorial15_finish folder as you look over this tutorial where page templates are created. You can observe the steps used for creating templates in Acrobat Professional and follow steps in the next tutorial for writing JavaScripts to spawn pages from templates.

2. **Open the** `15_application.pdf` **file from the Tutorial15 folder.**
   Note: The toolbars loaded in Session 14 should still be active in the Toolbar Well. If you reset the toolbars, load the Advanced Editing toolbar, Forms toolbar, and the Properties Bar, as described in Session 14.

3. **Click the Next Page tool in the Status Bar to navigate to page 2.**
   The open document contains four pages. Pages 2 through 4 are designed for amplifying answers to questions related to an applicant's education, special skills, and additional comments. Not all applicants need additional pages for amplifying answers to questions on page 1. However, as an applicant completes the form, s/he might want to add information. Hence, you'll create a form designed to create additional pages as needed by converting pages 2 through 4 to template pages and adding a JavaScript to spawn pages from the templates via a link or button action.

4. **Choose Advanced→Forms→Page Templates.**
   The Page Templates dialog box opens.

5. **Type** additionalEducation **in the Name field box.**

6. **Click the Add button.**
   By default, the current page in view is targeted as a Page Template. Page Templates can be visible or hidden. When you click the Add button, you see an eye icon placed in the box to the left of the template name in the list window. To hide the template, click the eye icon.

7. **Click the eye icon in the box to the left of the template name in the list window.**
   When a template is hidden, the total pages in the file appear in the Status Bar without counting hidden templates. As you click the eye icon the template page is hidden and the total pages reported in the Status Bar is three. You are returned to page 1 in the Document pane after clicking the eye icon.

8. **Click the Close button.**

9. **Click the Next Page tool to view page 2 in the document. (Notice page 2 is 2 of 3 pages in the file).**

10. **Choose Advanced→Forms→Page Templates.**
    The Page Templates dialog box opens again.

11. **Type** specialSkills **in the Name Field box.**

12. **Click Add.**

13. **Click the eye icon to hide the template. Click Close to return to the Document pane.**

14. **Click the Next Page tool to navigate to the last page in the file (page 2 of 2). Repeat the same steps to create a new template and hide the template. Type** comments **for the template name.**
    When you return to the Document pane you should see 1 of 1 reported in the Status Bar. The document contains one page and three template pages.

15. **Choose File→Save As and save the file to the Tutorial15_finish folder as** 15_application_finish.pdf.

16. **Keep the file open to follow the steps in the next tutorial.**

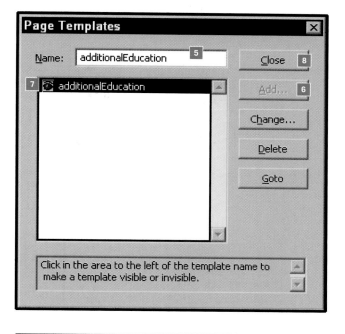

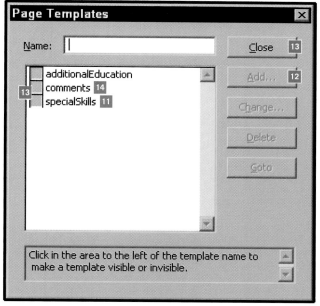

Tutorial
» Creating JavaScripts

JavaScript is a scripting language that enables you to add a number of automated steps in the form of actions which, in many cases, are not available with Acrobat tools. You can add JavaScripts to calculate field data with complex formulas, add interactive features for viewing pages and files, perform many operations found in the Acrobat menus, create new pages from templates, and a host of other tasks that add much more functionality to your PDF viewing and forms completion. In this tutorial you learn how to write a JavaScript to create new pages from the template pages you created in the last tutorial.

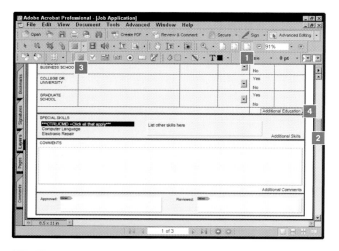

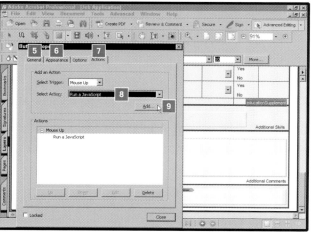

1. **Click the Fit Width tool.**

2. **Scroll to the bottom of the page by dragging the scroll bar to the bottom of the scroll box.**

3. **Click the Button tool.**
   Acrobat Standard users cannot create page templates nor can you create button fields. However, Acrobat Standard users can write JavaScripts and you can add JavaScripts to links. If you use Acrobat Standard, use the Link tool and follow the steps for adding a JavaScript to a link action where button actions are described in this tutorial.

4. **Drag a marquee around the text *Additional Education*.**
   Acrobat Standard users use the Link tool and create a rectangle around the same text. The Button Properties/Create Link dialog box opens. If you're creating a link, click Custom Link and click OK to open the Link Properties dialog box.

5. **Click the General tab and name the field/link**
   educationSupplement.

6. **Click the Appearance tab and set Border Color and Fill Color to no color.**
   The border color and fill colors are set to no color by clicking the swatches and clicking No Color from the pop-up palette options.

7. **Click the Actions tab.**

8. **Open the Select Action pull-down menu and choose Run a JavaScript.**

9. **Click the Add button.**
   The JavaScript Editor dialog box opens. In this dialog box you write JavaScripts according to the proper protocol and syntax acceptable to the Adobe Acrobat implementation of JavaScript.

10. In the JavaScript Editor, type the following code:

```
1. var f = this.getTemplate("additionalEducation");
2. f.spawn ({
3. nPage:this.numPages,
4. bRename:true,
5. bOverlay:false
6. });
7. this.numPages=this.numPages-1
```

Note: The line numbers shown above are not added in the code. They are used here to describe the lines of code used in the script. In the above code notice the name of the template targeted for spawning the page (line 1) is the additionalEducation template you created in the last tutorial. Be certain the name appearing within the quotes matches the template name exactly, including the exact letter case. Line 3 places the new page spawned from the template at the end of the file. Line 4 instructs Acrobat to rename fields to unique field names. Line 5 creates a new page. If line 5 reads bOverlay:true, the new page would be superimposed over the first page in the file. Line 7 opens the last page in the document. After a page is spawned, a user is likely to begin working on the page. In line 7 the new spawned page opens in the Document pane.

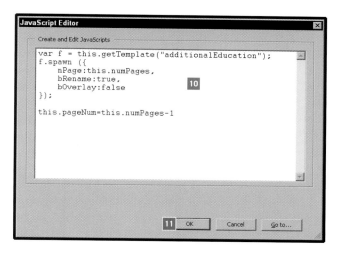

11. Click OK.

The JavaScript Editor dialog box closes.

Writing JavaScripts

In this tutorial you learned how to write a JavaScript on a button/link action. All the actions options for links, fields, bookmarks, and page actions make use of the Run a JavaScript action type. In addition, JavaScripts can be added to Document Actions (when pages close, save, and print) in either Acrobat Standard or Acrobat Professional. In Acrobat Professional you have another option for adding document-level JavaScripts.

Writing JavaScripts requires you to spend time learning the scripting language. One of the best ways to learn more about JavaScript in Acrobat is to explore PDF documents found on the Internet and examine scripts written by others. You can copy and paste JavaScripts by opening the JavaScript editor and pasting text in the editor window or by copying links and buttons that contain scripts.

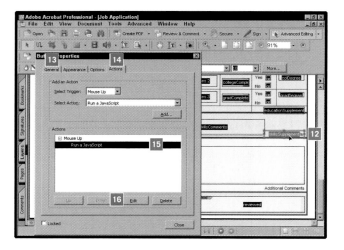

12. **Press Control/Option-click and drag the field/link down to the text** *Additional Skills.*
    Pressing the Control/Option key while dragging the field dupli-cates it. The JavaScript action is also duplicated with the field.

13. **Click the General tab and change the name to** skillsSupplement.

14. **Click the Actions tab.**

15. **Click Run a JavaScript.**

16. **Click the Edit button.**
    The JavaScript Editor opens showing you the script written for the first button/link. Rather than write a complete new script, you can edit the script in the JavaScript Editor to spawn a page from a different template page.

17. **Change the template name in the first line of code from** ("additionalEducation") **to** ("additionalSkills") **so that it appears as follows:**

    ```
    var f = this.getTemplate("additionalSkills");
    ```

18. **Click OK.**

19. **Duplicate the new button/link and change the first line of code in the JavaScript to** ("comments") **so that it appears as follows:**

    ```
    var f = this.getTemplate("comments");
    ```

20. **Click Close.**
    The JavaScript Editor dialog box closes.

21. **Choose File➔Save As and overwrite the file in the Tutorial15_finish folder.**

22. **Test the buttons/link by clicking the Hand tool. Click each button to be certain the respective page is spawned and that you see the new spawned page in the Document pane.**

23. **Close the file without saving.**

» Session Review

In this session you learned how to create page templates and write a JavaScript to spawn new pages from templates. Answer the following questions to review the session. Answers are found in the tutorial noted in parentheses.

1. How do you create a page template? (See Tutorial: Creating Page Templates (Acrobat Professional Only).)

2. How do you hide page templates? (See Tutorial: Creating Page Templates (Acrobat Professional Only).)

3. Where do you find JavaScripts? (See Tutorial: Creating JavaScripts.)

4. Where do you write a JavaScript? (See Tutorial: Creating JavaScripts.)

5. How do you open the page you spawned from a template with a JavaScript? (See Tutorial: Creating JavaScripts.)

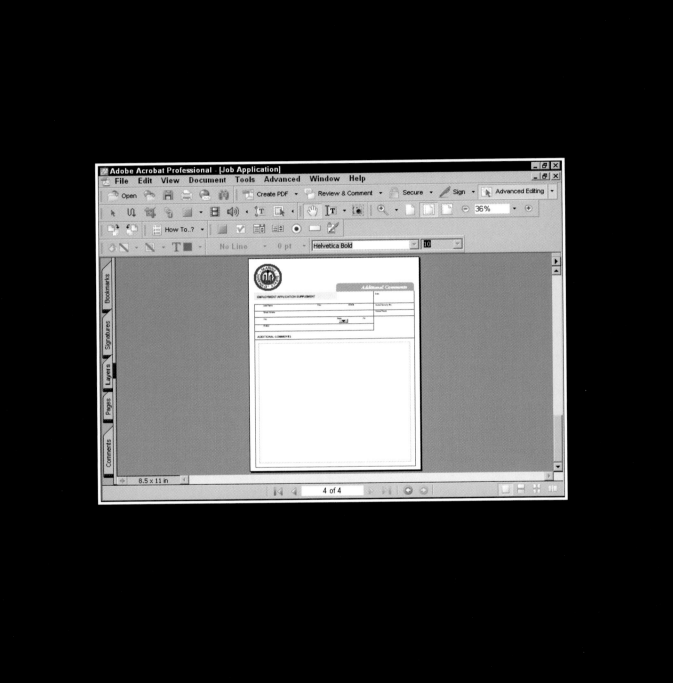

Part VIII

Signing and Securing PDF Documents

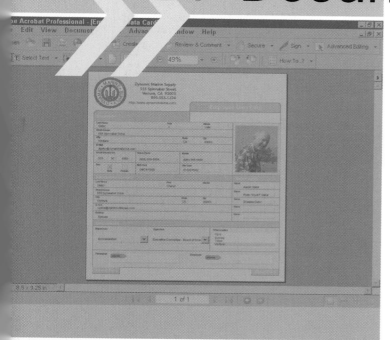

Securing
Documents

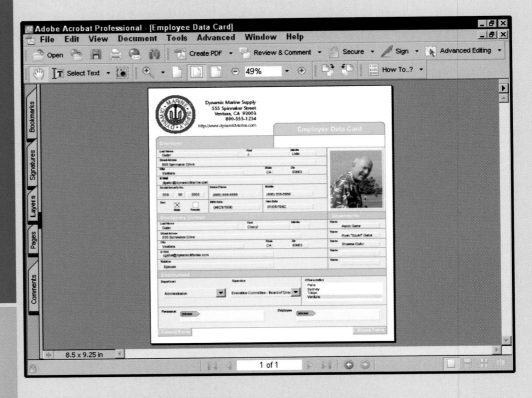

Tutorial: **Password-Protecting PDF Documents**   Tutorial: **Securing Content**

Session Introduction

Acrobat offers you several means of securing your PDF documents. Using Acrobat security, you can protect files against unauthorized viewing, unauthorized editing, or combinations of either. In this session you learn how to encrypt documents using Acrobat security.

TOOLS YOU'LL USE
Secure task button, Password Security – Settings.

CD-ROM FILES NEEDED
16_employeeData.pdf (found in the Sessions/Session16/ Tutorial16 folder).

TIME REQUIRED
45 minutes

Tutorial

» Password-Protecting PDF Documents

Acrobat PDF documents can be secured against viewing and/or editing through the use of Acrobat's built-in security features or through the use of third-party signature handlers. When you add security to a document, you have options for the level of security and different variations for Acrobat compatibility. Depending on which compatibility level you choose, options and encryption levels vary. In this tutorial you learn how to protect a document against unauthorized viewing.

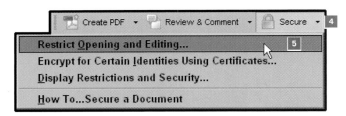

1. **Mount the CD-ROM located in the back of this book. Drag the folder Session16 from inside the Sessions folder to your desktop. Launch Acrobat by double-clicking the program icon.**

2. **Open the** 16_employeeData.pdf **file from the Tutorial16 folder.**

3. **Open a context menu on the Toolbar Well and choose Reset Toolbars from the menu options.**
   Adding security is handled with menu commands, dialog boxes, and the default task buttons. You don't need to load toolbars to secure documents.

4. **Click the down arrow from the Secure task button to open a pull-down menu.**

5. **Choose Restrict Opening and Editing.**
   The Password Security – Settings dialog box opens.

6. **Leave the default compatibility setting to Acrobat 5.0 and later.**
   From the Compatibility pull-down menu you have options for
   Acrobat 3, 5, and 6 compatibility. If you use Acrobat 3 compatibility, the encryption is 40-bit encryption. Using the lower
   encryption level enables users of earlier Acrobat viewers to
   open your files; however, the higher 128-bit encryption provides more options and a higher level of encryption. If you
   know your documents are viewed by users of Acrobat viewers
   version 5 and above, use the Acrobat 5 or 6 compatibility
   level.

7. **Click the check box for Require a Password to Open the
   Document.**

8. **Type** password **(lowercase) in the Document Open Password
   field box.**
   When you check the box for Require a Password to Open the
   Document, the field box below the text becomes active. Checking
   the box and adding a password protects the document from
   opening in Acrobat without a user supplying a password. When
   you add passwords to protect files, use passwords of at least
   eight characters. Using eight or more characters makes it
   harder to decrypt files if someone attempts to break your
   document encryption using programs to decrypt files.

9. **Leave the check box for Use a Password to Restrict Printing and
   Editing of the Document and its Security Settings disabled.**
   The Password Security – Settings dialog box offers options for
   securing a file against opening and options for printing and
   editing permissions. If you want to protect a file against unauthorized viewing only, leave the check box disabled. If you
   want to add two levels of security (one for opening the file and
   another for printing/editing permissions), you check the box
   and make choices for printing/editing permissions.

10. **Click the OK button.**
    The Adobe Acrobat – Confirm Open Document Password dia-
    log box opens. In this dialog box, you retype your password to
    confirm the characters added in the Document Open Password
    field box.

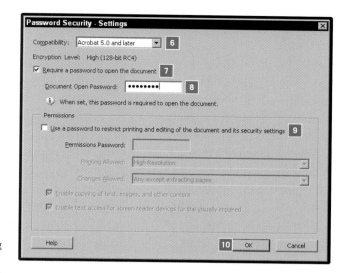

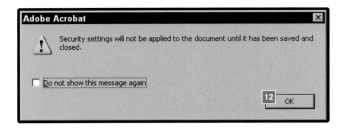

11. **Type** password **again in the dialog box and click OK.**
    A dialog box opens informing you the password settings are
    applied only when you save the file.

12. **Click OK in the Adobe Acrobat informational dialog box.**

13. **Choose File→Save As and save the file to the Tutorial16_finish
    folder as** `16_employeeData_finish.pdf`.

14. **Close the file.**

15. **Click the Open button and open the** `16_employeeData_
    finish.pdf` **file.**
    The Password dialog box opens. The file doesn't appear in the
    Document pane until you supply the password to open the file.
    When typing a password in the Password dialog box, you must
    use the exact password, including the same letter case.

16. **Type** password **(all lowercase characters).**

17. **Click OK.**
    The file opens in the Document pane.

18. **Leave the document open to follow the steps in the next tutorial.**

< T I P >

Acrobat is a great tool for protecting any kind of document. You can
attach files to PDF documents using the Attach File tool described
in Session 9 and add security to protect files from opening. When
users have no access to the PDF, they are prevented from accessing
file attachments.

Tutorial
» Securing Content

You may want to distribute documents that any user can open, but you don't want users to be able to edit your file. Acrobat security offers you options for determining the user permissions that relate to the amount of editing you want to grant to users as well as whether users can print your documents. In this tutorial you learn how to secure files to prevent users from editing the page content.

1. **Choose Restrict Opening and Editing from the Secure task button pull-down menu.**
   The Password Security – Settings dialog box opens.

2. **Uncheck the box for Require a Password to Open the Document.**
   You can add a password for opening a document and another password for setting permissions. When a user has the permissions password, the security can be discarded from the file. If a user has only the Document Open Password, access is granted to open the file, but printing and editing is limited to the permissions you set when protecting the file and the security cannot be changed.

3. **Check the box for Use a Password to Restrict Printing and Editing of the Document and its Security Settings. Type a password in the Permissions Password field box.**

4. **Open the pull-down menu for Printing Allowed and choose Low Resolution (150 dpi).**
   You have three choices for printing permissions. You can secure files against printing by clicking None, allow users to print low resolution copies at 150 dpi by clicking Low Resolution (150 dpi), or grant full printing permissions by clicking High Resolution.

5. **Open the Changes Allowed pull-down menu and choose Filling in Form Fields and Signing.**

6. **Click Enable Text Access for Screen Reader Devices for the Visually Impaired.**
   If you create documents with accessibility, be certain to enable this check box.

7. **Click OK.**
   A dialog box opens informing you that some restrictions may be bypassed using third-party products.

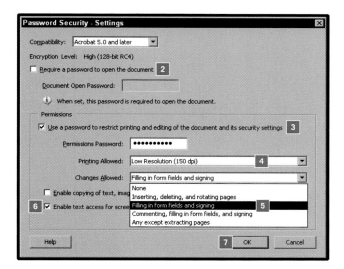

<NOTE>
You have several options for the type of permissions you want to grant when users open your document. The permissions choices change according to the compatibility level you select from the options in the Compatibility pull-down menu. When selecting Acrobat 5 compatibility, the options include: *None* – no editing is permitted in the document. *Inserting, deleting, rotating pages* — prevents users from editing pages; *Filling in form fields and signing* — grants permissions for filling in forms and digitally signing forms, but users cannot edit the form fields with the form tools; *Commenting, filling in forms, and signing* — adds to the form fill-in permissions the capability to add comments to the document; *Any except extracting pages* — grants permissions for all editing features but prevents users from extracting pages from the document.

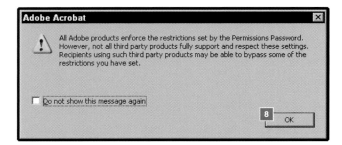

8. **Click OK in the informational dialog box.**

9. **You are prompted to confirm your password. Retype the password and click OK.**

10. **Close the document and reopen it.**

11. **Choose File→Save As and save the file to the Tutorial16_finish folder, overwriting the previous save.**

12. **Open a context window from the Toolbar Well and choose Advanced Editing. Return to the context menu and choose Commenting and Advanced Commenting to open the toolbars.**

13. **Open a context menu on the Toolbar Well and choose Dock All Toolbars.**
    Notice the Advanced Editing and Commenting tools are grayed out. The permissions restrictions prevent you from using the tools to edit the file. If you want to make changes in the file, you need to open the Password Security – Settings dialog box and disable the permissions check box. Gaining access to the security settings requires you to have the password used to secure the file.

14. **Quit Acrobat.**

» Session Review

In this session, you learned how to secure PDF document using Acrobat's built-in security features. To review the session, answer the following questions. Answers are found in the tutorial noted in parentheses.

1. What compatibility setting do you use if you share files with Acrobat 4 users? (See Tutorial: Password-Protecting PDF Documents.)

2. How do you prevent users from opening PDF documents? (See Tutorial: Password-Protecting PDF Documents.)

3. How do you prevent users from printing PDF documents? (See Tutorial: Securing Content.)

4. How do you prevent users against all editing? (See Tutorial: Securing Content.)

5. How do you remove security settings? (See Tutorial: Securing Content.)

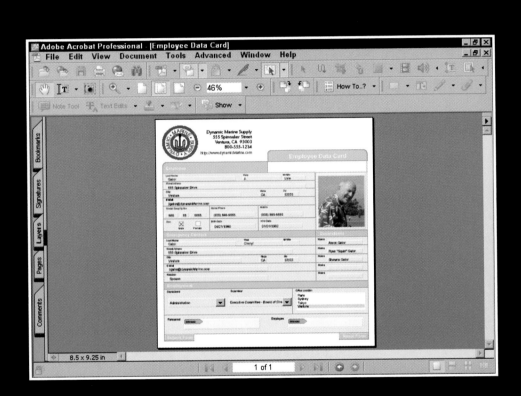

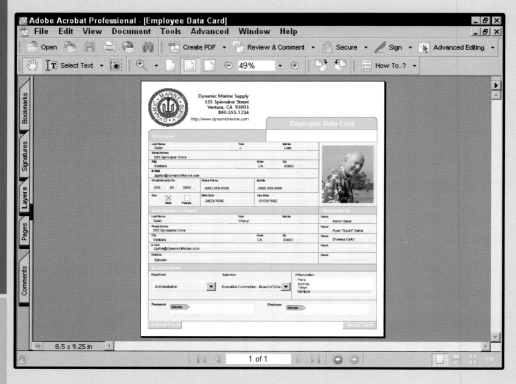

Tutorial: **Creating a Digital ID**

Tutorial: **Creating Signature Appearances**

Tutorial: **Signing Documents**

Tutorial: **Certifying Documents**

Session Introduction

Digital signatures enable you to electronically sign documents as well as add security to files. To begin using digital signatures you need to create a personal digital ID. You can use digital IDs to electronically sign PDF documents, to certify documents with a digital signature, and to encrypt files using digital signatures. In this session you learn how to create a digital ID and add digital signatures to PDFs for signing and securing files.

TOOLS YOU'LL USE
Sign task button, Manage Digital IDs command, Save as Certified Document command.

CD-ROM FILES NEEDED
17_ceoLetter.pdf, 17_employeeData.pdf, and 17_signature.pdf (found in the Sessions/Session17/ Tutorial17 folder).

TIME REQUIRED
90 minutes

Tutorial
» Creating a Digital ID

To begin using a digital signature, you need to create a digital ID. Digital IDs are then used to electronically sign PDF documents, to certify documents with a digital signature, and to encrypt files using digital signatures. In this tutorial you learn how to create a digital ID.

1. **Mount the CD-ROM located in the back of this book. Drag the Session17 folder from inside the Sessions folder to your desktop. Launch Acrobat by double-clicking the program icon.**

2. **Open the** `17_employeeData.pdf` **file from the Tutorial17 folder.**

<N O T E>
You start this session with a file open; however, creating digital IDs does not require you to open a file.

3. **Open a context menu from the Acrobat Toolbar Well and choose Reset Toolbars.**

4. **Choose Advanced→Manage Digital IDs→My Digital ID.**
   The Manage My Digital IDs dialog box opens.

5. **Click Add.**
   The Add Digital ID dialog box opens. In this dialog box you have three options. The Get a Third Party Digital ID button enables you to open a Web page hosted on Adobe's Web site where you obtain information on acquiring third-party digital IDs. Using a third-party digital ID from a reputable vendor provides you with maximum security. The Create a Self-Signed Digital ID button enables you to use Acrobat to create a personal digital ID. The Import Digital ID File button enables you to browse your hard drive to find a digital ID created in Acrobat or acquired from a third party.

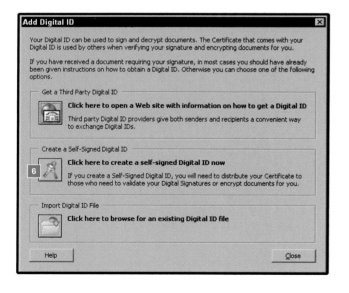

6. **Click the second button entitled Click Here to Create a Self-Signed Digital ID Now.**
   The Self-Signed Digital ID Disclaimer dialog box opens. This dialog box informs you that the digital ID might not be appropriate in some situations requiring third-party validation.

7. **Click Continue.**
   The Create Self-Signed Digital ID dialog box opens. In this dialog box, you add specific information related to your personal use for the ID.

8. **Fill in the fields using your personal information.**
   Note that Windows users have an option for adding the ID as a Windows Trusted Root whereby you can use the same ID in Windows applications supporting security handling. For this step, the check box is disabled.

9. **Click the Create button.**
   You are returned to the Manage My Digital IDs dialog box. Your digital ID is created and listed in the Digital IDs list window.

10. **Click the newly created digital ID in the Manage My Digital IDs list window and click the Settings button.**
    The Set Digital ID Usage dialog box opens. In this dialog box you make a choice for selection persistence.

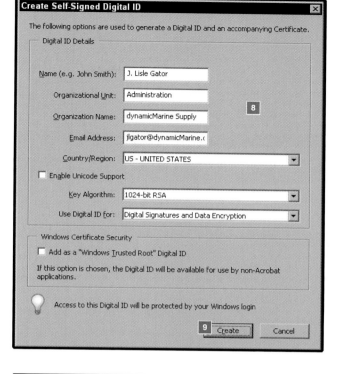

11. **Click the first radio button where you see Ask Me Which Digital ID to Use Next Time. If you create multiple IDs, Acrobat prompts you each time you sign a document for which ID to use for signing.**

12. **Click OK.**
    You are returned to the Manage My Digital IDs dialog box.

13. **Click Close in the Manage My Digital IDs dialog box.**

14. **Keep the file open to follow the steps in the next tutorial.**

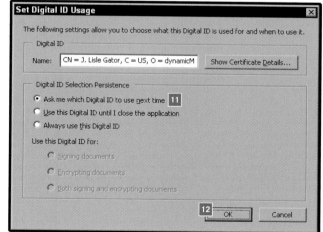

Tutorial
» Creating Signature Appearances

When you sign a document, Acrobat creates an appearance from various options you elect to use for your appearance settings. In addition to the text items Acrobat provides, you can also use an imported graphic image. You might want to scan your analog signature, use a logo or symbol, or use another kind of image as part of your signature appearance. In this tutorial you learn how to change signature appearances.

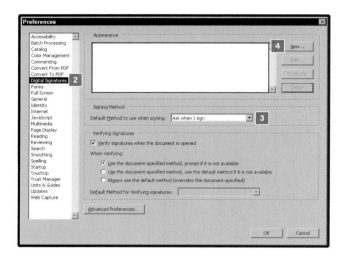

1. **Choose Edit→Preferences (Windows) or Acrobat→Preferences (Macintosh).**
   The Preferences dialog box opens.

2. **Click Digital Signatures in the left pane.**

3. **Open the pull-down menu and choose Ask When I Sign from the Default Method to Use When Signing.**

4. **Click New.**
   The Configure Signature Appearance dialog box opens.

5. **Click the Imported Graphic radio button.**

6. **Click the PDF File button.**
   Although the button implies only PDF files can be imported as a graphic, you can use file formats compatible with the Create PDF From File menu command. Clicking the button opens the Select Picture dialog box where you click Browse to navigate your hard drive and locate the file to import. Click the file to import in the Open dialog box and click Select to return to the Select Picture dialog box.

7. **Click Browse in the Select Picture dialog box. Choose the file to import in the Open dialog box and click Select.**
   Choose any file you want to use for an appearance. If you have a scanned image of your signature, use it. If no file is readily available, use the 17_signature.pdf document in the Tutorial17 folder. A thumbnail preview is placed in the dialog box to show you the image preview before applying it to the signature appearance.

8. **Click OK in the Select Picture dialog box.**
   You are returned to the Configure Signature Appearance dialog box.

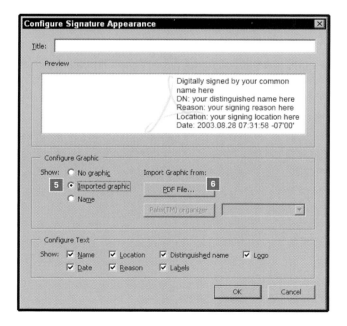

9. **Type a title in the Title field at the top of the dialog box.**
The title you add here appears in the Apply Signature to Document dialog box when you sign a document. Add a descriptive name for the signature you created in the last tutorial.

10. **Click OK.**
By default, the items at the bottom of the dialog box are all enabled. You toggle off options by disabling any of the check boxes. When all check boxes are enabled, your signature appears from a graphic file and the respective text items are enabled in the Configure Signature Appearance dialog box.

11. **Click OK in the Preferences dialog box.**
The signature appearance is ready to use with your digital ID.

12. **Keep the file open to follow the steps in the next tutorial.**

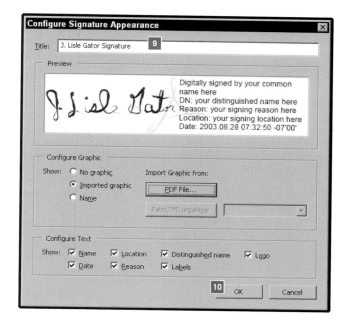

Tutorial
» Signing Documents

After creating your digital ID file and defining an appearance, you're ready to sign documents. PDF files can be signed in a number of ways. You can sign a document using a digital signature field present on a form, sign a document without any signature field, and certify documents using a digital ID. In this tutorial you learn how to sign a document using a digital signature field on an existing form.

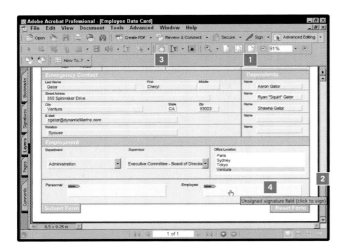

1. **Click the Fit Width button.**

2. **Scroll to the bottom of the page by dragging the scroll bar down.**

3. **Click the Hand tool.**

4. **Place the cursor over the signature field in the lower-right corner of the document and click the mouse button.**
   You'll remember in Session 16 you added security to the open file. You set permissions for restricting editing but enabled form fill-in and signing. Therefore, the secure document open in the Document pane cannot be edited without removing security, but it can be signed. When you click the signature field, an alert disclaimer dialog box opens.

5. **Click Continue Signing in the Alert – Document is Not Certified dialog box.**
   The Data Exchange File – Digital ID Selection dialog box opens.

6. **Click your digital ID in the list window and click OK.**
   The Apply Signature to Document dialog box opens.

7. **Open the pull-down menu for Reason for Signing Document: (select or edit) and click I Attest to the Accuracy and Integrity of this Document.**

   From the pull-down menu, you have preset choices for the reason for signing the document or you can edit the line where *<none>* appears and type your own reason for signing.

8. **Open the Signature Appearance pull-down menu and click the title you added in the last tutorial.**

   The title you provided for the appearance setting you set in the digital signatures properties appears in the pull-down menu.

<NOTE>

If the button below the pull-down menu for selecting the reason for signing the document reads Show Options, click the button to open the options so the signature appearance can be selected.

9. **Fill in the location and contact information in the last two fields.**

   Note these items are optional. As a matter of practice, add information respective to your location and e-mail address.

10. **Click the Sign and Save As button.**

11. **Save the file as** `17_employeeData.pdf` **to the Tutorial17_finish folder.**

12. **Close the file.**

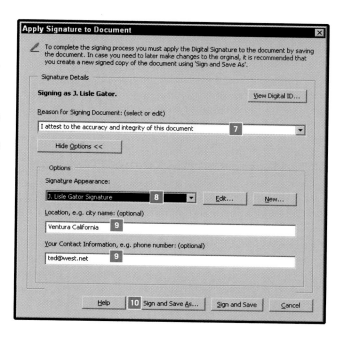

Using Public Certificates

Public certificates are used to validate signatures and encrypt files using trusted identities. When you create a digital ID file, the file is saved to your hard drive and used for your personal signing purposes. If you want other users to verify your signature after signing a document, you need to create another file referred to as your *public certificate*.

To export a public certificate, choose Advanced→My Digital IDs→My Digital ID. The Manage My Digital IDs dialog box opens. Click your signature in the list window and click the Export button. The Data Exchange File – Export Options dialog box opens.

In this dialog box you have options for e-mailing your certificate to another user or saving the public certificate to a file that can later be e-mailed or copied to a network server.

When you receive files from other users, you load the files as trusted identities. To load public certificates from other users, choose Advanced→Manage Digital IDs→Trusted Identities. Click Add. You add identities in the Select Contacts to Add dialog box, which enables you to browse your hard drive and load files.

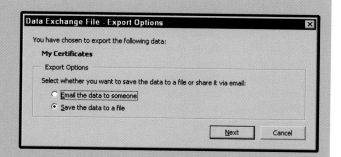

Once you have a list of trusted identities, you can encrypt files for individuals with individually assigned permissions. The steps to walk through the process are outlined in the Acrobat Help document. View the Complete Acrobat Help file to learn more about validating signatures and encrypting files using trusted identities.

Tutorial

» Certifying Documents

Certifying documents enables you to encrypt files using your digital signature. You can add security to prevent unauthorized editing and display a certificate on the signed document. In this tutorial you learn how to certify documents using your digital ID.

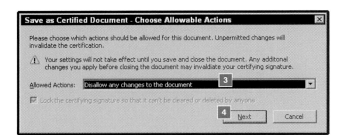

1. **Open the file** `17_ceoLetter.pdf` **from the Tutorial17 folder.**

2. **Choose File→Save as Certified Document.**
   The Save as Certified Document dialog box opens. Again this is a disclaimer informing you that using third-party signature handlers is more secure than using Acrobat's certificate authority. Click OK in the alert dialog box. The Save as Certified Document – Choose Allowable Actions dialog box opens.

3. **Choose Disallow Any Changes to the Document from the Allowed Actions pull-down menu.**
   Other options you can choose from the menu choices are allowing only form fill-in or allowing form fill-in and commenting.

4. **Click the Next button.**
   The Save as Certified Document – Select Visibility dialog box opens. This dialog box offers you options for either displaying a certificate on the PDF page or not showing the certificate after certification.

5. **Click the Show Certification on Document radio button.**

6. **Click Next.**
   A dialog box opens, providing you with instructions on how to add the certification. Click OK in the dialog box before you attempt to draw a marquee for the certification appearance.

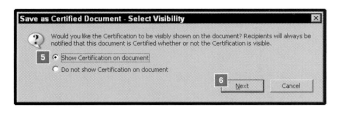

7. **Click OK.**

   The cursor changes to a plus symbol. You drag a marquee with the cursor to define the size of the certificate appearance.

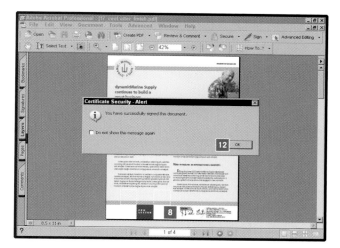

8. **Draw a marquee in the lower-right corner of the document.**

   When you release the mouse button, the Save as Certified Document – Sign dialog box opens.

9. **Open the pull-down menu for Reason for Signing Document: (select or edit) in the Save as Certified Document – Sign dialog box and click I Have Reviewed this Document.**

10. **Click the Sign and Save As button.**

11. **Save the file to the Tutorial17_finish folder as** `17_ceoLetter_finish.pdf`.

12. **The Certificate Security – Alert dialog box opens. Click OK to dismiss the dialog box.**

13. **Close the file.**

14. **Reopen the file by clicking** `17_ceoLetter_finish.pdf` **in the File menu (Windows) or by choosing the File→Open Recent File submenu (Macintosh).**

    Note that the certificate is not visible until you sign, save, close, and reopen the file.

15. **Quit Acrobat.**

» Session Review

In this session you learned how to create a digital ID and electronically sign and certify files. Review this session by answering the following questions. Answers are found in the tutorial noted in parentheses.

1. Where are signature appearance settings made? (See Tutorial: Creating Signature Appearances.)

2. How do you search for third-party signature handlers? (See Tutorial: Creating a Digital ID.)

3. How do you import a digital ID? (See Tutorial: Creating a Digital ID.)

4. Where do you change digital ID settings? (See Tutorial: Creating a Digital ID.)

5. How do you e-mail a public certificate? (See Tutorial: Signing Documents.)

6. How do you encrypt a document using a digital ID? (See Tutorial: Certifying Documents.)

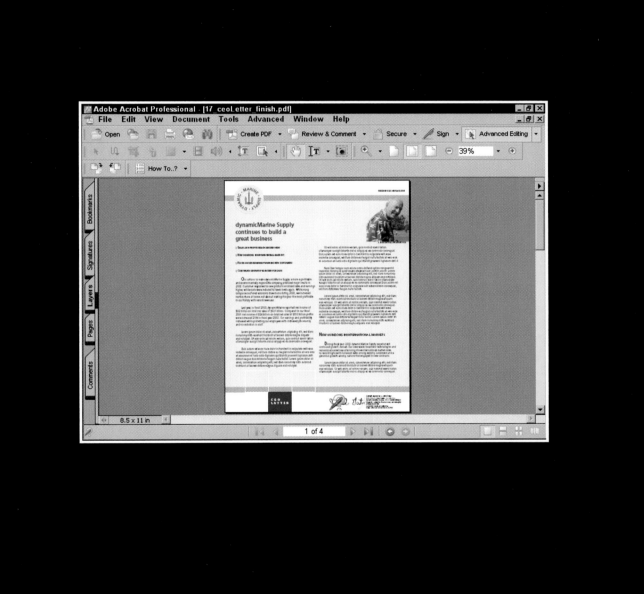

Appendix A

What's on the CD-ROM

This appendix provides you with information about the contents of the CD-ROM that accompanies this book. For the latest and greatest information, please refer to the readme file located at the root of the CD-ROM. Here is what you will find:

» System requirements

» Using the CD-ROM with Windows

» Using the CD-ROM with Macintosh

» What's on the CD-ROM

» Troubleshooting

System Requirements

Make sure that your computer meets the minimum system requirements listed in this section. If your computer doesn't match up to most of these requirements, you might have a problem using the contents of the CD-ROM.

For Windows 98, Windows 2000, Windows NT, Windows Me, or Windows XP:

» PC with a Pentium III class or better processor

» At least 128MB of total RAM installed on your computer

» At least 100MB of free hard drive space

» A color monitor with at least 800×600 resolution and a 16-bit video card

» A CD-ROM drive

For Macintosh:

» Macintosh OS computer with a G4 PowerPC processor running Mac OS X (10.2.4 or above)

» At least 128MB of total RAM installed on your computer

» At least 100MB of free hard drive space

» A color monitor with at least 800×600 resolution and a 16-bit video card

» A CD-ROM drive

Using the CD-ROM with Windows

To install the items from the CD-ROM to your hard drive, follow these steps:

1. Insert the CD-ROM into your computer's CD-ROM drive.

2. The interface will launch. If you have auto-run disabled, choose Start→Run. In the dialog box that appears, type **D:\setup.exe**. Replace *D* with the proper letter if your CD-ROM drive uses a different letter. (If you don't know the letter, see how your CD-ROM drive is listed under My Computer.) Click OK.

3. A license agreement appears. Read through the license agreement, and then click the Accept button if you want to use the CD—after you click Accept, the License Agreement window will never bother you again.

4. The CD interface Welcome screen appears. The interface coordinates installing the programs and running the demos. The interface basically enables you to click a button or two to make things happen.

5. Click anywhere on the Welcome screen to enter the interface. This next screen lists categories for the software on the CD.

6. For more information about a program, click the program's name. Be sure to read the information that appears. Sometimes a program has its own system requirements or requires you to do a few tricks on your computer before you can install or run the program, and this screen tells you what you might need to do, if necessary.

7. If you don't want to install the program, click the Back button to return to the previous screen. You can always return to the previous screen by clicking the Back button. This feature allows you to browse the different categories and products and decide what you want to install.

8. To install a program, click the appropriate Install button. The CD interface drops to the background while the CD installs the program you chose.

9. To install other items, repeat Step 8.

10. When you've finished installing programs, click the Quit button to close the interface. You can eject the CD now. Carefully place it back in the plastic jacket of the book for safekeeping.

<NOTE>

If you're on a Windows operating system other than Windows XP, you'll have to change the read-only status of the copied tutorial files. Otherwise, you won't be able to write over the files as you work through the tutorials. To do so, select all the files in a folder that you've copied to your computer. Right-click one of the files and choose Properties. In the Properties dialog box, uncheck the read-only box.

Also, I suggest that you instruct Windows to display the filename extensions of the copied tutorial files (if it isn't already set up to show them) so that you can see the file formats (.psd, .tif, .jpg, and so on). Find your Folder Options dialog box. (It's located in a slightly different place in different versions of Windows. In Windows XP, it's in the Appearance and Themes Control Panel; in Windows 2000, it's in the My Computer→Tools folder; in Windows 98, it's in the My Computer→View folder.) Click the View tab. Uncheck Hide File Extensions for Known File Types, which is checked by default.

Using the CD-ROM with the Macintosh OS

To install the items from the CD-ROM to your hard drive, follow these steps:

1. Insert the CD-ROM into your CD-ROM drive.

2. Double-click the icon for the CD-ROM after it appears on the desktop.

3. Double-click the License Agreement icon. This is the license that you are agreeing to by using the CD. You can close this window once you've looked over the agreement.

4. Drag the Sessions folders to your desktop as you work on each session.

What's on the CD

The following sections provide a summary of the software and other materials you'll find on the CD.

Author-Created Materials

All author-created materials from the book, including files and samples, are on the CD in the folder named Sessions. Inside the Sessions folder are individual folders for each session in the book. Session folders are referred to as *Session01*, *Session02*, *Session03*, and so on. Inside each session folder there are other folders where the tutorial files are found. These folders include:

» **Tutorialxx: (where xx refers to the Session number):** The Tutorialxx folders contain the raw data files that are used to follow steps in each tutorial.

» **Tutorialxx_finals:** Many sessions contain sequences of steps to produce a result. If you miss some steps and have a struggle accomplishing the proper sequence, the files contained in the *final* folders show you the results of each sequence followed in the tutorials.

» **Tutorialxx_finish:** You are asked to save files to a folder called Tutorial_finish. In most cases the folder is empty and only appears inside the sessions folder for you to be certain to save to the proper folder. In some cases you may be asked to open a file found in this folder to begin steps in a tutorial. Be certain you copy the respective session folder to your desktop as you work through sessions and all three subfolders will be copied.

In addition to the sessions folders, another folder titled *finalsSummarized* contains files in final form after properly executing steps in the tutorials. Open the finalsSummarized/finishedFiles.pdf and you'll find links to documents as they should appear in final form. Click the text listed in the two columns to open respective links.

Applications

The free Adobe Reader software is included on the CD-ROM. However, to follow all the tutorials in the book, the commercial version of either Adobe Acrobat Standard or Adobe Acrobat Professional is required. For more information about Adobe Reader and purchasing Adobe Acrobat visit http://www.adobe.com/products/acrobat.

Troubleshooting

If you have difficulty installing or using any of the materials on the companion CD-ROM, try the following solutions:

» **Turn off any antivirus software that you have running.** Installers sometimes mimic virus activity and can make your computer incorrectly believe that it is being infected by a virus. (Be sure to turn the antivirus software back on later.)

» **Close all running programs.** The more programs you're running, the less memory is available to other programs. Installers also typically update files and programs; if you keep other programs running, the installation might not work properly.

» **Reference the readme:** Please refer to the readme file located at the root of the CD-ROM for the latest product information at the time of publication.

If you still have trouble with the CD-ROM, please call the Wiley Publishing Customer Care phone number: (800) 762-2974. Outside the United States, call 1 (317) 572-3994. You can also contact Wiley Publishing Customer Service by e-mail at techsupdum@wiley.com. Wiley Publishing will provide technical support only for installation and other general quality control items; for technical support on the applications themselves, consult the program's vendor. For technical support on the author files contained on the CD-ROM, contact the author at ted@west.net.

Index

»D«

employee manual document, 225

encryption, 299, 313

Enlarge Page Thumbnails command, 78

Eudora, 201

Excel, 97

Execute a Menu Item action, 221, 256

Expand This button, 240

Explorer toolbar, 113–114

exporting comments, 204

Extract Pages command, 148

extracting

file attachments, 185

pages, 148

»F«

facing pages view, 69

Facing view, 71

favorites, 193

FDF file, 203–204

FDF file extension, 203

field tab order, 278–279

File Attachment Properties dialog box, 184–185

file attachments, 184–185

File menu (Windows), 54, 315

file types, converting to PDF files, 58

File→Close command, 42, 54, 60, 61, 270

File→Create PDF From Web Page command, 111

File→Create PDF submenu, 90

File→Document Properties command, 22, 72, 73, 82, 122, 124, 125, 157, 248, 256, 266, 269

File→New→Mail Message command, 116

File→Open command, 11, 46, 47, 54, 55, 58, 60, 68, 101, 113, 146, 163, 184

File→Open Recent File command, 74

File→Open Recent Files (Macintosh) command, 54, 315

File→Preferences (Windows) command, 72

File→Print command, 102, 115

File→Properties command, 263

File→Quit command, 115

File→Save as Certified Document command, 314

File→Save As command, 17, 22, 61, 73, 123, 132, 145, 185, 248

File→Save command, 61, 124

files

appending Web pages, 111–112

attachments, 184–186

compression, 88

converting to PDF documents, 44

deleting pages from, 60–61

drag-and-drop, 142

encrypting, 313

extracting pages, 148

opening saved in different formats, 56–57

optimizing, 62

saving, 17, 58–61

tiling on-screen, 139

tracking edits, 61

Files of Type (Windows) pull-down menu, 14, 88

Files to Combine window, 59

filling in forms, 282

fills, 181–182

Final stamp, 187

First Page tool, 13, 71, 80, 181, 185, 267

Fiscal Report bookmark, 270

Fit Page tool, 13–14, 22, 38, 68, 70, 75, 156, 218, 244, 267

Fit Page view, 68, 70, 72, 74–75, 79, 123–124, 246

Fit Page View (Control/Command+0 (zero)) keyboard shortcut, 75

Fit Width tool, 38, 154, 158, 174, 219, 223, 229, 240, 249, 255, 290, 312

Fit Width view, 22

Fit Window tool, 225

Float animation scheme, 262

floating toolbars, 38–39

fonts, 127, 129, 157–159

footers, 127–128, 130

Formatting palette (Macintosh), 95

forms, 278–282

Forms Data Format, 203

Forms Preferences dialog box, 282

Forms toolbar, 288

frames, 247–248

From Clipboard Image command, 93

From File command, 14, 88, 94

From Multiple Files command, 58, 98, 99, 138

From Web Page command, 108

» T «

About Seybold Seminars and Publications

Seybold Seminars and Publications is your complete guide

to the publishing industry. For more than 30 years it

has been the most trusted source for technology events,

news, and insider intelligence.

Workflow \
Media Te
Creation D
Manageme
Digital As:
Fonts an
Digital M
Content M
Manageme
Workflow \
Media Te
Creation D
Manageme
Digital As
Fonts an
Digital M
Content -M
Manageme
Workflow
Media Te
Creation D
Manageme

SEYBOLD
CONSULTING PUBLICATIONS

SEYBOLD
SEMINARS

Produced by

KM Key3 Media Group

PUBLICATIONS

Today, Seybold Publications and Consulting continues to guide publishing professionals around the world in their purchasing decisions and business strategies through newsletters, online resources, consulting, and custom corporate services.

○ **The Seybold Report: Analyzing Publishing Technologies**
The Seybold Report analyzes the cross-media tools, technologies, and trends shaping professional publishing today. Each in-depth newsletter delves into the topics changing the marketplace. *The Seybold Report* covers critical analyses of the business issues and market conditions that determine the success of new products, technologies, and companies. Read about the latest developments in mission-critical topic areas, including content and asset management, color management and proofing, industry standards, and cross-media workflows. A subscription to *The Seybold Report* (24 issues per year) includes our weekly email news service, *The Bulletin,* and full access to the seyboldreports.com archives.

○ **The Bulletin: Seybold News & Views on Electronic Publishing**
The Bulletin: Seybold News & Views on Electronic Publishing is Seybold Publications' weekly email news service covering all aspects of electronic publishing. Every week *The Bulletin* brings you all the important news in a concise, easy-to-read format.

For more information on **NEWSLETTER SUBSCRIPTIONS,**
please visit **seyboldreports.com**.

CUSTOM SERVICES

In addition to newsletters and online information resources, Seybold
Publications and Consulting offers a variety of custom corporate services
designed to meet your organization's specific needs.

○ **Strategic Technology Advisory Research Service (STARS)**
The STARS program includes a group license to *The Seybold Report* and
The Bulletin, phone access to our analysts, access to online archives at
seyboldreports.com, an on-site visit by one of our analysts, and much more.

○ **Personalized Seminars**
Our team of skilled consultants and subject experts work with you to create a
custom presentation that gets your employees up to speed on topics spanning
the full spectrum of prepress and publishing technologies covered in our publications. Full-day and half-day seminars are available.

○ **Site Licenses**
Our electronic licensing program keeps everyone in your organization, sales
force, or marketing department up to date at a fraction of the cost of buying
individual subscriptions. One hard copy of *The Seybold Report* is included with
each electronic license.

For more information on **CUSTOM CORPORATE SERVICES,**
please visit **seyboldreports.com.**

EVENTS

Seybold Seminars facilitates exchange and discussion within the high-tech publishing community several times a year. A hard-hitting lineup of conferences, an opportunity to meet leading media technology vendors, and special events bring innovators and leaders together to share ideas and experiences.

Conferences

Our diverse educational programs are designed to tackle the full range of the latest developments in publishing technology. Topics include:

- Print publishing
- Web publishing
- Design
- Creative tools and standards
- Best practices
- Multimedia
- Content management
- Technology standards
- Security
- Digital rights management

In addition to the conferences, you'll have the opportunity to meet representatives from companies that bring you the newest products and technologies in the publishing marketplace. Test tools, evaluate products, and take free classes from the experts.

For more information on **SEYBOLD SEMINARS EVENTS,**
please visit **seyboldseminars.com**.

Wiley Publishing, Inc.
End-User License Agreement

READ THIS. You should carefully read these terms and conditions before opening the software packet(s) included with this book "Book". This is a license agreement "Agreement" between you and Wiley Publishing, Inc. "WPI". By opening the accompanying software packet(s), you acknowledge that you have read and accept the following terms and conditions. If you do not agree and do not want to be bound by such terms and conditions, promptly return the Book and the unopened software packet(s) to the place you obtained them for a full refund.

1. **License Grant.** WPI grants to you (either an individual or entity) a nonexclusive license to use one copy of the enclosed software program(s) (collectively, the "Software") solely for your own personal or business purposes on a single computer (whether a standard computer or a workstation component of a multi-user network). The Software is in use on a computer when it is loaded into temporary memory (RAM) or installed into permanent memory (hard disk, CD-ROM, or other storage device). WPI reserves all rights not expressly granted herein.

2. **Ownership.** WPI is the owner of all right, title, and interest, including copyright, in and to the compilation of the Software recorded on the disk(s) or CD-ROM "Software Media". Copyright to the individual programs recorded on the Software Media is owned by the author or other authorized copyright owner of each program. Ownership of the Software and all proprietary rights relating thereto remain with WPI and its licensers.

3. **Restrictions on Use and Transfer.**

   (a) You may only (i) make one copy of the Software for backup or archival purposes, or (ii) transfer the Software to a single hard disk, provided that you keep the original for backup or archival purposes. You may not (i) rent or lease the Software, (ii) copy or reproduce the Software through a LAN or other network system or through any computer subscriber system or bulletin-board system, or (iii) modify, adapt, or create derivative works based on the Software.

   (b) You may not reverse engineer, decompile, or disassemble the Software. You may transfer the Software and user documentation on a permanent basis, provided that the transferee agrees to accept the terms and conditions of this Agreement and you retain no copies. If the Software is an update or has been updated, any transfer must include the most recent update and all prior versions.

4. **Restrictions on Use of Individual Programs.** You must follow the individual requirements and restrictions detailed for each individual program in the About the CD-ROM appendix of this Book. These limitations are also contained in the individual license agreements recorded on the Software Media. These limitations may include a requirement that after using the program for a specified period of time, the user must pay a registration fee or discontinue use. By opening the Software packet(s), you will be agreeing to abide by the licenses and restrictions for these individual programs that are detailed in the About the CD-ROM appendix and on the Software Media. None of the material on this Software Media or listed in this Book may ever be redistributed, in original or modified form, for commercial purposes.

5. **Limited Warranty.**

   (a) WPI warrants that the Software and Software Media are free from defects in materials and workmanship under normal use for a period of sixty (60) days from the date of purchase of this Book. If WPI receives notification within the warranty period of defects in materials or workmanship, WPI will replace the defective Software Media.

   (b) WPI AND THE AUTHOR(S) OF THE BOOK DISCLAIM ALL OTHER WARRANTIES, EXPRESS OR IMPLIED, INCLUDING WITHOUT LIMITATION IMPLIED WARRANTIES OF MERCHANTABILITY AND FITNESS FOR A PARTICULAR PURPOSE, WITH RESPECT TO THE SOFTWARE, THE PROGRAMS, THE SOURCE CODE CONTAINED THEREIN, AND/OR THE TECHNIQUES DESCRIBED IN THIS BOOK. WPI DOES NOT WARRANT THAT THE FUNCTIONS CONTAINED IN THE SOFTWARE WILL MEET YOUR REQUIREMENTS OR THAT THE OPERATION OF THE SOFTWARE WILL BE ERROR FREE.

   (c) This limited warranty gives you specific legal rights, and you may have other rights that vary from jurisdiction to jurisdiction.

6. Remedies.

(a) WPI's entire liability and your exclusive remedy for defects in materials and workmanship shall be limited to replacement of the Software Media, which may be returned to WPI with a copy of your receipt at the following address: Software Media Fulfillment Department, Attn.: *Adobe Acrobat 6 Complete Course*, Wiley Publishing, Inc., 10475 Crosspoint Blvd., Indianapolis, IN 46256, or call 1-800-762-2974. Please allow four to six weeks for delivery. This Limited Warranty is void if failure of the Software Media has resulted from accident, abuse, or misapplication. Any replacement Software Media will be warranted for the remainder of the original warranty period or thirty (30) days, whichever is longer.

(b) In no event shall WPI or the author be liable for any damages whatsoever (including without limitation damages for loss of business profits, business interruption, loss of business information, or any other pecuniary loss) arising from the use of or inability to use the Book or the Software, even if WPI has been advised of the possibility of such damages.

(c) Because some jurisdictions do not allow the exclusion or limitation of liability for consequential or incidental damages, the above limitation or exclusion may not apply to you.

7. U.S. Government Restricted Rights.
Use, duplication, or disclosure of the Software for or on behalf of the United States of America, its agencies and/or instrumentalities "U.S. Government" is subject to restrictions as stated in paragraph (c)(1)(ii) of the Rights in Technical Data and Computer Software clause of DFARS 252.227-7013, or subparagraphs (c) (1) and (2) of the Commercial Computer Software - Restricted Rights clause at FAR 52.227-19, and in similar clauses in the NASA FAR supplement, as applicable.

8. General.
This Agreement constitutes the entire understanding of the parties and revokes and supersedes all prior agreements, oral or written, between them and may not be modified or amended except in a writing signed by both parties hereto that specifically refers to this Agreement. This Agreement shall take precedence over any other documents that may be in conflict herewith. If any one or more provisions contained in this Agreement are held by any court or tribunal to be invalid, illegal, or otherwise unenforceable, each and every other provision shall remain in full force and effect.